The Definitive
PONTIAC GTO
GUIDE 1964–1967

David Bonaskiewich

CarTech®

CarTech®, Inc.
838 Lake Street South
Forest Lake, MN 55025
Phone: 651-277-1200 or 800-551-4754
Fax: 651-277-1203
www.cartechbooks.com

Edit by Paul Johnson
Layout by Monica Seiberlich

ISBN 978-1-61325-385-4
Item No. CT618

Library of Congress Cataloging-in-Publication Data

Names: Bonaskiewich, David author.
Title: The definitive Pontiac GTO guide : 1964-1967 / David Bonaskiewich.
Description: Forest Lake, MN : CarTech Books, [2018] | Includes index.
Identifiers: LCCN 2018007855 | ISBN 9781613253854
Subjects: LCSH: GTO automobile–History. | Pontiac automobile–History.
Classification: LCC TL215.G79 B65 2018 | DDC 629.222/2–dc23
LC record available at https://lccn.loc.gov/2018007855

Written, edited, and designed in the U.S.A.
Printed in China
10 9 8 7 6 5 4 3 2 1

DISTRIBUTION BY:

Europe
PGUK
63 Hatton Garden
London EC1N 8LE, England
Phone: 020 7061 1980 • Fax: 020 7242 3725
www.pguk.co.uk

Australia
Renniks Publications Ltd.
3/37-39 Green Street
Banksmeadow, NSW 2109, Australia
Phone: 2 9695 7055 • Fax: 2 9695 7355
www.renniks.com

Canada
Login Canada
300 Saulteaux Crescent
Winnipeg, MB, R3J 3T2 Canada
Phone: 800 665 1148 • Fax: 800 665 0103
www.lb.ca

CONTENTS

ACKNOWLEDGMENTS

Working a full-time job as an automotive painter while simultaneously writing a comprehensive book such as this is no simple task, and to say that it was a labor of love is a gross understatement. My own hobbies, including wrenching on my 1970 Pontiac LeMans and 1976 Pontiac Grand Safari station wagon, were put on hold while I researched, photographed, and wrote about the iconic 1964–1967 GTO cars that I absolutely love. It was my passion for the GTO model that kept me focused, with the desire to deliver a superior product; one that I hope you, the reader, will thoroughly enjoy.

Throughout this process, I've had to rely on numerous people within the Pontiac community. First and foremost is my mentor, Don Keefe, whose vast repository of Pontiac history is invaluable; I could send him any Pontiac-related question via text and receive a thoughtful, accurate reply within minutes. Don, along with Ann Caster Haines, founded *Poncho Perfection* magazine, an in-depth, monthly periodical that covers the entire scope of the Pontiac hobby. I've contributed numerous articles and photography to *Poncho Perfection* since its inaugural issue, and I hope to supply many more.

Other highly skilled and fervent photojournalists have also shared their expertise and/or lent the use of their photos to me for this project, and I am forever grateful. Chris Phillip, Rocky Rotella, and Tom DeMauro, along with Don Keefe, are heroes within the Pontiac community and their contributions to the hobby are unparalleled.

I must not forget to include the late Eric White and Paul Zazarine, whose books were of immense value to reference whenever I was in doubt of a certain statistic. Both *The GTO Association of America's Pontiac GTO/GT-37 Illustrated Identification Guide* by White and the Zazarine/Chuck Roberts collaboration, *Pontiac GTO Restoration Guide 1964–1970,* are excellent works that should be included in any Pontiac enthusiast's collection.

Jim Mott, owner of Jim Mott Restorations in Kimberly, Idaho, and 1965 GTO technical advisor to the GTOAA, was a great resource for the finer details concerning these legendary machines. Jim also provided numerous engine bay photos of award-winning GTOs, which can serve as templates for owners currently restoring their own cars to factory specifications. Special thanks are extended to Jim and his team.

Seasoned aficionados John Viale, Andre Rayman, Alan Swearingen, and Ken Nagy have also provided much-needed insights, evaluations, and photos. Their dedication to the GTO model and its legacy ensures that the Pontiac hobby will continue to thrive for years to come. John Kyros at the General Motors Media Archive was helpful and knowledgeable, and my longtime friend John Shade Vick was great company on the lengthy road trips required to photograph some of these cars. A great deal of thanks is bestowed upon these individuals.

The GTO story would be incomplete without including a detailed section about the muscle cars produced by other GM divisions, all of which arose as a result of the GTO's success. CarTech author Dale McIntosh was helpful and knowledgeable when I reached out to him regarding the Chevelle Malibu Super Sport. He, along with Rich Cummings, Bill Whorley, Derrick Knapp, and Ted Loranz, also provided excellent photos of the Malibu Super Sport and Oldsmobile 4-4-2 models.

My lovely wife, Jenn Bonaskiewich, often proofread and assisted with organizing several drafts of this project. Thanks to this wonderful lady for all that she did for this project and for me personally.

Then, there are the owners of these legendary cars; without them, this book would not have been achievable. My gratitude extends to Brian Thomason, Terry Bagby, Mike Speck, Bill Branly, Andre Rayman, Steve McNutt, Jack Suarez, Jerry Bulger, Larry Steele, Dave Erhardt, Jimmy Johnson, Lee Wintrode, Bob Wilcox, Tim Perry, Tom Harper, Robert Bennett, Guy Naylor, Gary Harrison, Mark Cronk, Eric Foehr, Mark Best, and Abram Scherbekow.

Jim Mattison of Pontiac Historical Services (PHS) should be recognized for his massive contribution to the Pontiac hobby. For the uninitiated, by submitting the VIN of your classic Pontiac and paying a modest fee, Jim will send you a detailed history of the car, including a list of its original equipment. This is especially valuable for 1964 and 1965 GTOs, which used LeMans VIN tags and cowl data plates; it will determine conclusively if the car is a legitimate, factory-produced GTO.

Although I've spent a considerable amount of time photographing cars and conducting research for this project, an inadvertent mistake or occasional typo may slip through the cracks. I feel I have done my due diligence, but I am not infallible. If you should come across any statistic or historical fact that you find questionable, please contact me through CarTech Books; I would very much like to hear what you have to say about the beloved 1964–1967 Pontiac GTO. Thank you and enjoy the book.

CHAPTER ONE

SETTING THE STAGE FOR THE GTO

Throughout the 1940s and much of the 1950s, Pontiac was building dependable yet mostly uninspired vehicles. By 1955, the result was a sixth-place market position behind Chevrolet, Ford, Buick, Plymouth, and Oldsmobile. In the span of just one year, from 1955 to 1956, sales penetration had dropped from 7.4 percent to 6.0 percent. This brought about rumors that the more successful Oldsmobile brand could absorb Pontiac. Pontiac needed to shed its "grandpa's car" image and find its niche if it was going to survive the decade. Consumers were now searching for something more exciting than a car that simply took them from Point A to Point B. New automotive trends were evolving, focusing on style and performance, not merely basic transportation.

Bold moves by Harlow Curtice, Semon "Bunkie" Knudsen, Pete Estes, John DeLorean, and others not only resuscitated Pontiac Motor Division but also directed it toward the most prosperous and memorable period in the brand's history. Iconic machines, such as the fuel-injected 1957 Bonneville, the completely redesigned 1959 Wide-Track Pontiacs, the tastefully appointed Grand Prix, and the first true muscle car, the Pontiac GTO, were made

On January 24, 1963, Pontiac Motor Division announced that all 389 and 421 Super Duty engines were canceled, and no new orders would be accepted, effectively removing Pontiac from any further racing involvement. As a result, Pete Estes and John DeLorean focused their efforts on street performance, and the Pontiac GTO was born.

An inline flathead-style 8-cylinder engine powers this 1950 Pontiac; inline-6 engines were also used. Dubbed the "Silver Streak 8," it was adequate for the time period, but it was replaced with the 287-ci V-8 in 1955. (Photo Courtesy Don Keefe)

This pristine 1950 Pontiac convertible highlights the dramatic styling changes that occurred throughout the 1950s. Compared with the 1959 Pontiac, it's hard to believe they were built in the same decade. (Photo Courtesy Don Keefe)

possible by the hard work and exceptional vision of each of these men.

When Harlow Curtice, president of General Motors, appointed Bunkie Knudsen as Pontiac's general manager in 1956, Knudsen filled the most critical role at the most dire time in the history of the brand to that point. At age 43, Knudsen was also the youngest general manager in GM history.

Semon Knudsen, the son of former GM president William S. Knudsen, was born October 2, 1912, in Buffalo, New York. His father is said to have given him the nickname "Bunkie," which was World War I jargon for "bunkmates," or close friends. Bunkie had an interest in automobiles from a very young age, even assembling his first car from pieces his father had laid out as a test of his abilities. Knudsen accepted and completed this and many other challenges throughout his lifetime. He attended Dartmouth College in Hanover, New Hampshire, for one year, then transferred to and eventually graduated in 1936 from the Massachusetts Institute of Technology with an engineering degree. After graduation, he found employment with local machine shops before landing at General Motors in 1939 as a tool engineer.

To assist Knudsen, Curtice also promoted Frank Bridge to general sales manager at Pontiac. With Pontiac on the verge of extinction, Knudsen was assigned the task of improving sales and given free rein to do whatever was needed to save the brand. He recruited the talents of Elliott Marantette "Pete" Estes from the Oldsmobile division as chief engineer and John DeLorean, from Packard, as director of advanced design. It's not an overstatement to say that the creative thinking, hard work, and enthusiasm of Knudsen, Estes, and DeLorean saved Pontiac from a much earlier demise than the brand ultimately experienced in 2010.

At the Automobile Manufacturers Association (AMA) meeting in June 1957, Harlow Curtice, president of General Motors, considered a voluntary ban on factory racing involvement. This was due in part to the tragedy at the 1955 24 Hours of Le Mans race, where a car piloted by Pierre Levegh careened into the stands, killing more than 80 people and injuring dozens more. Curtice reasoned that this self-imposed measure would prevent the US government from issuing a stricter, mandatory ban. Some automakers adhered closely to the new racing policy, but Knudsen, needing every advantage if he was to resuscitate Pontiac, ultimately chose to go racing.

With the trio of Knudsen, Estes, and DeLorean now firmly established, Pontiac focused its attention on younger car buyers who were looking for something new and exciting. Knudsen once said, "You can sell a

The 1955 Pontiac models sold poorly when new, but today they are collectible pieces of American automotive history. The 287-ci V-8 engine was standard equipment in 1955. (Photo Courtesy Don Keefe)

Tailfins, the heavy use of chrome trim, and two-tone paint were trademarks of mid-1950s American automotive styling. Although Pontiac was still suffering from a bland image, the introduction of the 287-ci V-8 showed promise, and, through increases in bore and stroke, grew to 389 ci by 1959. (Photo Courtesy Don Keefe)

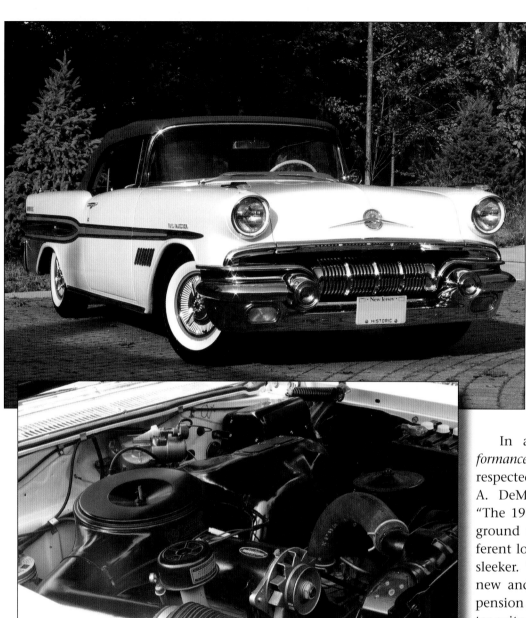

One of Bunkie Knudsen's first actions as general manager of Pontiac was to eliminate the silver streak trim that had adorned the hoods of countless Pontiacs of prior years. It was a symbolic gesture that signified that the brand was no longer tied to its past image. This 1957 Bonneville convertible would be a cherished addition to any collection. (Photo Courtesy Don Keefe) Inset: The 1957 Bonneville was equipped with a 347-ci engine topped with a Rochester mechanical fuel-injection system. Only 630 of the 1957 Bonnevilles were produced, making them extremely valuable in today's collector car marketplace. (Photo Courtesy Don Keefe)

young man's car to an old man, but you can't sell an old man's car to a young man." Knudsen and his youthful colleagues' first major accomplishments were the 1959 "Wide-Track" Pontiacs, which were a radical departure from the 1957 and 1958 models. This complete redesign included all-new sheet metal, and it was edgier and more streamlined than ever before. It also introduced the now iconic split grill design featured on every Pontiac except the 1960 models. The 1959 Wide-Tracks name came from the fact that the wheels were moved outward about 5 inches, a design sparked by Charles M. Jordan that resulted in a more aggressive appearance and an automobile that handled much better than its predecessors.

In an interview for *High Performance Pontiac* magazine with respected Pontiac journalist, Thomas A. DeMauro, Knudsen remembers, "The 1959 model was new from the ground up and had an entirely different look. It was wider, longer, and sleeker. The chassis was completely new and used an updated rear suspension system and was much better suited to racing than the previous model." The 1959s were well received, earning *Motor Trend*'s Car of the Year award and fueling sales growth of more than 56 percent, which placed Pontiac in fourth position for overall sales.

Despite the voluntary 1957 AMA racing ban, Knudsen was able to maintain Pontiac's strong presence at NASCAR and drag-racing venues across the country. Racing legends Smokey Yunick, Fireball Roberts, Mickey Thompson, and many others took Pontiacs to the winner's circle and helped shed the old Pontiac image. With a performance reputation now steadily growing, new car sales continued to increase, propelling Pontiac to third place in overall sales in 1962, behind only Chevrolet and Ford.

In recognition of his proven success at Pontiac, Bunkie Knudsen was promoted to general manager of

All 1958 GM full-size cars were one-year-only designs and conveyed a transitional styling from the more rounded shapes of previous years to the edgier, more masculine designs that would soon follow. The bold two-tone paint and large chrome accents on this beautiful 1958 Bonneville soon gave way to a more restrained, understated aesthetic in 1959. (Photo Courtesy Don Keefe) Inset: Nearly 60 years after it debuted, the interior of this 1958 Pontiac Bonneville remains as stunning as when the car was new, showcasing the ornate styling that Pontiac employed in the late 1950s. (Photo Courtesy Don Keefe)

The 1959 Pontiac lineup was completely redesigned and represented the first cars completed fully under the leadership of Bunkie Knudsen. Sales increased sharply from 217,303 in 1958 to 383,320 in 1959, proving that Knudsen and his team were guiding Pontiac in the right direction. (Photo Courtesy Don Keefe) Inset: By 1959, the Pontiac V-8 displaced 389 ci and remained a steadfast powerplant until it was superseded by the 400 ci in 1967. This highly detailed example resides in a 1959 Bonneville convertible. (Photo Courtesy Don Keefe)

Semon "Bunkie" Knudsen poses with two 1961 Pontiacs. Knudsen, along with Pete Estes and John DeLorean, rejuvenated Pontiac Motor Division, saving the brand from being absorbed by the more successful Oldsmobile division. The trio's tireless efforts resulted in dominating victories at NASCAR races and drag-racing events in the late 1950s and early 1960s. Estes and DeLorean later built upon that success, which led to the creation of the first muscle car, the Pontiac GTO. (Photo Courtesy GM Media Archive)

Chevrolet in 1961, while Pete Estes assumed that role for Pontiac, and John DeLorean moved to chief engineer at 36 years old, the youngest person to ever hold that position.

Elliott Marantette "Pete" Estes was born in southwest Michigan and began studying at the General Motors Institute in 1934 at the age of 18. It was there that Estes acquired the nickname "Pete." Estes recalled, "When I walked up to the crib in the shop where I had a job running a screw machine, the old boy (stock clerk) said,

'What's your name?' I told him. He let out half a laugh and said, 'You look like a Pete to me.'"

In 1940, Estes graduated with a degree in mechanical engineering from the University of Cincinnati. Estes excelled at school and also worked at GM Research Laboratories under Charles Kettering. Kettering was a brilliant scientist and engineer who cofounded what would become AC-Delco and was credited with 300 patents. Working alongside Kettering did pose some challenges, and in an interview with the *Detroit Free Press*,

Under Bunkie Knudsen's guidance, Pontiac was distancing itself from large, Indian-themed ornaments such as this. The 1959 Pontiacs clearly showed a departure from such adornments.

The large hood ornaments of the 1940s and 1950s Pontiacs were tastefully sculpted, but the focus was an effort to revitalize Pontiac's image and downplay the use of such features.

During his time at Oldsmobile, Estes played a key role in the brand's multiple carburetion setups. He later had a key impact on Pontiac's Tri-Power induction system, which debuted in 1957 on the 347-ci engine. Air filter elements on this 1957 Star Chief are aftermarket pieces.

When Pontiac ceased production of 389-ci and 421-ci (shown) Super Duty engines in early 1963, it effectively ended the fruitful racing involvement that the brand had enjoyed since the late 1950s.

Estes stated, "Ket would come in sometimes late at night, grab a screwdriver out of your hand, and fiddle with the engine until we had to do our work all over again." Estes went on to say, "Once he stalled a car in Detroit's Washington Boulevard traffic, then called me and said, 'Pete, I'll give you five minutes to come down and get this pile of junk off the street.'"

Estes became a senior engineer at GM Research Laboratories in 1945 and soon began working for the Oldsmobile division of General Motors. It was at Oldsmobile where Estes played a significant role in developing one of the first commercially viable overhead-valve V-8 engines.

Estes had been instrumental in the development of Oldsmobile's triple-carburetion systems. Knudsen then convinced him to leave the more exciting and successful Oldsmobile division for the floundering Pontiac brand, a move that eventually benefited both men, as Estes applied much of what he learned to Pontiac's Tri-Power in 1957.

When Knudsen's move to Chevrolet left a vacancy for Pontiac's top position in 1961, Estes filled that role and continued to build upon the success of his predecessor. Estes presided over one of the most successful periods in Pontiac's history, and sales improved each year of

his tenure, contributing to the revival of the brand. It was also during this time that the GTO was conceived, a project that almost certainly would not have made it past GM's management had it not been for Estes's enthusiasm and confidence in the car and his team at Pontiac.

A meeting of GM's upper management was held on January 21, 1963, and while there was no outright ban placed on corporate-backed racing, the corporation renewed its dedication to the 1957 AMA agreement. Days later, a memo was issued to "All Zone Car Distributors" that stated, "Effective today, January 24, 1963, 389 and 421 Super Duty engines are canceled, and no further orders will be accepted (421 HO engines are still available). Suggest you advise dealers who normally handle this type of business verbally." This is what most enthusiasts now refer to as the "1963 General Motors ban on racing." Initially, this was perceived as a monumental setback to Pontiac, which had worked feverishly in the late 1950s and early 1960s to cultivate and maintain a high-performance image. However, the collective efforts of Pete Estes, John DeLorean, and Jim Wangers would redirect the knowledge gleaned from Pontiac's racing success and apply it to the street, and a legend was soon created: the Pontiac GTO.

The Pontiac GTO helped define the careers of Pete Estes and John DeLorean during their tenure at General Motors. Like Bunkie Knudsen did before them, both men eventually served as general manager at Pontiac and, later, at Chevrolet.

Rightfully considered the first muscle car by scores of aficionados, the Pontiac GTO was the culmination of Pontiac's successful racing heritage as well as the engineering and marketing savvy displayed by Pete Estes, Bill Collins, and John DeLorean.

CHAPTER TWO

1964 GTO Genesis of the Legend

Pontiac's Tempest lineup dates to 1961, when it was a much different automobile than the 1964 model that became the platform for the legendary GTO. The Chevrolet Corvair, which had debuted in 1960, signified a radical departure from anything General Motors had produced to that point. The rear-mounted engine and transaxle along with the European-influenced styling represented a bold move for an American manufacturer. Powered by an aluminum air-cooled 140-ci horizontal 6-cylinder engine, the 1960 Corvair sold more than 250,000 units and proved to other American car companies that there was a demand for small, inexpensive cars in the United States. Hoping to capitalize on the Corvair's momentum, General Motors decided that Buick, Oldsmobile, and Pontiac would each produce a small, economy-minded vehicle.

Conceived by John DeLorean, the 1961 Tempest displayed a front engine and rear-mounted transaxle,

eliminating the transmission "hump" in the floor pan, thereby increasing passenger leg room. This layout also helped the car achieve an almost 50-50 weight distribution and removed the need for universal joints. Power was transmitted via a flexible driveshaft (often referred to as rope drive) housed within a separate tunnel called a torque tube, differentiating it from the otherwise similar Buick Special and Oldsmobile F-85, each of which featured a conventional front-mounted engine and transmission. Like the Chevrolet Corvair, the Pontiac Tempest used four-wheel independent suspension, whereas the Buick Special and Oldsmobile F85 had independent front suspension but a more traditional, solid rear axle.

The February 1961 issue of *Motor Trend* magazine highlighted road tests of the Buick Special, Oldsmobile F-85, and Pontiac Tempest. It praised Pontiac's innovative layout. "Pontiac's Tempest is far different than its parent line, but the differences go further than only size

The success of the Chevrolet Corvair prompted General Motors to have Pontiac, Buick, and Oldsmobile manufacture their own afford-able, compact cars.

The 1962 LeMans convertible was a handsome automobile. Pontiac Motor Division was quite proud of its Tempest/LeMans lineup, and the 1962 sales brochure boasted, "Pontiac craftsmanship at its best." Large, 15-inch wheels were standard.

At first glance, the 195-ci 4-cylinder engine, which was exactly one-half of Pontiac's 389-ci engine, could easily be mistaken for a V-8. Known as the Trophy 4, it was an adequate powerplant, but prone to perceptible vibration issues.

The all-aluminum Buick 215-ci V-8 was an optional engine for the 1961 and 1962 Pontiac Tempest. Installed in slightly more than 1 percent of Tempests, they are exceedingly rare in today's collector car marketplace. The 215-ci engine was also available in the Oldsmobile F-85, shown here, called the Rockette 8.

and styling. Strip the Tempest down to its bare essentials of powertrain and running gear, and the compact is radically different from the standard-size line." The writers were clearly impressed with the Tempest, touting the curved driveshaft, transaxle, and independent rear suspension, stating, "Overall, the Tempest's riding qualities were judged superior, probably the best in its class, and very near the top of all domestic-made car. . . . The spring rate is relatively firm, which gives a smooth precise feel at highway speeds. The firmness also contributes to the better-than-average handling at all speeds." It was cutting-edge technology for 1961, and the Pontiac Tempest was covered at length by both automotive and technology enthusiast magazines.

In addition to the February 1961 issue of *Motor Trend* magazine, the Tempest was also the main subject of the March issue, and it received the prestigious Car of the Year Award. *Popular Science* and *Motor Life* magazines also covered the Tempest extensively, with both publications featuring in-depth analyses of Pontiac's engineering marvel.

Another innovative and resourceful move by the Pontiac team was the design of the 195-ci inline 4-cylinder engine, derived from the passenger-side cylinder bank of the venerable 389-ci V-8. Known as the Trophy 4, it effectively reduced manufacturing costs and gave Pontiac a unique powerplant not shared by other manufacturers within General Motors. The Trophy 4 was available in three configurations: a low-compression, 1-barrel

By 1963, the redesigned Tempest grew 5 inches in length and 2 inches in width. The 326-ci V-8 also debuted; with a true displacement of 336 ci, it was advertised as 326 ci to remain below GM's limit of 330 ci as standard equipment for its senior compact cars. In 1964, the engine was reconfigured to an actual displacement of 326 ci, making the 1963 version a one-year-only design. By 1964, Pontiac interpreted the 330-ci limit to allow the 389 ci as optional equipment, technically complying with the word but not the spirit of the mandate. With the popularity of the GTO, the edict was revised to allow engines up to 400 ci in intermediates. In 1970, it was revised to 10 pounds per hp, allowing the largest engines into the now-heavier A-body cars.

in length and 2 inches in width. While Pontiac's full-size lineup changed to the now-iconic stacked headlight design, the 1963 Tempest models retained the horizontal layout of previous years. Advertised as a Senior Compact, the 1963 Tempest could be optioned with Pontiac's new 326-ci V-8 engine, which produced 260 hp and 352 ft-lbs of torque. With an actual displacement of 336 ci, Pontiac advertised the engine as 326 ci to remain below the 330-ci limit for GM compact cars. The 1963 models kept the front engine and the rear transmission configuration of the 1961 and 1962 compacts, but they featured an upgraded transaxle to accommodate the increase in horsepower.

Later in 1963, Pontiac debuted the 326 High-Output (HO); equipped with a 4-barrel carburetor, it boasted 280 hp. By this time, Pontiac had begun to emphasize the performance attributes of the Tempest, with one print ad reading, "Stick your foot into the 4-barrel gasworks. Hark to the dark brown sound of 280 horses mumbling to themselves. And give a passing thought to dual exhausts and, on stick shifts, high-performance hydraulic valve lifters with their fast bleed-down." It was this type of advertisement, with horsepower figures proudly listed and creative verbiage that appealed to the potential buyer's imagination that would soon be used with increasing frequency across Pontiac's entire lineup. The 1963 Tempest and LeMans models were a one-year-only design, and clearly represented an evolution from the compact, economy-based 1961 and 1962 units to the larger 1964 midsize Tempest, setting the stage for what became one of the most significant automobiles of all time, the Pontiac GTO.

1964 Tempest and LeMans

The 1964 model year brought about substantial changes to the Tempest and LeMans lineup. No longer a compact car, the unibody construction was replaced with a full-perimeter frame, the wheelbase increased from 112 inches to 115 inches, and overall length extended to 203 inches. Consequently, the front-engine/rear transaxle

carburetor rated at 110 hp; a high-compression 1-barrel rated at 140 hp; and a high-compression 4-barrel putting out a peppy 155 hp. The engine was not without its drawbacks; as a large-displacement 4-cylinder, it was heavy and prone to harsh vibrations. Pontiac attempted to remedy the problem by using large rubber motor mounts, which absorbed some of the engine's shakiness.

A noteworthy option for the 1961–1962 Tempest line was the availability of Buick's aluminum 215-ci V-8, producing 155 hp and 220 ft-lbs of torque. Because it proved to be unpopular, fewer were produced, and Tempests equipped with the 215-ci engine are now coveted in today's collector car marketplace. In late 1961, Pontiac introduced the Tempest LeMans to potential buyers who desired a bit more style than the modest Tempest conveyed. Essentially a trim package, the Tempest LeMans featured front bucket seats in lieu of the standard bench seat and could be optioned for the two-door coupe or convertible model. By 1962, the Tempest was available in a full range of configurations: convertible, two-door coupe, four-door sedan, or four-door station wagon.

Even though the 1963 Tempest and LeMans shared the same 112-inch wheelbase as the 1961 and 1962 models, they exhibited all-new sheet metal, gaining 5 inches

The 1964 Pontiac Tempest shared little with its predecessors. Now using a full-perimeter frame, longer wheelbase, and restyled sheet metal, General Motors designated it the A-body. The term was also used for the Chevrolet Chevelle, Buick Skylark, and Oldsmobile Cutlass, all of which employed full-frame construction.

layout and independent rear suspension were supplanted with a front-mounted engine/transmission and a solid rear axle. A completely redesigned exterior gave the car a more assertive, masculine profile that proved to be ideal for the soon-to-be-developed GTO. Now designated as the A-body, the 1964 Tempest and LeMans shared the same chassis as the Chevrolet Chevelle, Buick Skylark, and Oldsmobile Cutlass, all of which featured the more conventional front-mounted engine and transmission arrangement.

A 215-ci inline-6 engine producing 140 hp and 206 ft-lbs of torque replaced the 195-ci 4-cylinder as the standard engine. The 1964 Pontiac Tempest sales brochure boasted, "Who's going to get excited about a 6-cylinder in this day and age? You are. Any time Pontiac brings out a new engine, it's something to get excited about. Especially when it's a husky 215-ci 140-hp 6 that runs (and runs and runs) on regular gasoline. It's a beautifully balanced, serenely smooth inline-6 that's a lot lighter than the 6s you're probably used to. A lighter car makes for more horses-per-pound and better weight distribution. Sound good? You should hear how quietly persuasive it is on the road!" Throughout the years, many 6-cylinder Tempests have been hot-rodded; most have the 326-ci or 389-ci engine (or sometimes a Chevrolet V-8 engine) residing between the fenderwells. As a result, locating a 1964 Tempest with its original 215-ci 6-cylinder can be quite challenging.

Even though the popular 326-ci V-8 remained in the 1964 lineup, its bore was reduced to 3.71875, yielding a true displacement of 326 ci, thus making the 1963 326-ci a one-year-only anomaly, and quite rare today. For 1964, the base 2-barrel 326-ci engine produced 250 hp and 333 ft-lbs of torque. Pontiac again offered the 326 HO engine for the Tempest and LeMans with the intent that this combination would equip a high-performance midsize car, but the 326 HO–powered LeMans was overshadowed when the GTO option debuted in late 1963. The 326 HO was a very capable powerplant. Rated at 10.5:1 compression,

Produced only in 1964 and 1965, the Pontiac 215-ci 6-cylinder was the base engine for Tempest and LeMans models. A close relative to the 230-ci Chevrolet 6-cylinder, it was a durable and reliable powerplant.

280 hp, and a stout 355 ft-lbs of torque, a Tempest equipped with the 4-speed manual transmission, 326 HO mill, and fitted 3.36:1 rear gears (standard when a manual transmission was selected) could certainly keep pace with a GTO fitted with the 389-ci 4-barrel, automatic transmission, and 3.08:1 rear end gears. Although the GTO owner could perhaps suffer a bruised ego, it certainly could have made for an entertaining drag strip comparison.

For 1964, Pontiac Motor Division offered three separate choices for its A-body lineup: the 20-Series Tempest, the 21-Series Tempest Custom, and the 22-Series Tempest LeMans. The differences between the models were somewhat subtle, most notably interior appointments and exterior trim; the inline-6 and various 326-ci V-8 engines could be had in any of the three series. The 20-Series Tempest was the most economical choice and featured a combination of cloth and Morrokide upholstery; *Morrokide* was Pontiac's name for a durable, long-lasting vinyl material available in a wide-range of colors. The 21-Series Tempest Custom was a step above the base Tempest and was furnished with all Morrokide seats and additional exterior trim along the belt line and across the rear of the decklid. The 22-Series Tempest LeMans was the most well-equipped Pontiac A-body in 1964 and included additional cabin lighting, partially carpeted door panels, Deluxe steering wheel, and front bucket seats. The LeMans also displayed blacked-out grilles and a unique tail panel design that would be shared with the GTO. The Tempest, Tempest Custom, and LeMans were strong sellers for Pontiac; 202,676 (not including the GTO) combined units were sold in 1964.

1964 GTO: A Legend Is Born

On Saturday mornings, John DeLorean held weekly "what if?" sessions at the GM Proving Grounds in Milford, Michigan. Bill Collins, Russell Gee, and other key Pontiac team members usually accompanied DeLorean to discuss ideas for new projects in an informal atmosphere. In his book, *Glory Days: When Horsepower and Passion Ruled Detroit,* Jim Wangers recalls the genesis of the GTO, "The birth of the GTO took place inside a Proving Grounds garage during one of these Saturday morning sessions. It was very early spring 1963. A prototype 1964 Tempest coupe equipped with a 326 engine was up on the lift. DeLorean, Collins, and Gee were under the car discussing the chassis. Collins casually mentioned, 'You know, John, with the engine mounts being the same, it would take us about 20 minutes to slip a 389 into this thing.' John looked at him, caught an approving nod from Gee, and without uttering another word, they were all in agreement." This defining moment could not only be thought of as the "birth of the GTO" but also the birth of the entire muscle car phenomenon, sparking dozens of performance models by numerous American manufacturers.

Indeed, it was a simple task for Gee and his experienced crew, and they had the 389 installed in the Tempest in time for the following week's test session. Collins remembers, "Russell Gee was in charge of engine and machine shops, and he and his guys did the installation. Pontiac was very small in those days and all of us had 'overall car experience,' not just one area of expertise,

This Marimba Red 1964 Tempest Custom is equipped with the optional Cordova top and Deluxe wheel covers. The Tempest Custom was one level above the base Tempest and featured additional trim along the side of the body and on the tail panel. This car is driven regularly, and its owner chose modern radial tires for better handling and safety.

JOHN DELOREAN

The storied life of John Zachary DeLorean began January 6, 1925, in the Motor City: Detroit, Michigan. DeLorean's father, Zachary, was a Romanian immigrant who worked for Ford Motor Company as a millwright, which entailed installing and maintaining heavy machinery in factories. His mother, Kathryn, worked as a tool assembler for the Carboloy Products Division of General Electric. Even though they were financially stable, at least by Depression-era standards, the DeLorean household was tumultuous, and the couple eventually divorced in 1942. In J. Patrick Wright's book, *On a Clear Day You Can See General Motors*, DeLorean recalled, "Part of my dad's inclination towards fisticuffs came from a deep frustration caused by his inability to communicate effectively and thereby capitalize on his mechanical genius. He was uneducated when he came to the United States and he couldn't speak English. Although he eventually mastered the language, he always spoke with a trace of an accent."

Despite considerable challenges at home, John was an exceptional student, earning a scholarship to the Lawrence Institute of Technology. However, because of World War II, his education was put on hold, and in 1943 he was drafted into the military, serving three years in the US Army. Upon returning home, he resumed his collegiate pursuits and graduated in 1948 with a degree in industrial engineering. At the behest of John's uncle, Earl Pribak, DeLorean entered the Chrysler Institute of Engineering and graduated in 1952 with a degree in automotive engineering. Chrysler employed him briefly before he accepted a position at Packard Motor Company, where he worked alongside Forest McFarland, then head of research and development. DeLorean held a strong admiration for McFarland, crediting him as "a patient and understanding man who taught me much."

By 1956, John DeLorean was already a valuable commodity and accepted a position at Pontiac as an assistant to general manager Bunkie Knudsen and chief engineer Pete Estes. DeLorean said, "I was offered jobs in five different divisions of General Motors and eventually decided on Pontiac. The main reason for my decision was the general manager of the division, Semon E. 'Bunkie' Knudsen." Knudsen and DeLorean soon forged a special relationship, with Knud-

A brilliant engineer with a flair for style and extravagance, John DeLorean was instrumental in the development of the Pontiac GTO (1966 model shown) and the redesigned 1969 Grand Prix. Financial and legal troubles mired DeLorean after his days at General Motors, and today he is best remembered for his namesake car: the DeLorean DMC-12. (Photo Courtesy GM Media Archive)

JOHN DELOREAN CONTINUED

It was John DeLorean himself who chose the name GTO for Pontiac's new midsize performance car, which stood for Gran Turismo Omologato, *a name that irritated many Italian sports car purists.*

sen seemingly going out of his way to educate DeLorean about the automobile industry. In the book, *On a Clear Day You Can See General Motors*, DeLorean recalled, "under Bunkie I grew in knowledge of the automobile business and General Motors. I owe him a lot. For some reason, he singled me out and decided to expose me to all of the facets of running a car business. He made a deliberate program out of the education of John DeLorean. I remember going with Bunkie to meetings with the corporate brass at the GM Tech Center and watching corporate management in action. He introduced me to legendary GM executives who were also some of the most prominent and powerful names in the world automobile industry: Harlow Curtice, Albert P. Bradley, Frederic G. Donner, and Alfred P. Sloan, Jr."

DeLorean advanced rapidly through the ranks, progressing to chief engineer at Pontiac in 1961. Due in part to the major success of the 1964 GTO, he was then appointed general manager of Pontiac Motor Division in 1965 at age 40, the youngest person to hold such a title. DeLorean was also instrumental in the development of the 1967 Firebird. Even though it shared the same basic layout as the Chevrolet Camaro, DeLorean and his team worked tirelessly to improve the car's handling characteristics and present each model within the Firebird lineup with its own unique personality.

DeLorean, in collaboration with Ben Harrison and Jack Humbert, redesigned the slumping Grand Prix for 1969 by successfully using the A-body chassis and lengthening the wheelbase from 112 to 118 inches. Because it shared many chassis components with the Tempest/LeMans/GTO, it saved both time and money and was brought to market in about 18 months from initial conception. Employing all-new sheet metal that incorporated a short deck and a long,

elegant hood, the car imparted a sleek, formal appearance. The 1969 Grand Prix was a winner, selling 112,486 units (versus just 37,711 copies of the 1968 model), which led to *Car Life* magazine naming it Car of the Year.

In his book, *Grand Prix: Pontiac's Luxury Performance Car*, author Don Keefe stated, "Pontiac General Manager John DeLorean's stamp was unmistakable on this new Grand Prix. He chose to base the 1969 GP on an extended A-body chassis known internally as the G-body. It sported a wheelbase of 118 inches and the new-generation design took the long nose, short deck styling theme further than Pontiac ever had before. The 1969 Grand Prix was a striking combination of modern elegance, performance, and classic styling themes, all wrapped in a trim, athletic package that was every bit as true to the original GP theme as the original, perhaps even more so. In one fell swoop, Pontiac re-established itself as the leader in the luxury performance market. There was nothing around like it, nor even in the same league."

Due in large part to his contributions to the Pontiac GTO and the successfully redesigned 1969 Grand Prix, DeLorean was promoted to general manager of Chevrolet in 1969, where he oversaw the introduction of the 1970 Monte Carlo and 1971 Vega models. In J. Patrick Wright's book, *On a Clear Day You Can See General Motors*, DeLorean recalled, "From the first day I stepped into the Chevrolet Division, in 1969, it was obvious that the Vega was in real trouble. General Motors was pinning its image and prestige on this car, and there was practically no interest in it in the division. We were to start building the car in a little more than a year and nobody wanted anything to do with it." DeLorean implemented additional quality control measures to ensure that the Vega would be the best available car in its class. However, because of cost-cutting priorities, these were soon eliminated, and nearly 800 workers were laid off.

A union strike followed and it wasn't long before DeLorean's renegade mentality clashed with members of GM's upper management; he left the company in 1973.

A beautiful 1969 Pontiac Grand Prix speeds by the camera. The completely redesigned 1969 models were hugely popular, and Chevrolet would soon have its own version of a luxury sports car, the Monte Carlo, which debuted in 1970. (Photo Courtesy Don Keefe)

From this angle, the short deck design of the 1969 Grand Prix is evident. This elegant Expresso Brown example features a Cordova top and stylish Rally II wheels. (Photo Courtesy Don Keefe)

BILL COLLINS AND RUSSELL GEE

The Pontiac GTO almost certainly would not have existed without the contributions of both Bill Collins and Russell Gee. The ideas and technical expertise of Bill (a chassis engineer) and Russell (an engine specialist) were integral in the development of the car.

Bill Collins

Bill Collins's affinity for automobiles began at a very early age. His father was a mechanic at a Ford dealership and Bill remembers, "When I was a little kid, he would take me down there on Saturdays. I think that's where my interest in cars began." Bill later attained his mechanical engineering degree from Lehigh University in Bethlehem, Pennsylvania, and began his career at Pontiac Motor Division soon thereafter. He was testing acceleration and fuel economy on the "new for 1955" V-8 engines before serving two years in the US Army.

Upon returning to General Motors in 1958, Bill Collins recalls, "The difference between Pontiac in 1954 and 1958 was monumental. George Delaney was in charge of Pontiac in 1954 and he was very old-school and kind of set in his ways, where Pete Estes was much more current and performance-oriented." Collins was initially in charge of designing and testing the transaxles for the 1961 Tempest; he later oversaw the development of upgrades for the units, which were required to handle the power of the stout 421 Super Duty engines that were installed in 14 1963 Tempests. Most of these Tempests were drag race cars, but one was modified for circle track use. Collins recalls, "I was very involved with the 1963 Super Duty Tempests and the famous race at Daytona that included two Ferrari GTOs. The General Motors racing ban in 1963 eventually killed that series for us." That famous race was the Daytona 250-mile Challenge Cup,

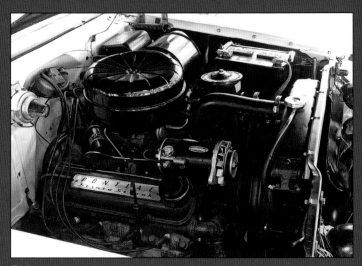

Before serving two years in the United States Army, Bill Collins was testing the 287-ci V-8 for performance and economy. The Strato Streak valve covers and 518024 cylinder head castings are correct for this engine. (Photo Courtesy Don Keefe)

and the 1963 Tempest driven by Paul Goldsmith not only lapped the Ferrari driven by David Piper but finished first, a full 5 miles ahead of second place finisher A. J. Foyt. Famed NASCAR driver Fireball Roberts finished fourth, behind the wheel of a Ferrari GTO. The Goldsmith-piloted Tempest had a top speed of 163 mph and led 74 of the 100 laps.

Bill Collins was promoted to assistant chief engineer at Pontiac in 1967 and stayed with the company until 1974. In a recent phone interview, he said, "I actually suggested that Pontiac drop the GTO after the 1974 model. They went from the LeMans body style in 1973 to the Nova X Body in 1974 as a way to further reduce costs. Sales departments were not performance-oriented and just wanted to sell cars." Col-

Bill Collins played a central role in the development of the transaxle unit used in 1961–1963 Tempest and LeMans models. This 1962 LeMans convertible is a beautiful example of one of these groundbreaking automobiles.

The 1963 Tempest and LeMans have become popular models to transform into high-powered drag race machines, inspired by the legendary Super Duty machines. Oftentimes, these cars are converted to a traditional front-mounted engine and transmission, as parts are more easily obtainable.

lins then went to work for John DeLorean, co-designing the iconic DMC-12 model, and later founded his own company, Vixen Motorhome, in 1981. Vixens, known as the "driver's RV," are well respected for their innovative design features that include a low center of gravity, a fuel-efficient engine, and the ability to be housed in a conventional garage.

Russell Gee

Russell Gee, an engine specialist, was another key component in the genesis of the 1964 GTO. In 1956, he was testing Pontiac's V-8 engine for durability when Bunkie Knudsen and Pete Estes approached him. Their goal was to enter Pontiac in stock-car racing, and they appointed Gee head of the program. Working with other engineers, Russell Gee succeeded in vastly improving the car's performance and increasing power output from the 347-ci engine, which was released the following year, in 1957. These efforts were also applied to the 370-ci engine in 1958 and the well-regarded 389-ci beginning in 1959. Gee and his team were rewarded for their efforts in the form of several NASCAR victories from 1957 to 1962.

With Gee now fluent in performance Pontiacs, he regularly accompanied John DeLorean and Bill Collins to the Pontiac (GM) testing facility. Staring at the 326 engine in a 1964 Tempest, Bill Collins said, "You know, John, it would take us about a half-hour to stick a 389 in this thing." With the external dimensions of the 326 and 389 being identical, it was a simple task for the crew, and the new engine was installed and ready for next week's session. Collins says, "Russell Gee was in charge of the engine and machine shops, and he and his guys did the installation. Pontiac was very small in those days and all of us had 'overall car experience,' not just one area of expertise, which was a big advantage."

An excerpt by Jim Wangers in the book, *The All-American Muscle Car*, recalls the thrill-seeking side of Gee, "Each division had private engineering garages at the Milford Proving Grounds, where they fiercely protected their innovations to the end. The development of the GTO was one of those closely and fiercely guarded secrets! After Gee and Collins had assembled the prototype, DeLorean took it for a test drive at the Proving Grounds. Upon his return, DeLorean instructed Gee to park the car in the corner of Pontiac's garage, cover it up, and not breathe a word about it, under the threat of losing his job!

"Gee did as instructed. However, knowing just how much fun driving the yet-to-be-named GTO was, he couldn't resist. As Gee recalled to (Dave) Anderson and me, 'It was an early Saturday morning when I decided to take the car for a drive on the grounds. I saw no other employees, so I felt secure in bringing the car out. As I accelerated, grabbing one gear after another, I looked down track only to see a senior Oldsmobile engineer standing along the wall. I said to myself, 'This is it! You are going to get fired!' I brought the car to a stop. He commented on how well the car seemed to perform and inquired if it was anything special. I told him we were testing a new camshaft design and he seemed to buy it. I put the car away, back under cover, and never brought it out again."

Gee stayed with Pontiac until 1979 when he accepted a position at Chevrolet as head of the racing and performance programs.

Russell Gee was tasked with extracting more power from the 1957 347-ci and 1958 370-ci engines for use in Pontiac's NASCAR racing efforts. This 370-ci Tri-Power mill resides in a beautifully restored 1958 Bonneville. (Photo Courtesy Don Keefe)

BILL COLLINS AND RUSSELL GEE CONTINUED

If you compare the 1964 Tempest (in this case, a Tempest Custom) with a 1964 GTO, it's obvious that the cars were built on the same platform. The mounting points on the chassis were identical, as were the external dimensions of the 326-ci and 389-ci V-8 engines. Each of these 1964 models is painted Marimba Red, which accentuates the similarities between the two Pontiacs.

As anyone familiar with the GTO knows, it truly is a driver's car. In the early stages of development, Russell Gee took the 1964 prototype for an unauthorized test drive at the Milford Proving Grounds, nearly being found out by an Oldsmobile engineer who was present at the time.

Most muscle car aficionados consider the 1964 Pontiac GTO to be the first of its kind. Showcasing a large-displacement V-8 engine in a midsize chassis, it was marketed directly to the youth-oriented performance segment and sparked fierce competition among all American automobile manufacturers.

The GTO option (code 382) added $295.90 to the price of a 1964 LeMans. A 389-ci engine topped with a 4-barrel carburetor producing 325 hp and 428 ft-lbs of torque was standard with the GTO package. This Gulfstream Aqua (code Q) model is equipped with the optional 348-hp Tri-Power engine.

External dimensions for the powerful 389-ci V-8 found in Pontiac's full-size cars were identical to the 326 ci used in the Tempest and LeMans. Pontiac engineer Bill Collins recognized this fact and casually mentioned it to John DeLorean at the GM Proving Grounds in early spring 1963. This moment is considered the genesis of the Pontiac GTO and the catalyst for the entire muscle car phenomenon. For 1964 models without air-conditioning, a fan shroud was not used.

which was a big advantage." Despite GM's recent ban on corporate-backed racing, Collins thought the 389-ci Tempest would be a good candidate for a NASCAR entry. "When I made the suggestion of installing the 389 in the Tempest, my idea was to adapt the car for NASCAR competition, but John DeLorean and Jim Wangers took it in a completely different direction." One can't help but wonder how a 1964 Tempest powered by a 389-ci engine would have fared on the NASCAR circuit, perhaps replacing the full-size Pontiacs used in previous years.

Pete Estes, president of Pontiac Motor Division, played a vital role in getting the GTO into production. At the time, General Motors had an internal policy declaring that a car could have no less than 10 pounds of vehicle weight per cubic inch of displacement. Using this formula, the GTO, which weighed approximately 3,500 pounds, would only be approved for an engine with a maximum displacement of 350 cubic inches. Fearing that top GM executives might reject the car, Estes and DeLorean marketed the GTO as an option package for the LeMans and not as a separate model, which would have to be approved by the conservative GM management. It was this type of creative thinking, and passion for the car, that was pushing DeLorean, Estes, and Wangers to the limits of what could be accomplished within the confines of GM's strict corporate policies. In *Glory Days: When Horsepower and Passion Ruled Detroit*, Jim Wangers wrote, "Certainly a great deal of credit must be given to Pete Estes, who put his GM career on the line. Had management taken a hard line and stuck to their rule, or had the GTO been an initial sales flop, it could have been a black mark on Estes' record. That didn't happen; nevertheless, Pete Estes is, in large part, responsible for the existence of the Pontiac GTO."

By checking the box for code 382 on the options list, which added $295.90 to the price of the LeMans, speed-seeking buyers received the GTO package, which included a 325-hp 389-ci engine equipped with a single Carter 4-barrel carburetor, dual exhaust, and 3.23:1 rear end gears. A 3-speed manual transmission came standard with a Hurst shifter and added to the car's racy image. A large-diameter front sway bar, stiffer springs and shocks, and 6-inch-wide wheels shod with redline tires were all part of the GTO package. Several other options could be ordered at additional charge to further enhance the car's performance.

By offering the GTO as an option on the LeMans and not a separate model, Pete Estes and his team were able to circumvent the GM policy that limited engines in midsize cars to 330 ci. This pristine Skyline Blue (code H) convertible would be a welcome addition to any collection. (Photo Courtesy Don Keefe)

Body

The 1964 GTO was available in three configurations: convertible, two-door hardtop, and two-door sedan, which Pontiac called a Sports Coupe. Designed as a performance car, the GTO was not available in four-door sedan or station wagon models.

Although it was the last body style into production, the two-door hardtop (style 37) proved to be the most popular version by far, with 18,422 units produced in 1964. The December 1963 issue of *Hot Rod* magazine had one of the first feature articles about the 1964 GTO, and it did not mention the hardtop, stating only, "Two body styles are offered with the GTO kit; two-door coupe and convertible."

On hardtop models, when the door and quarter windows are lowered, there is no visible structure between the two, and the result is very tidy and unobstructed. Even though Pontiac's full-size lineup had changed to a stacked headlight design in 1963, the Tempest, LeMans,

With 18,422 examples produced, the hardtop was the most common of the three bodies available for the 1964 GTO. Starlight Black with a black Cordova top and black interior; cars such as this are commonly referred to as "triple black."

Sometimes called a "post car," Pontiac referred to its two-door sedan as a Sports Coupe. By using steel window frames and reinforced B-pillars (the posts), the Sports Coupe was the sturdiest of the three body configurations and favored by many racers of the era.

Pontiac Motor Division built just 6,644 GTO convertibles in 1964, the lowest number of the three body styles. GTO convertibles are highly sought after by many classic car collectors, especially when combined with desirable options such as Tri-Power induction and a 4-speed manual transmission. Due to structural reinforcements, including boxed frame rails, convertibles were the heaviest of the three body styles. This stunning example is equipped with aftermarket Hurst wheels and an owner-added painted pinstripe.

and GTO did not acquire that feature until 1965. The four horizontal headlights of the 1964 model help differentiate it from the 1965–1967 units.

From a distance, the two-door Sports Coupe (style 27) appears very much like the hardtop, but a structural B-pillar, or post, separates the door and quarter area and displays a steel window frame, which remains visible even when the window is lowered. While many enthusiasts prefer the appearance of the hardtop, the Sports Coupe possesses the greatest structural rigidity and lightest weight of the three body styles. Pontiac produced just 7,384 Sports Coupes in 1964, and due to its lower production numbers, it is now one of the more desired GTO models among collectors.

In addition to the boxed frame, convertible models received other structural reinforcements, such as added bracing between the rear inner wheelhouses and quarter panels.

A 1964 Pontiac GTO convertible was (and still is) the perfect car for deliberately cruising down Main Street on Saturday night or motoring down the highway en route to the beach on Sunday morning. Pontiac produced 6,644 GTO convertibles (style 67) in 1964, making the convertible the rarest of the three configurations, and often, the most valuable.

Any convertible needs chassis reinforcements, such as boxed frame rails, to counter the effect of not having a solid roof structure. The added weight of the strengthened chassis resulted in the convertible being the heaviest of the three body types. A heavy-duty frame option (code 661) for the hardtop or Sports Coupe bodies was available, which used the sturdier, convertible boxed frame. This option was aimed at the serious performance enthusiast, and it would have been a wise upgrade for use in road- and drag-racing applications, for which structural integrity is paramount. All convertible tops on 1964 GTOs were power operated and featured a soft (plastic) rear window. They were offered in six colors: ivory, black, blue, aqua, beige, or saddle. Through a combination of low production numbers and its association with freedom and the American spirit, the 1964 GTO convertible has become one of the most desired automobiles in today's collector car market.

Visually, the 1964 GTO was quite similar to its lower-performing siblings within the Pontiac A-body lineup, particularly the LeMans, which shared the same taillight treatment as the GTO. The Tempest and Tempest Custom featured characteristic taillight lenses housed within

The 1964 Tempest Custom (pictured left) featured a tail panel similar, but not identical, to a base Tempest. (The Tempest Custom received additional trim.) The 1964 GTO (right) received the same tail panel treatment as the LeMans. Note how the GTO (and LeMans) displayed color-keyed quarter-panel extensions, whereas the Tempest and Tempest Custom exhibited their taillights in that location.

quarter-panel extensions attached at the rear of each quarter panel. On the Tempest Custom, stainless steel trim spanned the width of the rear body panel, interrupted by the fuel door, which was adorned by similar trim and a Pontiac emblem. (Base model Tempests did not receive this trim.) In contrast, the LeMans and GTO models displayed body-color quarter-panel extensions and distinctive taillight lenses that were located within the rear body panel itself. The lenses featured several chrome ribs in line with matching trim pieces, including the fuel filler door, which were highlighted with Marimba Red paint. This gave the LeMans and GTO a more formal appearance from the rear, with the illusion that the taillights were one continuous piece.

Exclusive to the 1964 models (and some very early production 1965 cars) was the use of body-color paint inside the trunk area; later years used varying shades of gray spatter paint, most likely a cost-cutting measure. A two-piece mat came standard, which helped to protect the glossy finish. A spare tire cover (code 572) could be added separately for an extra $2.58 or as part of the Protection Group (code 062), which added $64.66 to the hardtop and Sports Coupe models and $43.14 to the convertible. The lower price reflected the fact that the rear window defogger was not available on the convertible body.

The hood was unique to the GTO and featured two simulated or nonfunctional scoops highlighted by chrome-ribbed inserts, which magazine critics always grumbled about. A line from the March 1964 *Car and*

The fuel filler on the 1964 GTO was located behind a small door just above the rear bumper. In 1965, it was moved to behind the license plate.

For the 1964 GTO, the inside trunk area was painted body color; all subsequent years (with the exception of early production 1965 models) featured gray spatter paint. The two-piece mat was standard equipment. Trunk volume is 35.4 cubic feet.

The hood, which features two simulated scoops, was unique to the GTO and demonstrates the largest exterior difference between it and other Tempest and LeMans models. The Pontiac arrowhead was affixed to all units within the Tempest and LeMans lineup. Inset: Chrome ribbed Inserts adorn the hood scoops and are identifying characteristics of the 1964 GTO. Reproduction units are currently available for the Pontiac hobbyist.

Driver review read, "We find the GTO quite handsome, except for those phony vents that GM Styling's Bill Mitchell insists upon hanging on everything." Indeed, late in the 1965 model year, the GTO's hood scoop could be made functional with the optional Ram Air setup. The 1964 GTO hood is another one-year-only item, and quality used examples are increasingly difficult to find, often commanding high prices. While fiberglass reproduction hoods have been available for many years, recently, high-quality steel versions have become available.

Cordova vinyl tops were available in either ivory or black as an option for both the Sports Coupe and hardtop GTO in 1964. They featured a grain pattern and could be identified by either a 1 (ivory) or 2 (black) on the cowl data plate next to the exterior paint code. Although attractive, vinyl tops were not without problems; they tended to retain moisture, and this, combined with a propensity by most manufacturers to use less paint on the roof when a vinyl top was specified, often led to corrosion problems, especially around the rear window area. Any hobbyist in the market for a classic car equipped with a vinyl top should inspect the roof thoroughly for any signs of rust, as this could lead to costly paint and body repairs.

Exterior color choices for the 1964 GTO were: Starlight Black (code A), Cameo Ivory (code C), Silvermist Gray (code D), Yorktown Blue (code F), Skyline Blue (code H), Pinehurst Green (code J), Marimba Red (code L), Sunfire Red (code N), Aquamarine (code P), Gulfstream Aqua (code Q), Alamo Beige (code R), Saddle Bronze (code S),

Singapore Gold (code T), Grenadier Red (code V), and Nocturne Blue (code W).

Not commonly seen today, factory two-tone paint was also available for the 1964 GTO in a wide range of combinations. The two-tone paint option featured the main color on the lower portion of the body and a contrasting roof color adorned with the same type of trim that accompanied models equipped with a Cordova top. Again, by inspecting the cowl data plate, the owner can identify which color (or colors) his or her GTO was

A Cordova top, which was available in two color choices for 1964 (ivory and black), gave the car a slightly more formal aesthetic; it was garnished with additional trim. The top was a $75.32 option.

Two-tone paint was a $31.74 option for the 1964 GTO. This striking hardtop model is painted Grenadier Red (code V) with a Cameo Ivory (code C) roof. (Photo Courtesy Chris Phillip)

The grilles of the 1964 GTO received a semi-gloss blackout treatment except for the perimeter and one section that ran lengthwise through the grille centers. The driver-side grille contained a chrome GTO emblem with white enamel overlay. The influence of the 1962 Pontiac Grand Prix is apparent in the four horizontal head-lights and clean, uncluttered appearance.

painted by the factory. Excluding convertibles and cars equipped with a Cordova top, in most instances there are two letters designating the exterior color(s). For example, C C indicates that the car is Cameo Ivory, both top and bottom, while V C denotes the main color (lower) as Grenadier Red and the roof color as Cameo Ivory. Note: Due to variations from different manufacturing plants, occasional anomalies are found on cowl data plates.

With the GTO being so similar in appearance to the LeMans, Pontiac designers sought to ensure that it was distinguished by proper exterior identification; a GTO emblem was placed in the grille, one on each quarter panel toward the rear of the car, and one on the passenger side of the decklid. Stylish badges that boasted "GTO 6.5 Litre" were affixed on each fender, just behind the wheel opening. Notably, Pontiac was the first Amer-

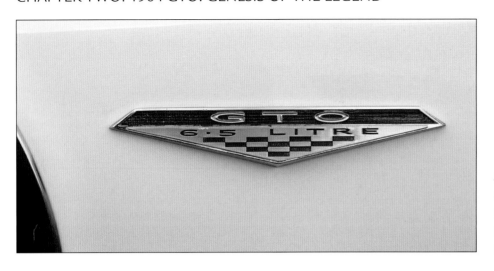

An emblem reading "GTO 6.5 Litre" was affixed to each fender behind the wheel opening. It's a beautiful piece in somewhat of a diamond shape with a checkered flag integrated into the design.

ican car manufacturer to use *litres* in some areas instead of the traditional cubic inch designations. A caption in the 1964 GTO sales brochure described the fender emblem with, "You'll find one of these on each side. If you don't think this is enough warning, you could always fly the skull and crossbones." The sales brochure was filled with creative and suggestive language, and it showcased the enthusiasm that Pontiac and its marketing team felt for the car.

Air-conditioning was the most expensive option for the 1964 GTO. Known as Tri Comfort air-conditioning (code 581), it added $345.60 to the price of the car, $50 more than the GTO option itself. Because of the added stress on certain components, cars equipped with an air conditioner automatically received the heavy-duty radiator and battery.

In today's world, cars are equipped from the factory with numerous high-tech safety devices, even on entry-level models. Back-up cameras, parking sensors, advanced braking systems, and air bags located throughout the cabin are but a few of the modern safety implements used to protect occupants. In the mid-1960s however, safety technology was not nearly as advanced, and many of the rudimentary protection items had to be special ordered. For the 1964 GTO, backup lamps were optional equipment, as was a driver-side mirror. The standard mirror was mounted on the left door, while the cable-operated remote mirror was affixed to the left fender. Research suggests that a passenger-side door mirror was available at the dealer. A dash pad (code 424) could be purchased separately for an extra $16.14, or as part of the 062 Protection Group. Seat belts did not become standard until

Air-conditioning was still considered a luxury in 1964, and quite rare on performance cars such as the GTO. It also added a substantial amount of weight to the front end of the car.

The dash area for cars equipped with air-conditioning received five vents: three in the dash itself and two just below. At $345.60, it was the most expensive option for the GTO. It adds a great deal of value in today's collector car marketplace.

Many, but certainly not all, GTOs were fitted with the optional instrument panel pad. It could be ordered separately (code 424) or as part of Protection Group 062, which included the instrument panel pad, door edge guards, rear window defogger (hardtop and Sports Coupe models only), spare tire cover, retractable front seat belts, and a complete set of floor mats.

January 1964 (though they could be special ordered before then).

Interior

In the early 1960s, Pontiac was producing clean, well-designed interiors throughout its entire model line. This trend continued for the 1964 Tempest and LeMans, and the GTO's cabin was nearly indistinguishable from the LeMans. Front bucket seats and a rear bench seat were standard on the LeMans and GTO and covered with Morrokide upholstery. The seat pattern was simple and tasteful, incorporating several ribs running from front to back. The bucket seats were a low-back design and did not feature headrests, which was common for the era. A power-operated driver's seat could be ordered (code 564) for an additional $71.02. (No passenger-side power option was offered.) Interestingly, it has been documented that a very small number of 1964 GTOs were special ordered with a front bench seat. A special order such as this was rather simple for the dealer and factory to fulfill, as it would have just required replacing the buckets with a Tempest front bench seat.

Simple yet tasteful would be a perfect way to describe the interior space of the 1964 GTO. Seat upholstery was made from Morrokide, a type of vinyl that was quite durable. Seat patterns changed every year of GTO production.

Identical to the LeMans pieces, the 1964 GTO's door panels were quite stylish and one of only two years that did not display a GTO emblem (1972 models with the LeMans Sport interior being the other). The carpeted portion at the bottom was usually color-keyed to the door panel, but in the case of Parchment interiors such as this, it was black. The 1964 Parchment interior color did not display the pearlescent quality of the 1965 and later versions.

The convertible's rear side panels (saddle, left) were quite different from those of the hardtop (black, bottom) and Sports Coupe models. The convertible's side panels extended approximately 3 inches inward at the rear and bottom portions to house the top mechanisms. Doing so created a "built-in" armrest (with ashtray), but decreased hip and shoulder room for rear seat passengers.

The rear panels for the hardtop and Sports Coupe GTOs were much simpler and featured a separate armrest with integrated ashtray. The rear seat in the hardtop and Sports Coupe afforded more room than the convertible.

Color-keyed rubber floor mats could be ordered to protect the GTO's carpet. Available separately or as part of Protection Group 062, they were both durable and stylish, displaying the Pontiac name as well as the arrowhead logo. Inset: This is the correct astral pattern (commonly referred to as "star pattern") for the headliner and sun visors in the 1964 GTO.

The automotive press was also pleased with the layout of the 1964 GTO interior, as the January 1964 issue of *Motor Trend* magazine stated, "Everything about the GTO had that just-right feeling. The steering wheel was low enough to see over, yet high enough to slip in under easily. Its relationship to the comfortable bucket seat was good, and even long drives didn't find us squirming around for a more comfortable position. The buckets gave reasonably good support to legs, hips, and back. The optional power seat allows an infinite number of positions that should suit everyone. Even the rear bench seat had adequate legroom for two people." A great deal of credit should be bestowed upon Pontiac's design team for producing a handsome interior that is as attractive today as it was in 1964.

Interior color choices for the 1964 GTO were: black (code 214), dark blue (code 215), saddle (code 216), dark aqua (code 217), medium red (code 218), and parchment (code 219). It should be noted that the 1964 parchment color did not display the pearlescent effect of the 1965 and later interiors.

The GTO's door panels, also covered with Morrokide, were the same pieces used on the LeMans, and did not display a GTO emblem. The panels featured an armrest with the door handle just to the front and a window crank near the vent window. The crank was for the main door window; simply unlatching and moving the window by hand operated the vent window. Both the seat pattern and door panel design changed every model year for the duration of the GTO's production.

Convertible models received special interior treatment to accommodate the hardware required to operate the top. A narrower rear seat was employed, along with uniquely designed rear interior side panels that featured courtesy lamps. The narrow rear seat reduced passenger hip room from 58.7 inches for hardtop and Sports Coupe models to 48.6 inches for convertibles. Because of the lack of a dome light, courtesy lamps were standard on convertibles and optional for hardtop and Sports Coupe models. In addition, the rear speaker option was not available on the convertible due to limited space and configuration of the top mechanism.

Loop-pile carpeting featuring an insulation layer was color-matched to the rest of the interior, excluding parchment interior cars, which received black carpet. Durable rubber floor mats were available at extra cost and greatly reduced wear and tear on the carpet. Available in assorted colors, the floor mats displayed the Pontiac name as well as the arrowhead logo. Quality reproduction floor mats are available from a host of restoration supply companies.

Most headliners for the 1964 models were color-matched to the rest of the cabin space, except black interior, which received a silver headliner, and red interior, which received an ivory headliner. It was thought that an all-black interior would be too dark, and Pontiac surmised that a lighter color headliner would brighten the otherwise black cockpit.

The engine-turned dash applique, which surrounded the four gauge pods and heater controls, was

The Deluxe steering wheel was standard issue for the 1964 GTO. A two-spoke design featured a chrome center section; the main part of the wheel was color-matched to other interior components and was quite a handsome piece.

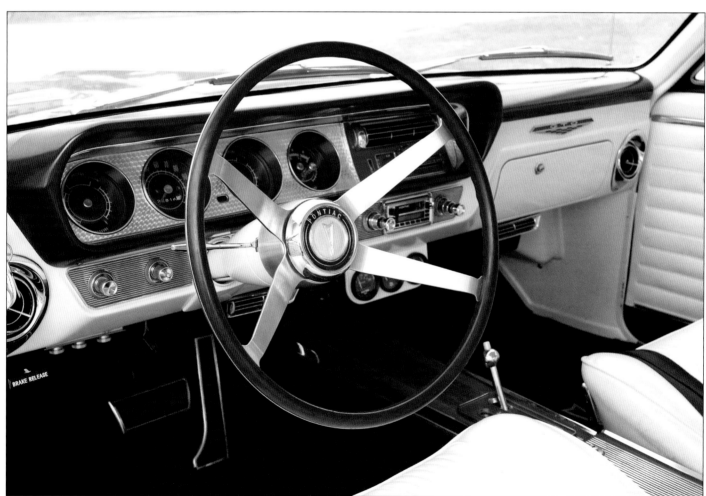

The Custom Sports steering wheel (code 524) was a $39.27 option and displayed four metal spokes and a simulated-wood rim. The piece was so attractive that some in the automotive press mistook it for an actual wood wheel.

A bold GTO emblem was placed on the dashboard just above the glove box door. This Cameo Ivory Sports Coupe also features a dash pad and air-conditioning.

The push-button AM radio (code 392 with manual antenna, code 393 with electric antenna) was one of two radio options for the 1964 GTO; the other was a manually controlled AM unit. The owner of this Pontiac fitted his car with a later, aftermarket FM receiver.

unique to the GTO and presented the dashboard with a race-inspired appearance. In addition, a bold GTO crest mounted above the glove box door alerted passengers that this was not merely a base model Tempest. The standard steering wheel for the 1964 GTO, known as the Deluxe, was a two-spoke color-keyed unit and was also available on Tempest and LeMans models. The wheel was attractive but it lacked the performance styling one might expect on a car such as the GTO, and many were removed in favor of aftermarket units. Now, with original appearance a priority, this trend has been reversed, and most GTOs are currently fitted with the Deluxe or Custom Sports steering wheel. A tilt steering column (code 454) was available for an additional $43.04 and required the buyer to also select the power steering option.

The Custom Sports steering wheel could be optioned for the GTO and featured four metal spokes surrounded by a simulated-wood rim. A stylish piece, many current owners desire the Custom Sports steering wheel even if their car was not originally so equipped, as they feel it is a key component to the GTO's identity and allure. The 1964 sales brochure boasted, "The Custom Sports wheel. Looks like wood but isn't. Stainless steel spokes. Optional." The 1964 Custom Sports steering wheel is a one-year-only design and currently not reproduced; it commands high prices ranging from $1,000 to more than $2,000, depending on condition.

Two radio options were offered for the 1964 GTO: a manually controlled AM unit or a push-button AM piece. Either of these could be ordered with the fixed, fender-mounted antenna or the power antenna located on the passenger-side quarter panel. By checking off one of the radio options, the buyer received a single dash-mounted speaker with the Sepra-Phonic (code

The engine-turned dash applique was unique to the GTO and one of few deviations from Tempest and LeMans cabin spaces. This car is factory equipped with the electric clock (code 604).

The electric clock (left) and tachometer (below) occupy the same space so the car could not be equipped with both items.

The tachometer was a $53.80 option (code 452) but had a reputation for being inaccurate; a new design appeared in 1965.

401) or Verbra-Phonic (code 474) rear-speaker options available at extra cost. Due to the complexity and size of the top mechanism, a rear-speaker option was not available for convertible models. If no radio was selected, a corresponding trim piece was installed in its place.

Instrumentation for the 1964 GTO, like the Tempest and LeMans, was stylish, with four large, round gauge pods, each serving distinct functions. Occupying the pod farthest to the left were simple battery voltage and oil pressure warning lights. To the right of that was the 120-mph speedometer with the fuel gauge and temperature warning light residing in the next pod. These warning lights did not supply nearly as much information as full gauges, only illuminating when the engine was perilously close to complete failure. Many 1964 GTO owners added aftermarket units to more closely monitor engine parameters and provide some level of reassurance while driving. Pontiac recognized this, and a Rally gauge set, including a tachometer, oil pressure, and coolant temperature gauges, was made available for the 1965 model year.

The far-right gauge pod came standard with a decorative block-off plate. If the clock or tachometer was checked off on the option list, it would occupy this space; therefore, the buyer would have to choose one or the other. The factory-issued tachometer was afflicted with visibility and accuracy issues, and many owners sought out aftermarket units to better observe the engine RPM. In addition, a console-mounted vacuum gauge could be specified. (Some sources suggest the vacuum gauge was a dealer-only option.) Although it is functional and coveted by today's collector, it wasn't the type of instrument demanded by the diehard enthusiast.

Driveline

The engine is the heart of any automobile, but this is especially true with a high-performance car such as the GTO. Pontiac's overhead valve V-8 engine dates to 1955, when it debuted as a 287-ci powerplant. Dubbed the Strato-Streak, the 2-barrel engine produced 173 hp; a 4-barrel version soon followed that developed 200 hp. Using a 3.75-inch bore and a 3.25-inch stroke, the design of the Pontiac 287 ci allowed engineers to increase displacement in future engines while retaining the same basic layout and exterior dimensions. This critical element is what eventually allowed the Pontiac team to seamlessly install a 389-ci engine into a 1964 Tempest where a 326 ci typically resided.

For 1956, Pontiac's V-8 was enlarged to 317 ci and rated at 205 hp. A special high-performance package was made available mid-year. It featured a higher compression ratio, two 4-barrel carburetors, and a distinct camshaft profile; this combination generated an impressive 285 hp. The 317 ci jumped to 347 ci in 1957 and delivered 227 hp in base trim. The optional Tri-Power induction system also debuted in 1957, using three 2-barrel carburetors and producing 290 hp.

Based on the 1958 370-ci engine, the Pontiac 389-ci engine debuted in 1959 and displayed a 4.0625-inch bore and a 3.75-inch stroke. Throughout the early 1960s, Pontiac continually improved the engine's performance characteristics, refining the cylinder head and camshaft design. For the 1964 GTO, engineers made further upgrades to transform the 389-ci into the ideal engine for Pontiac's new car and ignite the muscle car phenomenon.

Like other cars from the era, the 389-ci engine in the 1964 GTO employed a cast-iron engine block. An Arma-Steel crankshaft was fitted to the block that used 3-inch mains secured by two-bolt main bearing caps. Connecting rods measured 6.625 inches and were also constructed from Arma-Steel. Although technically not steel, Arma-Steel is GM's trade name for a type of durable cast iron that was used in numerous applications for many years. Standard cast-aluminum pistons were dependable in all but the most punishing conditions. However, Pontiac's Super Duty engines employed forged aluminum pistons for the added durability required by racing applications.

An efficient cylinder head design is paramount for achieving top performance. Pontiac engineers chose casting number 9770716 (often referred to as 716) cylinder heads for the 389-ci engine in the 1964 GTO. These

Pontiac used casting number 9770716 cylinder heads on the 389-ci engine in the 1964 GTO. These were the same pieces used on the 421 HO engine installed in some of Pontiac's full-size performance cars. The casting number is located on the two center exhaust ports, making them easy to identify.

Pontiac's 389-ci powerplant debuted in 1959 when it supplanted the previous year's 370-ci engine. Output for the 1964 GTO was 325 hp for 4-barrel and 348 hp for Tri-Power cars. The lack of a fan shroud is correct for non–air-conditioned 1964 GTOs. (Photo Courtesy Jim Mott)

This low-mileage 1964 GTO was professionally restored using nearly all of its original components and is a stellar example of a factory-spec engine compartment. Some Pontiac enthusiasts opine that the master cylinder should be cast-iron gray; however, an inspection of photos from articles in both the January 1964 issue of Motor Trend and the June 1964 issue of Car Life showed that both test cars clearly displayed black-painted master cylinders. (Photo Courtesy Jim Mott)

A Carter 500-cfm carburetor atop a cast-iron dual-plane intake manifold was the standard induction system for the 1964 GTO. Many Pontiac enthusiasts choose to install the Tri-Power setup on their cars, even if it's not factory-correct; therefore, locating a 1964 model with its original 4-barrel can be quite challenging.

The chrome-plated air cleaner was unique to the 4-barrel-equipped 1964 models. It showcased a large, single snorkel design that fed air directly to the Carter carburetor. Driven regularly, this GTO displays a few deviations from stock, most notably the dual-reservoir master cylinder.

were the same components used on the 421 HO engines that were available in some of Pontiac's full-size performance cars and featured 1.92-inch intake and 1.66-inch exhaust valves, as opposed to the smaller 1.88-inch and 1.60-inch valves found in Pontiac's lower-performing V-8 engines. These heads also contained larger intake and exhaust ports than the standard 389-ci engines, which, combined with the larger valves, allowed for more air and fuel, resulting in additional power. The 68-cc combustion chamber of these cylinder heads, along with the flattop pistons, yielded a compression ratio of 10.75:1.

The camshaft is another critical component in a performance engine and can perhaps be thought of as the engine's "brain." It operates the valves, and it controls how *long* they stay open (known as duration) and how *far* they open (known as valve lift). Camshaft profile greatly affects horsepower, torque, and the engine's RPM potential. The camshaft design or timing can affect idle quality and fuel economy dramatically. The engineers at Pontiac fitted the GTO's 389-ci with a hydraulic lifter cam, displaying 273/289 degrees duration and .407-inch valve lift (some sources list .410/.413) when used with the factory-issued 1.5:1 rocker arms.

The hydraulic lifters used in the 1964 GTO were an improvement over the units installed in standard 389-ci engines. These lifters showcased a unique internal design that consisted of a small check valve, which, when combined with the heavy-duty valve springs, increased the engine's high-RPM capability. However, research suggests

that the 389-ci engines for use in the GTO built prior to mid-November 1963 may not have been equipped with the heavy-duty valve springs, although all GTO engines produced after November 1963 did receive the stiffer valve springs. In addition, Pontiac V-8 engines equipped with the 9770716 cylinder heads used an oiling system that employed hollow pushrods and redesigned rocker arms to provide oil to the upper part of the valvetrain. The previous design, including other 1964 Pontiac V-8 engines, used hollow rocker arm studs that made them prone to failure in high-horsepower applications. Beginning in 1965, Pontiac adopted the new oiling system throughout its engine lineup, eliminating the hollow rocker arm studs.

The standard induction system on the 1964 GTO consisted of a single 500-cfm Carter AFB 4-barrel carburetor mounted on a dual-plane cast-iron intake manifold. The Carter AFB featured 1.438-inch primary and slightly larger 1.688-inch secondary throttle bores, and while it performed admirably, some Pontiac enthusiasts felt that the Carter carburetor was too small for the GTO's large, powerful 389-ci engine. The 4-barrel–equipped GTOs were topped with a chrome plated single-snorkel air cleaner exclusive to the 1964 model. Factory-issued chrome valve covers complemented the air cleaner and provided the owner with yet another reason to show off the engine. In fact, chrome valve covers were standard on all GTOs through the 1970 model year; engine-color pieces replaced them for 1971–1974.

A Delco single-point distributor was standard issue in 1964 for both the 4-barrel and Tri-Power engines. The ignition coil was mounted at the rear of the passenger-side cylinder head. Notice the pitting on certain components. This is not the result of harsh Northeast winters, but rather a close proximity to the Atlantic Ocean in South Florida.

Casting number 9775088 is the correct Tri-Power intake manifold for the 1964 GTO; it's located between the center and rear carburetors. A dual-plane design, they are constructed from cast iron and are quite heavy.

A Delco single-point distributor, with a transistor ignition (code 671) was available as a $75.27 option. The transistor ignition was more reliable at high RPM, which provided a more complete burn of the combustible mixture, resulting in more horsepower. The spent fumes exited via cast-iron exhaust manifolds into a true dual system featuring 2.25-inch head pipes and 2-inch tail pipes. The dual exhaust was standard equipment for the GTO package and a $30.88 option for the 326-ci equipped Tempest and LeMans models. In addition

to increasing power, the muscular exhaust note emanating from the pipes was essential to the GTO's success. Chrome exhaust extensions (code 422) were a $21.30 option.

The standard combination (4-barrel) was rated at 325 hp and 428 ft-lbs of torque and the potent engine excited many writers in the automotive press. In the January 1964 issue of *Motor Trend* magazine, writer Bob McVay testified, "Our first and lasting impression of the Tempest (GTO) was one of more-than-adequate power . . . our first acceleration run left our photographer standing in a huge cloud of blue rubber smoke, looking at a long black strip on the pavement."

Tri-Power

Pontiac debuted its Tri-Power induction system in 1957 as a performance option for the 347-ci engine. It was available every year through 1966, when General Motors decided to eliminate multiple carburetion setups on everything except the Chevrolet Corvette. Interestingly, 1967 was the first year for the Tri-Power–equipped Corvette, which used Holley carburetors instead of the Rochester units found on GTOs.

The Tri-Power system for the 1964 GTO (code 809) was a $115.78 option and featured three Rochester 2-barrel carburetors mounted on a cast-iron dual-plane intake manifold. The two outboard carburetors were vacuum operated and opened at approximately two-thirds of wide-open throttle. Thanks to the additional air and fuel provided by the Tri-Power, horsepower increased from 325 to 348. Curiously, torque output is rated at 428 ft-lbs for both the 4-barrel and Tri-Power engines, although at slightly different revs: 3,200 rpm and 3,600 rpm, respectively.

The 1964 Tri-Power system was not without its peculiarities; under typical driving conditions, air and fuel were supplied solely by the center carburetor. However, when the vacuum signal reached a certain point, both outboard carburetors opened fully and the acceleration surged. In addition, because of the remaining vacuum in the lines, the outboard carburetors could stay open momentarily, even after lifting off the accelerator. These idiosyncrasies could create a white-knuckled driving expe-

The Tri-Power option consisted of three Rochester 2-barrel carburetors that increased the 389-ci engine's power from 325 hp to 348 hp. The outboard units were vacuum operated; it was quite a complex system. Late in 1964, mechanical linkage was made available over the counter at the dealer. Note: This engine is not installed, and a throttle cable is not present. (Photo Courtesy Jim Mott)

Passenger-side rear view of the photo above. Carburetors, linkage, air cleaners, distributor, and spark plug wires are all factory-correct. The blue-painted carburetor studs are another accurate detail. (Photo Courtesy Jim Mott)

rience for anyone unfamiliar with these characteristics.

Three 2-barrel carburetors also proved to be more difficult for novice mechanics to tune compared to the simplicity of the single 4-barrel. One former owner relates, "I had a 1964 GTO with a 4-barrel, and if I was racing a guy with a Tri-Power setup, I'd give him one car length at the starting line. They could run strong when they were set up properly, but not many guys knew how to do that. The 4-barrel carbs were much simpler and more consistent. I knew that my Carter carb was going to run the same way on every pass." Mechanical linkage became available late in the 1964 model year as an over-the-counter item; it provided a more controlled, linear

transition from part throttle to full throttle. Capable GTO owners could install the new linkage themselves or choose to have their local Pontiac dealership make the conversion.

Three small, chrome-plated air cleaners containing dark gray, foam filtration elements adorned the GTO's Tri-Power induction system. Although these air filters were more restrictive than some of the larger units that other manufacturers used, they provided a bit of exotic flair under the hood and greatly enhanced the GTO's racy image.

Pontiac produced 24,205 4-barrel and just 8,245 Tri-Power GTOs in 1964, thus making original Tri-Power-

A Cameo Ivory Sports Coupe gleams in the sun along Florida's coastline. The very attractive combination of Custom wheel covers, redline tires, and exhaust splitters led to 32,450 total GTOs produced for the 1964 model year.

equipped cars much more desirable to collectors. Many present-day GTO owners consider the Tri-Power induction system an integral part of the GTO's allure, and have superseded the factory-issued 4-barrel with a Tri-Power configuration. It's a common swap, even on restored examples, and uncovering a 1964 GTO with its original Carter 4-barrel carburetor can be quite a task.

In his book, *Muscle Car Color History: GTO 1964–1967*, respected Pontiac author Paul Zazarine commented on the visceral thrill of the Tri-Power induction system. He wrote, "Normal operation was with the center two-holer, but at approximately 70-percent throttle the two outer carbs would open and produce a banshee-like wail as the 389 wound out to produce 348 hp at 4,900 rpm. Under wide-open throttle, the GTO accelerated like a rocket. The driver held on to the wheel and it was all he could do to remember to watch the tach and power-shift through the gears."

Indeed, the 389-ci engine generated tremendous amounts of low- and mid-range power; this, combined with the GTO's relatively light weight, gave Pontiac Motor Division exactly what it needed: a hot new car that would keep the brand relevant in the high-performance arena, even without factory-supported race efforts.

Transmission Options

"Three deuces and a 4-speed, and a 389!" boasted the song, "G.T.O.", by Ronny and the Daytonas. Past and present gearheads understand that the engine is only one part of the equation in a performance car, and that transmission and rear-end hardware are vital to winning races, both on and off the track. Pontiac offered four transmission options in 1964, including the M21 close-ratio 4-speed that arrived later in the year. A Muncie 3-speed manual transmission was standard equipment and featured a 2.58:1 first gear, 1.48:1 second, and 1:1 third gear. Even though the 3-speed was adequate, many performance enthusiasts opted for the M20 wide-ratio 4-speed. The extra gear resulted in quicker acceleration, and, when negotiating curves, it allowed the driver to select a gear that would keep the engine near its peak power range. Gear ratios for the 4-speed were 2.56:1 in first, 1.91:1 in second, 1.48:1 in third, and 1:1 in fourth. All manual transmissions employed a heavy-duty clutch with a 10.4-inch diameter.

Another 4-speed manual transmission, the Muncie M21 close-ratio, was made available later in the 1964 model year. This transmission featured gear ratios of 2.20:1 in first, 1.64:1 in second, 1.25:1 in third, and 1:1 in fourth. Due to the late availability and complexities in

the ordering process, 1964 Pontiac GTOs factory issued with the M21 close-ratio are extremely rare and valuable.

For potential buyers who did not wish to do their own shifting, a 2-speed automatic transmission was offered. The Super Turbine 300 displayed a 1.76:1 first gear and a 1:1 second gear: it was better suited to leisurely cruising than spirited performance driving. The shifter was either mounted on the steering column or housed in the center console, if so equipped. The availability of an automatic transmission assured Pontiac that the GTO could appeal to a wide range of auto enthusiasts, from speed-obsessed gear heads to more casual Sunday drivers.

The Super Turbine 300 unit installed in the 1964 GTO did receive a few upgrades over the standard unit. A high-output governor raised the wide-open throttle upshift to 5,200 rpm, and the forward clutch pack had

The shifter for the 2-speed automatic transmission is located in the center console, if so equipped. Otherwise, it would be mounted on the steering column. A 3-speed automatic transmission was not offered for the GTO until the 1967 model year, when the TH-400 debuted.

six pairs of discs, compared with five for 326-ci powered Tempest and LeMans models. The torque converter's stall ratio was also adjusted to 2.2:1 for use behind the GTO's stout 389-ci engine, compared with a 2.5:1 ratio for the 326-ci equipped Tempest and LeMans.

The Super Turbine 300 was water-cooled, with cooling lines running to and from the radiator on the passenger's side. Because it was a GM 2-speed automatic transmission, many hobbyists wrongly assume that it was Chevrolet's Powerglide unit, when, in fact, there are very few similarities between the two components. The Super Turbine 300 is considered inferior to the 3-speed automatic transmissions that Ford and Chrysler offered at the time.

UNRAVELING A MYSTERY: THE M21 CLOSE-RATIO TRANSMISSIO

Respected 1964 GTO hobbyist John Viale has conducted countless hours of research to unravel a topic that, to many Pontiac enthusiasts, has remained shrouded in mystery. Viale's explanation follows:

"The speedometer drive gear (internal to the Muncie 4-speed) needed for all Tempest applications, including the GTO, was an eight-tooth piece, with the only exception being if the order called for the 3.90:1 axle ratio. In that case, the speedometer drive gear needed to be a six-tooth unit. Since the speedometer drive gear was part of the transmission assembly, Pontiac needed Muncie to produce two specific versions of the wide-ratio M20: one for use with all applications except the 3.90 axle and one for use with the 3.90 axle.

Pontiac assigned part number 9774825 to the transmission assembly needed for all applications except 3.90 axle with the transmission code W, derived from sales code 77W. Part number 9774826 was assigned to the transmission assembly needed for all applications with 3.90 axle along with transmission code 9, drawn from the sales code 779; this transmission was identical to the code W except for the internal speedometer drive gear. The buyer never specifically ordered this transmission; he or she simply ordered the 4-speed option. The selection of one or the other was simply a result of the axle ratio being installed.

The M21 close-ratio was not available at the beginning of GTO production and was first mentioned in the second version of the GTO sales brochure, dated April 17, 1964. It was assigned part number 9777000, with sales code 778 and transmission code 8. It featured a six-tooth internal speedometer drive gear, like the code 9 M20. Incidentally, the part numbers were embossed on a small metal tag and bolted to the sidecover.

To order the M21 transmission, Pontiac made several optional components mandatory, which contributed to its limited production. The GTO package, Tri-Power, and 3.90:1 axle all had to be specified. The additional features that normally accompanied the 3.90:1 axle were also required and included metallic brake linings, Safe-T-Track rear end, heavy-duty fan, and heavy-duty radiator. The buyer did not have to order the close-ratio M21 to get the 3.90 axle. Until the M21 was released, you could order the 3.90:1 and 4-speed and receive the code 9 wide-ratio M20. The buyer could still order it that way after the M21 became available.

Further complicating matters was the now-famous March 1964 *Car and Driver* article that claimed that the 4-speeds in the two GTOs tested were Muncie units, stating, "It had the new GM Muncie 4-speed transmission." The article listed the transmission gear ratios; they are not Muncie M21 ratios, but BorgWarner ratios. Whatever the reason for the misinformation, that article spurred numerous sales of 3.90:1 axle GTOs built in March. Many buyers thought they were getting a close-ratio M21 because of what they read in *Car and Driver*; instead they received the code 9 M20, as the M21 was yet to be released. Even today, many GTO enthusiasts believe that ordering the 3.90:1 axle ratio got you the close-ratio M21 (that, and the fact that PHS still claims the code 9 is a close-ratio based on the old, erroneous published material). Whenever the original transmissions have been studied, they have always been found to be part number 9774826, code 9, M20 wide-ratio units, exactly as Pontiac Motor Division intended them to be.

To date, no 1964 GTO is known to still exist that was built with the M21. Viale states, "I am aware of one, but the car is gone; however, the VIN-matched original transmission does still exist along with the original tattered window sticker for the car. As a Fremont build, the window sticker not only identifies the trans as an M21, but also lists the sales code 778. Fremont 1964 window stickers listed options by UPC (M21 is a UPC) and Sales Code (778 in this case)."

Thanks to Viale's comprehensive research, in conjunction with input from other notable 1964 GTO experts, this description of the coding and availability of the M21 close-ratio 4-speed transmission is the most detailed and current information available to the 1964 GTO enthusiast.

Hurst Shifter

A Hurst shifter came standard on all manual transmission GTOs, thanks in large part to Jim Wangers, who knew it would appeal to the serious performance enthusiast. In his book, *Glory Days: When Horsepower and Passion Ruled Detroit,* he stated, "Pontiac got the jump on the rest of the industry because of my personal relationship with George Hurst, which developed out of our mutual interest in drag racing. After having my race car converted, I said to George, 'What a shame that every Pontiac owner can't enjoy this kind of shifting.' I discussed it with DeLorean, and he invited me to bring George in for a talk. Together they worked out a profitable agreement that resulted in the Hurst shifter being offered as standard equipment on every Pontiac equipped with a manual transmission." For the GTO, this arrangement lasted through the 1972 model year, after which

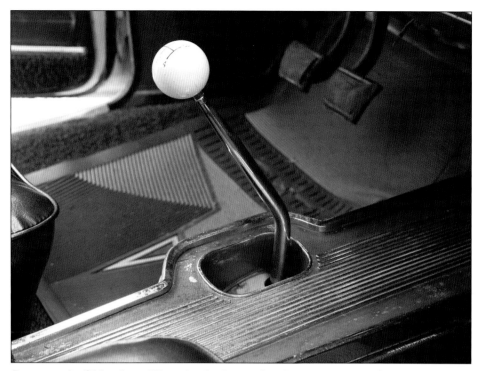

Because of a GM policy, shifters for the 3-speed and 4-speed manual transmissions did not display the Hurst name in 1964. This policy was revised for 1965 and later models when Jim Wangers conveyed that it would benefit Pontiac to allow the Hurst name on the units. A simple white ball displaying the shift pattern topped the shifter. This car is equipped with the optional center console (code 601).

Pontiac fitted Inland shifters in the 1973 and 1974 cars. At this point, America's muscle car obsession was on a downward trend, and the switch to the Inland shifter was likely a cost-cutting measure.

The shifter on the 1964 GTO is unique in the fact that it does not display the Hurst name. General Motors had a policy in place stating that any components (except tires) not manufactured by General Motors could not feature the supplier's name. Jim Wangers explained to Pete Estes that it would be beneficial to Pontiac to have the Hurst name on the shifter and the policy was revised starting with the 1965 models. The shifter was topped with a white, ball-type knob and the shift pattern engraved in black.

Rear Differential

The rear end of the 1964 models used an 8.2-inch diameter ring gear that contained an open differential as standard equipment. A 3.23:1 gear set was standard issue on 4-barrel cars and a 3.55:1 ratio was fitted when the Tri-Power option was specified. However, after January 1964, the Tri-Power cars received 3.23:1 gears, although the 3.55:1 gears remained as optional equipment. The 3.55:1 gear ratio was a good compromise between quick acceler-

The 10-bolt cover of Pontiac's 8.2-inch rear end displayed C-shaped notches in the nine o'clock and three o'clock positions. This example is equipped with the Safe-T-Track limited slip differential and the proper metal tag is affixed to the cover.

ation and highway drivability, and Pontiac reverted back to this gearing as standard issue for Tri-Power-equipped cars in 1965.

Rear-end gearing was available in 3.08:1 to 3.90:1 ratios from the factory, with 4.11:1 and 4.30:1 ratios available as dealer-installed items. The 4.11:1 and 4.30:1

Although probably best known for going fast in a straight line, Pontiac furnished the 1964 GTO with upgraded suspension components. Items such as firmer springs and shocks contributed greatly to better cornering and high-speed stability.

gear ratios empowered the car to accelerate much more quickly from an idle and were sought after by serious drag racers of the day. Disadvantages to such gears included poor fuel economy and, of more concern, very high RPM while driving at highway speeds; these put an enormous strain on engine and transmission components.

With the 389-ci doling out abundant amounts of power, attaining traction with an open differential was next to impossible. A Safe-T-Track limited-slip differential unit was offered as a performance option and was an essential piece of both drag and street racing hardware, as it effectively transferred power to both rear wheels, instead of just one, as is the case with an open differential. The 1964 Pontiac sales brochure stated the case quite well: "With 325-plus horsepower on tap, traction can be a sometime thing. We strongly recommend Safe-T-Track, our optional limited-slip differential." Even with the added benefit of the Safe-T-Track–equipped rear end, grip was still an issue with the factory-installed 7.50x14 tires, and long smoky burnouts became a trademark of GTO ownership.

Suspension and Braking Components

The GTO was much more than a Tempest with a high-powered engine, and the engineers at Pontiac outfitted the car with numerous handling upgrades. The December 1963 issue of *Hot Rod* magazine boasted, "GTO's suspension, designed for high road speeds and supplemented by the firmer shocks and fast steering, should make the car a natural for sports car rallies." Although the GTO is not typically thought of as a rally car, it was noticeably more agile and assertive in turns than the lower-priced Tempest models.

Unlike the unitized construction of previous years, the 1964 Pontiac Tempest was built around a full-perimeter frame, which it shared with the Oldsmobile Cutlass, Buick Skylark, and Chevrolet Chevelle. Although heavier, the full-frame construction increased chassis rigidity greatly and provided a solid foundation for mounting the various suspension components. This produced a much stronger car that fared better in most types of collisions. The full frame, combined with the redesigned suspension, gave the 1964 units a more stable ride with enhanced road feel, superior to that of earlier Tempest and LeMans models. This was also a far better configuration than the soon-to-be released Ford Mustang, which used the Ford Falcon's unitized construction and inferior suspension pieces.

Like the 1964 Tempest, the front suspension of the GTO was an A-arm type mounted with rubber bushings. Handling was further improved by using firmer coil springs and shocks that were standard equipment when the GTO option was specified. Likewise, the GTO came equipped with a large, .938-inch front sway bar, compared to the Tempest's .875-inch unit. Sway bars, or

The Saginaw steering gearbox for power steering–equipped 1964 GTOs displayed casting number 7826692 and featured a 17.5:1 ratio. Power steering (code 501) was a $96.84 option.

The available steering boxes on the GTO were Saginaw units that employed a recirculating ball-bearing steering gear. Ratios were 24:1 on manual steering cars and 17.5:1 when power steering was selected. A shock absorber for the steering linkage was optional for cars with manual steering and helped dampen vibrations to the steering wheel, delivering a smoother ride.

Handling Package

In addition to the GTO's already firm springs and shocks, an optional handling package could also be specified (code 612). This included stiffer shocks than the standard GTO units and a 20:1 steering gear ratio. The January 1964 issue of *Motor Trend* magazine revealed, "Our test car, the one with the stiffer suspension, had a just-about-right feeling under most driving conditions. Cornering felt stable without excessive body lean or understeer, the GTO's power steering gave us a good road feel yet was fairly quick and light in action; and the car didn't nose-dive or squat to any great extent during hard acceleration or braking." Critical praise such as this was vital for informing the prospective buyer that the GTO could do much more than go fast in a straight line.

"anti-sway bars," control lateral movement and increase vehicle stability, especially while cornering. Pontiac would not offer a rear sway bar on the GTO until the 1970 model.

The rear suspension configuration, again equivalent to the Tempest's, was a four-link type, with rubber bushings used to mount the upper and lower control arms. Like the front of the GTO, the rear received firmer springs and shocks. Air shocks were also available for the rear; dubbed the Superlift option, it was designed for towing rather than performance.

Braking System

A 4-wheel manual braking system, which featured 9.5-inch drums and a single-reservoir master cylinder, was standard equipment for the 1964 GTO. (Front disc brakes were not available until the 1967 model.) The

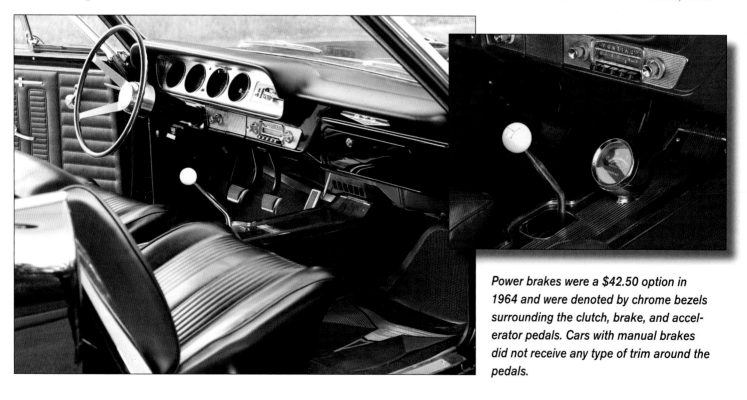

Power brakes were a $42.50 option in 1964 and were denoted by chrome bezels surrounding the clutch, brake, and accelerator pedals. Cars with manual brakes did not receive any type of trim around the pedals.

Detailed view of rear brake assembly. GTOs equipped with standard brake linings (shown) received different-colored springs than those optioned with metallic linings. Standard linings were riveted to the backing plates, while metallic versions were glued. (Photo Courtesy Jim Mott)

front brake shoes measured 2.5 inches wide, while the rears were 2 inches wide. The braking components of the 1964 GTO were the same pieces used on all Tempest and LeMans models, even the base model 6-cylinder Tempest. Power brakes were an available option for the GTO (code 502) and were denoted by chrome bezels surrounding the accelerator, brake, and clutch pedals (if so equipped).

An anomaly for the 1964 power-brake-equipped GTOs is the emergency brake pedal, which did not receive the chrome bezel trim, though this piece *was* included on 1965 and later models. While the power brake option did reduce the driver's pedal effort required to stop the car, it did not necessarily translate into shorter stopping distances.

Considering the high-speed situations that the car and its owner would likely find themselves in, some critics alleged the braking system to be the weakest aspect of the GTO. In the January 1964 issue of *Motor Trend* magazine, writer Bob McVay noted that the brakes "felt adequate during normal driving yet heated up and showed considerable fade after half a dozen high-speed stops, but recovered fairly quickly." Brake fade can occur after repeated or heavy use of the braking system and can ultimately lead to complete brake failure. Semi-metallic brake shoes were optional hardware and helped to reduce brake fade but they tended to be noisy and many new GTO owners chose the standard brake linings. Even the 1964 GTO sales brochure noted, "Metallic brake linings are available as a separate option with all axle ratios except 3.08:1 but are recommended only for extreme duty service since they have the usual metallic brake ailments of squeaks, grunts, and high pedal pressure when cold."

Even though they were common for the era, the single-reservoir master cylinder had one major drawback. In the event of a brake fluid leak at any point in the hydraulic system, all fluid could be lost, and complete brake failure would soon follow. To remedy this problem, a dual-reservoir master cylinder made its debut for the 1967 model year. This feature kept the front and rear braking systems isolated and allowed at least some braking ability in the event of a fluid leak. The dual-reservoir system was an important safety advancement, and all GTOs from 1967 onward used this arrangement.

This highly detailed 1964 GTO engine compartment highlights the power brake booster and black-painted single-reservoir master cylinder. A fan shroud is correct for cars equipped with air-conditioning. This car won Best of Show at the 2014 GTOAA Nationals. (Photo Courtesy Jim Mott)

Although simple in design, the standard hubcaps present the 1964 GTO with an understated muscular attitude. High-quality reproductions are now available for the hobbyist who wishes to return his or her car to original specifications. The standard hubcap design lasted through the 1971 model year.

Wheels and Tires

To further improve handling, the 1964 GTO came standard with 14x6 steel wheels (compared to 14x5 for the Tempest and LeMans) and displayed small hubcaps covering the center of the wheels. These hubcaps, frequently referred to as "poverty caps" or "dog dishes," presented the car with a simple, street-tough attitude. GTOs painted Yorktown Blue, Pinehurst Green, Singapore Gold, Gulfstream Aqua, and Saddle received color-keyed wheels when the standard hubcap was specified; all other exterior colors were adorned with Regent Black painted wheels.

Even though a styled steel wheel was not available for the 1964 GTO, there were four different wheel cover choices for the buyer. The appearance of the car could be altered considerably depending on which wheel covers were selected. (Some Pontiac literature refers to wheel covers as wheel discs.) The Deluxe wheel cover (code 462) featured 10 simulated spokes and covered the entire wheel. This understated piece was less aggressive in appearance than the standard hubcaps.

The more familiar Custom wheel cover (code 521) displayed eight cooling slots and a spinner center section. Stylish and highly detailed, Custom wheel covers are seen today on many 1964 GTOs, even if they were not factory equipped, as many current owners regard them as the best-looking of all choices for 1964. Seldom seen, and therefore highly sought after by collectors, are the wire wheel covers. These pieces gave the car a more elegant appearance, as opposed to the more muscular look of some of the other choices. Original sets of wire wheel covers in excellent condition often command more than $1,000.

U.S. Royal Super Safety 800 "Tiger Paw" redline tires featuring a 7.50-inch width and nylon cords were standard issue on the 1964

Deluxe wheel discs were a $15.60 option for the GTO, making them the least expensive wheel cover option in 1964. The Deluxe wheel discs were changed drastically in 1965, making the 1964 versions easily identifiable.

GTO, marking one of the first instances where redline tires were available on an American car. According to Coker Tire, American automobile manufacturers wanted a more aggressive looking tire to better complement the appearance of their new 1964 models, and the redline design was a perfect fit. Whitewall tires with rayon cords were also available on the 1964 GTO at no additional charge, and many GTO buyers opted for them. However, many current 1964 owners choose redline tires, Tri-Power induction, and 4-speed manual transmission, even if not factory issued, because this combination seems to epitomize a 1964 Pontiac GTO.

For enthusiasts who regularly drive their GTOs, companies such as Coker Tire and BFGoodrich now produce redline tires using modern radial technology in sizes compatible with original equipment wheels. These tires offer superior performance compared to the bias-ply construc-

tion of the originals while maintaining a classic appearance.

Despite a few shortcomings, the 1964 Pontiac GTO possessed the necessary hardware to be one of the best all-around performance cars of its time and it launched the muscle car era. An excerpt from the famed March 1964 issue of *Car and Driver* magazine asserted, "This car does what so many others only talk about; it really does combine brute, blasting performance with balance and stability of a superior nature."

Marketing the 1964 GTO

Choosing the GTO name itself was an audacious move by John DeLorean, as Ferrari was already using it on one of the most exotic and high-performing automobiles ever constructed: the Ferrari 250 GTO. In Italian, GTO means *Gran Turismo Omologato*, which translates to

A favorite within the Pontiac community, Custom wheel discs presently adorn many 1964 GTOs. Commonly referred to as "spinners" or "spinner hubcaps," they were a $35.50 option. This car is also fitted with modern radial redline tires.

U.S. Royal Super Safety 800 redline tires were standard issue on the 1964 GTO and featured a 7.50-inch width. Redline tires are now so closely associated with the model, many casual enthusiasts forget that whitewall tires were a popular, no-cost option.

Wire wheel covers (code 411) were a $69.40 option in 1964. These pieces, combined with the two-tone paint of this GTO, present the car with a decidedly upscale appearance. (Photo Courtesy Chris Phillip)

Amazingly, this Cameo Ivory convertible is still in the possession of its original owner. Driven regularly thanks to year-round cruising weather in South Florida, the owner was drawn to his GTO because he "wanted a powerful convertible with a 4-speed gear box." The M20 4-speed manual transmission added $188.30 to the price of the car.

Grand Touring Homologated. The name simply means that a manufacturer has produced at least 100 cars to compete in the Grand Touring class of international road racing. Interestingly, Ferrari did not produce enough of its GTOs to officially qualify for the Grand Touring series, but it circumvented the rule by numbering the chassis out of sequence, thereby giving the impression that more cars existed than actually did.

Another obstacle for DeLorean and his crew was that General Motors had a strict policy stating that no intermediate-size car could have an engine larger than 330 ci. The clever team at Pontiac was able to sidestep this regulation by offering the GTO as an option for the LeMans, and not as a separate model. Once again, DeLorean and Wangers pushed the boundaries of what could be accomplished within the tight framework of General Motors.

Arriving in October/November 1963, the GTO was a late addition to the 1964 Pontiac lineup. Because of the car's late arrival and the apprehensiveness of GM's upper management, initial advertising was modest, even restrained, when compared to what it eventually became.

In a dealer training film on the 1964 Tempest and LeMans series, the GTO is only given brief mention, and the narrator simply stated, "The styling and engineering features of this option result in the finest rally-type American production car available." Many details of the GTO were not disclosed, and the overall emphasis appeared to be merely informing salesmen of the available body configurations for the 1964 model year, not the performance characteristics of the new GTO option.

Another dealer instructional film for the 1964 Pontiacs went into great detail on the new Tempest and LeMans models, even touting the performance of the 280-hp 326-ci V-8 engine. However, the GTO was conspicuously absent. This was likely because the film was produced in early to mid-1963 while the GTO was still in the development and planning stages. It's interesting to note that Pontiac emphasized a smooth and quiet ride quality. This theme was repeated throughout the duration of the film, with the narrator stating, "The Pontiac is not just a little bit quieter and smoother than other makes, it's very noticeably quieter and easier riding." These are two aspects that the performance-minded enthusiast perhaps would not consider to be positive characteristics.

Pontiac first used the tiger theme in advertisements for the 1963 Tempest. One print piece depicted two cars, one with the 4-cylinder engine and the other with the new 260-hp 326-ci V-8. It stated, "Can you tell which Tempest is the tiger?" Another print advertisement for the 1963 Tempest features four young people in a Tempest convertible accompanied by four action photos with a layout quite similar to the GTO ads that soon followed. The text is aggressive, challenging the potential buyer to "turn on a Tempest and make off with all the fun."

A device for shrinking time and distance
Pontiac GTO

The now-famous 1964 GTO sales brochure boasted the brilliant tag line, "A device for shrinking time and distance." A second version, dated April 17, 1964, was issued to reflect the availability of the M21 close-ratio 4-speed transmission. (Photo Courtesy GM Media Archive)

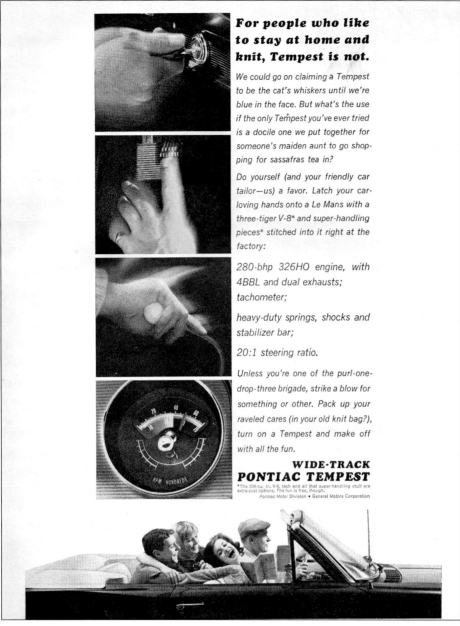

For people who like to stay at home and knit, Tempest is not.

We could go on claiming a Tempest to be the cat's whiskers until we're blue in the face. But what's the use if the only Tempest you've ever tried is a docile one we put together for someone's maiden aunt to go shopping for sassafras tea in?

Do yourself (and your friendly car tailor—us) a favor. Latch your car-loving hands onto a Le Mans with a three-tiger V-8* and super-handling pieces* stitched into it right at the factory:

280-bhp 326HO engine, with 4BBL and dual exhausts; tachometer;

heavy-duty springs, shocks and stabilizer bar;

20:1 steering ratio.

Unless you're one of the purl-one-drop-three brigade, strike a blow for something or other. Pack up your raveled cares (in your old knit bag?), turn on a Tempest and make off with all the fun.

WIDE-TRACK PONTIAC TEMPEST

*The 326-cu. in. V-8, tach and all that super-handling stuff are extra-cost options. The fun is free, though.
Pontiac Motor Division • General Motors Corporation

Pontiac had begun using the tiger theme in 1963 to advertise the 280-hp 326 HO Tempest, which was called a "three-tiger V-8." The tiger motif carried over to the soon-to-be-released GTO and remains popular to this day.

Esso brand gasoline and Uniroyal Tires were also using tiger imagery to promote their products, with Esso declaring, "Put a tiger in your tank!" In Jim Wangers's book, *Glory Days*, he recalls, "When U.S. Royal [Uniroyal] approached us about using their new 'Tiger Paw' on every new GTO, the opportunity for an advertising tie-in was a natural. We had already considered using the tiger theme for the GTO, since it had been used in some 1963 Tempest/LeMans advertising." Some Pontiac historians opine that the Tiger Paw tires were chosen at least partially for their ability to spin and produce clouds of tire smoke

quickly, further portraying the GTO as an untamable street beast. That theory was echoed by Wangers himself in a 2003 interview for the television show, *American Muscle Car*. "One of the things we used to laugh about is, if we wanted to burn rubber for an effect in an ad, all we had to do is just get a Uniroyal Tiger Paw and start burning rubber and you could burn til infinity. You know, it would never stop, until you let off," he said. Due to the large amount of horsepower and torque put down by the 389-ci engine, it's safe to say that tires produced by any manufacturer from this era (except dedicated drag slicks) would also "burn til infinity."

With limited time and resources, Jim Wangers suggested early GTO advertisements be placed in automotive magazines such as *Hot Rod* and *Car Craft*, figuring Pontiac could directly reach the type of potential buyer for whom the GTO was built without raising too many eyebrows at the top executive level. Wangers recalls, "I always seemed to be fighting an uphill battle with upper management, they seemed to be afraid of what we wanted to do, it was all so new to them. It's amazing we got anything past them."

One clever print ad from this period bragged, "GTO is for kicking up the kind of storm that others just talk up." It featured various photos of gear slamming and spinning tires accompanied by text that simply listed the standard and optional performance equipment. It was a perfect example of what Wangers and the rest of Pontiac's marketing team were trying to accomplish, promoting the GTO directly to the performance-minded car buyer within the constraints set by the conservative upper management at General Motors.

Another early print ad for the GTO depicts its various performance components and a photo of the car at speed with the line, "For the man who wouldn't mind riding a tiger if someone'd only put wheels on it: Pontiac GTO." It was one of the first instances of the tiger

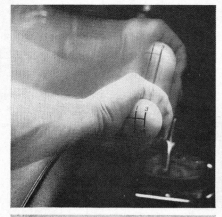

GTO is for kicking up the kind of storm that others just talk up.

Standard Equipment: engine: 389-cu. in. Pontiac with 1-4BBL; bhp—325 @ 4800; torque—428 lb-ft @ 3200 rpm/dual-exhaust system/3-speed stick with Hurst shifter/heavy-duty clutch/heavy-duty springs, shocks, stabilizer bar/special 7.50 x 14 red-line high-speed nylon cord tires (rayon cord whitewalls optional at no extra cost)/14 x 6JK wide-rim wheels/high-capacity radiator / declutching fan / high-capacity battery (66 plate, 61 amp. hr.)/chromed air cleaner, rocker covers, oil filler cap/bucket seats/standard axle ratio 3.23:1 (3.08, 3.36*, 3.55* to 1 available on special order at no extra cost). **And some of our extra-cost Performance Options:** engine: 389-cu. in. Pontiac with 3-2BBL (Code #809); bhp—348 @ 4900; *Available only with heavy-duty options at slight additional charge.

torque—428 lb-ft @ 3600; 3.55:1 axle ratio standard with this engine option/4-speed with Hurst shifter (gear ratios 2.56:1, 1.91:1, 1.48:1, 1.00:1, and 2.64:1 reverse)/2-speed automatic with 2.20:1 torque converter/Safe-T-Track limited-slip differential (Code #701)/3.90:1 axle ratio available on special order with metallic brake linings, heavy-duty radiator and Safe-T-Track/handling kit—20:1 quick steering and extra-firm-control heavy-duty shocks (Code #612)/high-performance full transistor (breakerless) ignition (Code #671)/tachometer (Code #452)/custom sports steering wheel (Code #524)/exhaust splitters (Dealer installed)/wire wheel discs (Dealer installed)/custom wheel discs, with spinner and brake cooling holes (Code #521)/console (Code #601).

the GTO makers—Pontiac

PONTIAC MOTOR DIVISION • GENERAL MOTORS CORPORATION

Print ad for the 1964 GTO touting its performance hardware accompanied by exciting action photography, a formula that Pontiac employed successfully until the 1967 model year when General Motors placed a renewed emphasis on safety and curtailed the use of aggressive action photography.

theme being used to promote the GTO. Tiger imagery ultimately became synonymous with the car, and various promotional items such as tiger tails and license plates were made available to the Pontiac enthusiast.

The now famous issue of *Car and Driver* magazine from March 1964 depicted a Pontiac GTO in hot pursuit of the Ferrari 250 GTO, with a line that read: "Tempest GTO: 0 to 100 in 11.8 seconds." Wangers envisioned a head-to-head duel between the Pontiac and Ferrari GTOs, whereby a winner would be crowned following a series of

performance tests in Daytona Beach, Florida. In *Glory Days,* Wangers stated, "One of the best promotions we ever put together was our first one, with *Car and Driver* magazine. . . . We agreed to supply two Pontiac GTOs, one a stock Sports Coupe with standard suspension, a 348-hp Tri-Power engine, a wide-ratio 4-speed gearbox, and a limited slip 3.55:1 rear end. . . . The second GTO, which became known as the 'red car' since it was painted Grenadier Red, also had the 348 Tri-Power engine, but used a close-ratio 4-speed, and a 3.90:1 limited slip rear end."

Even though a Ferrari GTO never actually participated in the experiment, it still proved to be a triumph for Wangers, as both Pontiacs performed admirably and the "red car" absolutely stunned the editors from *Car and Driver* with its brute force. Acceleration tests were measured by simple stopwatches, which left a lot of room for operator error, and many automotive critics suspected that the results of the *Car and Driver* tests could not possibly be accurate, or that there was more than a well-tuned 389-ci engine under the hood of the red GTO. In *Glory Days,* Wangers confessed, "I'm here to admit that more than three decades after the fact, that yes, I did install a 421 HO Tri-Power engine in the red Royal Bobcat *Car and Driver* test car," confirming what many enthusiasts had long believed.

In April 1984, *Car and Driver* magazine revisited its original concept, this time finding two willing 1964 GTO owners, one Pontiac and one Ferrari, to participate in the comparison tests. The Pontiac was a convertible model equipped with the 348-hp Tri-Power engine backed by a 4-speed manual transmission but did not include power steering or power brakes. The Ferrari, not surprisingly, was much more race ready than its Pontiac counterpart, displaying a 3.0-liter 12-cylinder engine with single overhead cams, six Weber carburetors, and a dry sump oiling system. The car was also

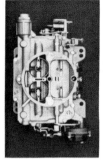

From early on, Jim Wangers and his team created specific, aggressive print advertisements for the GTO. Featured in publications such as Hot Rod magazine, the ads directly targeted the speed-obsessed youth market and contributed greatly to the car's street-tough image. (Photo Courtesy GM Media Archive)

For the man who wouldn't mind riding a tiger if someone'd only put wheels on it—Pontiac GTO

This piece of machinery is something our Engineering Department slipped a motherly big Pontiac 389-incher into and named the GTO.

It comes in hardtop, sports coupe and convertible form, based on the Le Mans—only sleekened down some and fitted with a special set of red-circle high-performance tires.

The looks you can see for yourself. The big deal is under the hood: 325 bhp at 4800 rpm and 428 lb-ft of torque at 3200 rpm. That's just the standard 4BBL engine. There's also a version with 348 bhp* at 4900 rpm and 428 lb-ft of torque at 3600 rpm.
*optional at extra cost.

This one does deep-breathing exercises through a 3-2BBL setup. Both make bad-tempered noises through dual pipes. As illustrated above, pairs of exhaust splitters on each flank, just behind the rear wheels, are available dealer installed*.

A 3-speed transmission is standard, stirred by a Hurst shifter on the floor. Extra-cost variations include an automatic with shift on the column . . . an all-synchro 4-speed on the floor . . . or a choice of any one of them sprouting out of a console.

Give yourself a blast of tonic. Sample one of these here big pussycats.   PONTIAC MOTOR DIVISON ● GENERAL MOTORS CORPORATION

Tempest Ad No. T64-1030
1 page—7 x 10 inches—B&W
Motor Trend—December, 1963
Car Life—December, 1963
Hot Rod—December, 1963
Car & Driver—December, 1963
Road & Track—December, 1963
(A) Mechanix Illustrated—December, 1963
(A) Popular Science Monthly—December, 1963
(A) Popular Mechanics—December, 1963
MacMANUS, JOHN & ADAMS, Inc.
26817—W-F—9-26-63 (00)

fitted with Dunlop disc brakes and a 5-speed manual transmission. For safety and comparison reasons, both cars were shod with Michelin XWX radial tires. Legendary race car driver Dan Gurney put both GTOs through their paces at the Laguna Seca road course in Salinas, California. (Note: the article cites track length at 1.9 miles while the Laguna Seca Raceway website states 2.238 miles.)

Gurney first got behind the wheel of the renowned Ferrari and put down a best time of 1:20.5 with an average speed of 85 mph. After his laps in the Italian-spec GTO, Gurney stated, "You can tell it's a race car, something meant to be driven hard. It will rev to eight [8,000 rpm] with ease. It feels smooth as the dickens most of the time, but occasionally the carburetors aren't giving it what it wants."

Next, Gurney took the Pontiac around the course and managed a best time of 1:28.1 with an average speed of 78 mph. Because this Pontiac retained its factory configuration (no Royal Bobcat trickery), it was almost 8 seconds slower than the Ferrari. Gurney said, "It feels like an aircraft carrier. You start it turning, and this great big long polar-moment deal takes over. It does everything all right; it's just sort of pendulous and heavy. The progressive throttle linkage is something you have to dial into." This certainly wasn't the type of fervent acclaim that Jim Wangers and the rest of Pontiac Motor Division received in the March 1964 article, but it did represent

A common sight in the 1960s as well as today, a novelty tiger tail hanging from the rear of this 1964 model showcases how deeply the tiger theme permeated the Pontiac market.

a much more accurate portrayal of the capabilities of each car. Even so, the Pontiac impressed the magazine editors when they took it out for some hot laps; they relayed, "During our turn on the track, we're surprised by the feeling of sheer fortitude in the Pontiac. It's too big and heavy for this duty, but this car has guts. The Hurst shifter and the Muncie four-speed are pure magic.

The chassis feels particularly unflappable, ready to soak up the massive torque from the engine, the firm pull of the brakes, and the impressive cornering forces of the Michelin XWXs."

The article ends with a nostalgic epilogue by David E. Davis Jr., citing that *Car and Driver* became a "real grown-up magazine" with the March 1964 issue. Davis went on

Taken at Lime Rock Park in Lakeville, Connecticut, the famous Royal Bobcat GTO from the March 1964 issue of Car and Driver magazine stands proudly next to a Ferrari of the same name. (Photo Courtesy Don Keefe)

Long after automotive critics surmised that there was much more than a "tuned" 389 ci between the fenders of the Grenadier Red GTO, Jim Wangers admitted in his book Glory Days that there was, in fact, a 421 HO under the hood. Soon after the Car and Driver tests, Milt Schornack fabricated a cowl-style Ram Air system and installed large diameter headers. (Photo Courtesy Don Keefe)

Yorktown Blue (code F) was only available for the 1964 model year; it contrasts well with the black interior of this GTO convertible. Redline tires, Custom wheel covers, and chrome exhaust extensions add an upscale flavor to the car.

Although it's a factory-issued hue, Sunfire Red (code N) is a magnificent, vibrant color not commonly seen on GTOs. The brilliant paint combined with standard hubcaps, redline tires, and lack of exhaust splitters, results in a unique appearance. Regent Black wheels are correct for this car. (Photo Courtesy Rich Cummings)

to say, "We owe a great debt to Jim Wangers and his Pontiac GTO." This simple statement is proof that the Pontiac GTO had far-reaching effects, perhaps even more so than those individuals directly involved could have imagined.

Pontiac's performance advertising soon began to include the full-size models within the brand, building upon the early success of the GTO. One such ad from 1964 displayed a photo of an empty garage at night with the line, "There's a tiger loose in the streets." Pontiac must have been quite confident with the performance image it had cultivated to that point, as there was no photo of the car or its components, which only added to the mystique of the piece. The text described an exciting late-night drive and ended with, "Have you tried one of our 421s?"

The GTO was rapidly becoming a cultural sensation, and well-known rock and roll acts were soon writing songs about Pontiac's hot new car. Surf-rock band Ronny and the Daytonas scored a number-four hit with their song, "G.T.O." Released in January 1964, it featured lyrics such as, "Three deuces and a four speed, and a 389. Listen to her tachin' up now, listen to her whine. Come on and turn it on, wind it up, blow it out, GTO!" Set to an energetic rhythm and showcasing soaring vocals, it was the perfect song to further hype Pontiac's new performance model. Similarly, popular surf-rock duo Jan and Dean released "My Mighty GTO" in June 1964, which bragged, "On the way to the strip, ya know she shows lots of style, but nobody takes her in the quarter-mile. With three pots on the manifold and louvers in the hood, and the competition steering wheel is made outta wood." These musical tributes highlighted the fact that the GTO was much more than just another car; it was an attitude, part of an all-encompassing lifestyle that set it apart from other performance cars of the era.

Proud 1964 GTO owner Andre Rayman relates, "The 1964 Pontiac A-body was one of the first cars of the modern era. It was a combination of the full-size Pontiacs and the smaller, trans-axle midsize cars of earlier years. By combining the best attributes of its predecessors, this intermediate was powerful and nimble, yet could be optioned to be as luxurious as the owner desired." Rayman goes on to state what most people in the classic car hobby can agree upon, no matter where their brand loyalty lies, "It is rightfully considered the first muscle car, and a legend in American automotive history."

General Motors initially projected that just 5,000 1964 GTOs would be sold, but total production for 1964 resulted in 32,450 units, proving that DeLorean and Wangers had their fingers on the pulse of the young car-buying public. The advertising campaign for the Pontiac GTO eventually became enthusiastic and hard-hitting, portraying the car as a powerful and desirable machine craved by the trendsetting youth of America. It's interesting to note that the early success for the 1964 GTO was achieved without the aid of television advertisements, the first being for the 1965 models.

From late 1964 to 1970, the various advertising campaigns for the Pontiac GTO, along with inclusions in television, movies, and popular music, became some of the most memorable in automotive history. Such promotions greatly enhanced the youth-oriented image that was being cultivated by the creative experts within Pontiac Motor Division.

The January 1964 issue of *Motor Trend* magazine summed up the 1964 GTO very well, proclaiming; "Our GTO Tempest was quite a car. Not only did it have gobs of brute horsepower, but it looked well-built and had a luxurious, comfortable all vinyl interior. In addition, it rode and handled like a high-performance car should. It was controllable and gave us a feeling of safety under most conditions, although it would require special care and handling when the road's wet or icy."

A Cameo Ivory (code C) 1964 hardtop appears ready for action against the industrial background. The profile of the inaugural year GTO has endured as one of the most iconic and favorite designs of all machines from the muscle car era.

CHAPTER THREE

1965 GTO More Horsepower, More Star Power, and More Tri-Power

Pontiac sold 32,450 GTOs in the car's inaugural year, easily surpassing the 5,000-mark predicted by GM's management. It was evident that John DeLorean and his team had engineered a winning formula: fitting a large, powerful V-8 engine into a midsize chassis and executing a hard-hitting, enthusiastic promotional campaign.

Sales literature for the second year borrowed heavily from the print advertisements created for the 1964 model: cars in motion, burning rubber, and gear jamming were highlighted alongside technical details such as horsepower ratings and performance options. They clearly demonstrated that Pontiac management was no longer reticent about advertising the GTO. The 1965 brochure proudly boasted, "Ever wondered what it feels like to be shot from a cannon? The GTO comes in three models—the Hardtop, the Sports Coupe, and the Convertible. Both engines for it are 389-cubic inchers, the standard one putting out 335 hp and the high-performance one 360 hp." It was a marketing recipe that Pontiac Motor Division refined endlessly and perfected until the muscle car phenomenon reached its zenith in 1970. Even as American performance cars were declining in popularity in the 1970s and 1980s, Pontiac continued to employ exciting, relevant advertisements for its new models, particularly the Trans Am and Fiero, with great success.

For the 1965 GTO, mechanical improvements generated more horsepower from both the 4-barrel and Tri-Power-equipped 389-ci engines, and transmission choices

The 1965 Pontiac GTO built upon the success of the 1964 model. However, thoughtful exterior refinements and greater power made it more exciting than the previous year's offering. The 1965 version is beloved by scores of enthusiasts worldwide and is often considered the epitome of Pontiac style and performance.

expanded to include a fully synchronized 3-speed manual unit manufactured by Ford Motor Company (Dearborn). The 1965 model was more powerful and, to many enthusiasts, a more exciting overall package than the 1964 version.

In *Glory Days*, Wangers recalled, "For the GTO, all the things that should have been done to the 1964 car, were done to the 1965. These included new front and rear styling, [optional] full instrumentation, a new camshaft, better cylinder heads, a new intake manifold, and a little more sophistication in the suspension. We also

introduced a new styled wheel just for the A-body cars, called the Rally Wheel. The GTO however, was still sold as an option, only available on the LeMans."

Indeed, it was these enhancements that led many Pontiac aficionados to opine that the 1965 model was, and still is, the epitome of a GTO. An article by Richard Lentinello that appeared in the August 2004 issue of *Hemmings Muscle Machines* echoed Jim Wangers's assessment of the 1965 GTO: "Sleek styling. Compact proportions. And just plain handsome good looks. These are

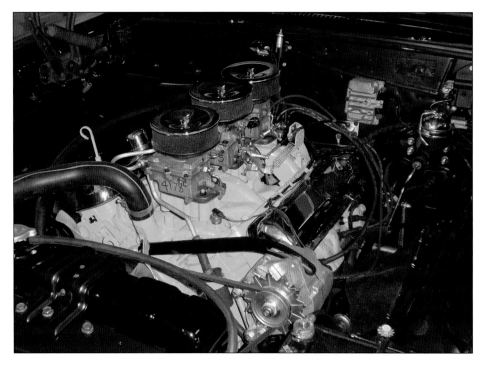

The 1965 389-ci Tri-Power engine produced 360 hp. Mechanical linkage is correct for 4-speed cars (shown); automatic transmission GTOs retained vacuum-operated setup. Note the optional transistorized voltage regulator. (Photo Courtesy Jim Mott)

The stacked headlight design was a new feature for the GTO in 1965, but it had been used on Pontiac's big cars since 1963. The GTO would keep this arrangement until the 1968 model.

Perhaps sensing a trend in automotive styling, other manufacturers began to implement the vertical headlight layout. The front-end treatment of the 1965 Ford Galaxie was clearly similar to the Pontiac design.

just a few of the hallmark characteristics that identify Pontiac's GTO for 1965. In fact, if you poll GTO owners, or even muscle car fans in general, chances are the 1965 GTO would top everyone's list." Lentinello added, "When Pontiac stylists redesigned the GTO's front end with stacked quad headlamps for the 1965 model year, they created an instant classic."

Rival manufacturers were well aware of the impact of the GTO (and larger performance models such as the 2+2) on the car buying public, and the market was soon flooded with stylish full- and intermediate-size cars fitted with large-displacement high-horsepower engines. Ford Motor Company took a page from Pontiac's automotive styling book when it adopted a stacked headlight configuration for its 1965 full-size Galaxie, a feature that Pontiac had used with great success since 1963. The 1965 Galaxie (available in many configurations, including two-door, four-door, station wagon, and convertible) proved to be a strong seller for Ford, with 420,379 units produced for the model year. This clearly demonstrated the powerful influence of the Pontiac design team on the American automotive industry. The following year, Ford restyled the Fairlane model in a similar fashion and installed a 390-ci engine rated at 335 hp. The Fairlane GT, which was considered direct competition for the GTO and represented one of many manufacturers' attempts to cut into GTO sales, sold 37,342 units in 1966.

Pontiac seized this momentum and redesigned the entire lineup for 1965. The wheelbase on full-size models grew 1 inch, and overall length increased 1.5 inches. The cars wore completely new sheet metal, and the "Coke-bottle" shape from the previous two years was accentuated further, resulting in a very sleek and sexy appearance. In past years, full-size cars fitted with large-displacement high-horsepower engines were the only Pontiac offerings available to car buyers seeking maximum performance, but the success of the GTO reconfigured the entire lineup, and the GTO soon became the top choice. Pontiac author and historian Don Keefe commented on this change in his book, *Grand Prix: Pontiac's Luxury Performance Car*, stating, "The GP was becoming a bit more patrician, and for the first time, could even be ordered with a bench seat in place of the buckets and console.

"The truth be told, Pontiac's performance image was being carried very capably by the GTO and 2+2. There quite simply wasn't any tangible need to position the car as a pavement burner, although it certainly could be if the proper option boxes were checked." The mid-1960s would prove to be one of the most prosperous eras in the history of Pontiac Motor Division. The second-year GTO impressed both the buying public and automotive press, with *Motor Trend* magazine giving its Car of the Year award to the entire 1965 Pontiac lineup, stating, "This year, 1965, will be another banner sales year for

Body

The 1964 full-size lineup had been an enormous success for the brand, with 480,135 Catalina, Star Chief, Bonneville, and Grand Prix models sold that year. The redesigned 1964 Tempest series also boasted higher production than previous years, moving 235,126 units, including the GTO. Together, they yielded Pontiac's best sales results to date: an impressive 715,261 new cars. Notably, the Tiger theme, in conjunction with the effective wide-track marketing hook, helped Pontiac appeal to a much younger and impassioned audience. As a result, by 1965, Pontiac Motor Division was regarded as a leading American automotive manufacturer, combining style, innovation, and performance like no other.

Pontiac's use of the tiger theme to promote the GTO was so popular that it began to carry over to the full-size performance cars such as this 1965 2+2 model. The BIGGTO license plate reinforces this notion.

THE CHEVROLET CHEVELLE, OLDSMOBILE 4-4-2, AND BUICK GRAN SPORT

Some of the Pontiac GTO's greatest rivals came from other divisions within General Motors. Cars such as the Chevrolet Chevelle Malibu Super Sport, Oldsmobile 4-4-2, and Buick Gran Sport, all based on the same A-body platform as the Tempest/LeMans/GTO and sharing numerous chassis and suspension components, eventually competed for the coveted performance-minded youth demographic.

The stiffest competition from within the GM stable undoubtedly came from Chevrolet and its Malibu Super Sport. Presently, when muscle car enthusiasts conjure up images of a Malibu Super Sport, they envision a 396-ci big-block engine, 4-speed manual transmission, and rear-end gearing that could rotate Earth with a push of the accelerator pedal. However, during the first two years of production (1964 and 1965), the Super Sport series was much more appearance-focused than performance-oriented. The base engine for the 1964 Malibu Super Sport was a 194-ci inline-6 rated at 120 hp, with a 230-ci inline-6 producing 155 hp as optional equipment. Small-block 283-ci V-8 engines were available in 195-hp and 220-hp arrangements. These two engines were quite similar, except that the 220-hp version

featured a Rochester 4-barrel carburetor, recurved distributor, and dual exhausts. From inception in 1964, the Malibu Super Sport series included full instrumentation (oil pressure, coolant temperature, and ammeter gauges), features that were not available on the 1964 GTO and were only offered as optional equipment from 1965 onward.

For the first several months of the Malibu Super Sport's inaugural year, the 220-hp 283-ci engine was the most powerful offered, falling quite short of the 1964 GTO's 325-hp and 348-hp engines. Witnessing the success of the Pontiac GTO firsthand, Chevrolet's general manager Bunkie Knudsen knew that he and his team would need to offer a more powerful combination to remain competitive in the performance car segment. In March 1964, Malibu Super Sport buyers could opt for the 250-hp 327-ci engine, and a few months later, a 300-hp 327-ci engine became available. Because these engines were added so late in the model year, only 6,598 buyers opted for the 250-hp engine and a scant 1,737 performance enthusiasts received the 300-hp mill. Today, the low production numbers of the 250-hp and 300-hp 1964 Malibu Super Sports make them highly sought after by muscle car aficionados.

The 1964 Chevrolet Malibu and the 1955 Chevrolet shared many of the same dimensions, a similarity that the brand leveraged to promote the "new for 1964" Malibu. This Ermine White example was built at the Van Nuys, California, assembly plant. (Photo Courtesy Malibu SS Registry)

Stylistically, the 1965 Malibu Super Sport changed very little from the previous year, with the grille, bumpers, and taillights being the most noticeable differences. This Cameo Beige convertible is a prime example of a 1965 Malibu Super Sport. (Photo Courtesy Bill Whorley)

The Chevrolet 283-ci small-block was the base V-8 engine for the 1965 Malibu Super Sport; it put out 195 hp. Small-block 327-ci engines were available in 250-hp, 300-hp, and 350-hp versions. (Photo Courtesy Bill Whorley)

tor, big valve heads, and a stout 11:1 compression ratio, finally empowered Chevrolet with a midsize performance car capable of challenging Pontiac's GTO, which, for 1965, was rated at 335 hp for 4-barrel-equipped cars and 360 hp for Tri-Power units.

A Chevrolet print advertisement from 1965 was aimed directly at the GTO, stating, "350-hp Chevelle by Chevrolet, the perfect squelch. That's a potent squelch to all those others who keep talking about lions, tigers, and such." Much like Pontiac's ads from the era, it also stated the horsepower and torque output of the L79 327-ci engine, as well as other available performance hardware, including the 4-speed manual transmission and Positraction rear end. It closed with another not so subtle dig at the GTO, claiming it would have "a silencing effect on all the tigers and tamers."

While the 350-hp 327-ci engine was formidable, Chevrolet realized that it would need to offer larger, more powerful engines to remain viable in the increasingly crowded muscle car market. Later in 1965, the Mark IV 396-ci Chevrolet big-block engine debuted and a 375-hp version was created specifically for the Malibu Super Sport. The L37 375-hp 396-ci engine was part of the Z16 package, which cost

For the 1965 Malibu Super Sport, the base engine remained the meager 120-hp 6-cylinder, and the 195-hp 283-ci endured as the base V-8. The 250-hp and 300-hp 327-ci engines continued as the top powerplant options until the potent 350-hp 327-ci arrived shortly into the 1965 model year. Dubbed the "Big-Block Killer," the L79 327-ci engine generated an impressive 350 hp and 360 ft-lbs of torque. The L79, which featured a Holley 4-barrel carbure-

THE CHEVROLET CHEVELLE, OLDSMOBILE 4-4-2, AND BUICK GRAN SPORT *CONTINUED*

This angle highlights the revised grille and front bumper for 1965; both pieces come to a slight point in the center. This Madeira Maroon Super Sport is equipped with the 350-hp 327-ci L79 option. (Photo Courtesy Rich Cummings)

tachometer, 160-mph speedometer, dash-mounted clock, and an AM/FM stereo with four speakers. The 14x6 steel wheels were shod with 7.75x14 tires and special mag wheel–style wheel covers. Chevrolet purposely limited production of its new super car, and thus, only 201 Malibu Super Sports were produced with the Z16 package.

Throughout 1964 and part of 1965, Chevrolet was seemingly searching to find a niche for the Chevelle Malibu Super Sport, but the exciting Z16 package caused quite a stir among performance enthusiasts and automotive critics. In the July 1965 issue of *Motor Trend* magazine, John Ethridge wrote, "The way horsepower figures are bandied about nowadays, we never know what to expect. But this one's got it; from idle to redline, it's definitely got it. There's no brief range where it feels like it comes on the cam. It puts out gobs of romping, stomping torque throughout the entire range of useful RPM."

Although the 1965 Z16 package was expensive and exclusive, it launched the Malibu Super Sport into the muscle car stratosphere. Chevrolet built upon its big-block success in 1966, when the Chevelle SS 396 was offered only with 396-ci big-block power, which was available in 325-hp, 360-hp, and 375-hp versions. Inline-6s and small-block V-8 engines were no longer offered in Super Sport trim, which strengthened the car's high-performance motif. While the 1966 Super Sports featured less exotic hardware than the iconic 1965 Z16 models, they were much more affordable and sold extremely well, totaling 72,272 cars. However, this was not enough to surpass the GTO, which had its strongest year ever in 1966, moving 96,946 units off of showroom floors.

The L79 327-ci engine was rated at 350 hp at 5,800 rpm with 360 ft-lbs of torque at 3,600 rpm. It was a highly potent package in 1965. (Photo Courtesy Rich Cummings)

a hefty $1,501.05 and included other high-performance items, such as a stiffer boxed frame, heavy-duty shocks and springs, 12-bolt axle housing that used an 8.875-inch diameter ring gear, 3.31:1 axle ratio, and an open differential. Larger 11-inch diameter brake drums (used on Chevrolet's full-size cars) were employed for improved braking ability. Interior appointments included a padded dash, 6,000-rpm

With only 201 produced, the 1965 Malibu Super Sport Z16 is one of the most desirable muscle cars in the world. Created as both a response to the enormous popularity of the GTO and a clever way to promote the new Mark IV 396-ci big-block engine, these cars were presented to high-profile race car drivers and celebrities to maximize the promotional impact. Inset: The 396-ci big-block engine in the Z16 was officially rated at 375 hp with 420 ft-lbs of torque. However, most enthusiasts estimate the true output to be about 450 hp. This restored example recently brought $280,500 at auction in Kissimmee, Florida.

The potential buyer of a 1966 Chevelle SS 396 could have any engine he desired, as long as it was a 396-ci big-block. Offered in 325-hp, 360-hp, and 375-hp versions, the Chevelle SS 396 joined the Pontiac GTO as one of the top muscle cars of 1966. (Photo Courtesy Dale McIntosh)

THE CHEVROLET CHEVELLE, OLDSMOBILE 4-4-2, AND BUICK GRAN SPORT CONTINUED

Oldsmobile too, made a strong foray into the muscle car market in 1964 with its renowned 4-4-2 model. The 4-4-2 designation signified 4-barrel carburetor, 4-speed transmission, and dual exhaust. The 4-4-2 was available in various body styles, including a four-door sedan, in its debut year. In fact, a print advertisement for the 4-4-2 from mid-1964 depicted an illustration of two police officers in a four-door 4-4-2 and read, "Police needed it . . . Olds built it . . . Pursuit proved it! Put this one on your WANTED list!" The 1964

models were powered by a 330-ci engine producing 310 hp, 15 less than the 325-hp 4-barrel-equipped 1964 GTO. When General Motors lifted the 330-ci displacement limit on intermediates in 1965, Oldsmobile outfitted the 4-4-2 with a powerful 400-ci engine rated at an impressive 345 hp and 440 ft-lbs of torque. A somewhat conservative appearance hampered early 4-4-2 sales, but with a tuned suspension featuring stiff springs and shocks, boxed rear lower control arms, and a rear anti-sway bar, they handled exceptionally well.

The 1964 Oldsmobile 4-4-2 was equipped with a 330-ci engine that delivered 310 hp. It was attractive but the styling was less sporty than that of the GTO, which contributed to low sales figures. The low production numbers of the 1964 4-4-2 have resulted in high collectability today. (Photo Courtesy Ted Loranz)

For the 1966 models, Oldsmobile equipped its 4-4-2s with a 400-ci engine that produced 350 hp and 440 ft-lbs of torque, 15 more ponies than the 1966 GTO and eclipsing the torque output by either 9 ft-lbs or 16 ft-lbs, depending on whether the GTO was a 4-barrel car or Tri-Power equipped. In addition, Oldsmobile offered Tri-Power induction for the 1966 models, the one and only year such an option was available on the 4-4-2, making for a rare and desirable collector car. The addition of the Tri-Power raised horsepower output to 360, equaling the 1966 389-ci Tri-Power found in GTOs.

In the late 1960s, Oldsmobile developed the Doctor Oldsmobile character to promote the brand's performance models. He was an imposing, mad scientist type, clad in a lab coat and often surrounded by spooky sidekicks who served as his assistants. The premise centered on constantly improving the performance of the Cutlass and 4-4-2 W-Machines to stay ahead of the competition. Pontiac ad man Jim Wangers loved the concept, stating in a recent interview, "I thought it was 'right on,' and was insanely jealous; of course, they had a good product. The GTO was in a class by itself,

The 1966 Oldsmobile 4-4-2 was a formidable contender to the GTO's muscle car throne; this was the only year a Tri-Power induction system was available on the 4-4-2. This example is shod with later-style Oldsmobile Rally wheels and modern radial tires.

In the late 1960s, Oldsmobile created the "Doctor Oldsmobile" character, often shown in a smoky laboratory or garage standing proudly next to one of Oldsmobile's W-Machines. This modern re-creation with a 1968 Oldsmobile Cutlass S pays tribute to those memorable advertisements.

but the 4-4-2 was close and that son of a bitch RAN. It was a well put together car and campaign."

Having undergone complete restyles in 1966, 1968, and 1970, the Oldsmobile 4-4-2 evolved into a beautifully sculpted performance machine that is now highly collectible in today's classic car market; many in the automotive community opine that the 1970–1972 versions are some of Detroit's best designs of the era.

When General Motors redesigned the A-body in 1973, most enthusiasts felt that the 4-4-2 was the most attractive of the Chevrolet, Buick, Pontiac, and Oldsmobile offerings. This style lasted through the 1977 model year, when the entire lineup was downsized in 1978 and dubbed the G-body. Again, the 4-4-2 was one of the more attractive designs, highlighted by bolder stripes and graphics than any of its corporate rivals. Today, collectors and performance enthusiasts recognize the G-body 4-4-2 models as a true American muscle car.

While the Oldsmobile 4-4-2 models and the 250-hp and 300-hp versions of the Chevrolet Malibu Super Sport arrived late in the 1964 model year, Buick waited until 1965 to unveil its new muscle car, the Skylark Gran Sport. Fitted with the 401-ci nailhead engine, it provided ample power, with 325 hp and 445 ft-lbs of torque. Buick used a Wildcat 445 air cleaner decal to showcase this impressive torque output, rather than follow other manufacturers in emphasizing horsepower. Like the early 4-4-2 models, the

inaugural Buick Gran Sports featured more of a formal aesthetic and lacked the intense marketing campaign that benefited the Pontiac GTO. In the May 1965 issue of *Hot Rod* magazine, writers Eric Dahlquist and Pat Brollier conducted an in-depth review of a 1965 Skylark Gran Sport. The article noted, "One of the many items that separate this car from its standard brethren is the heavier-gauge, fully-boxed convertible frame used on all Gran Sport Skylark models to handle the hotter engine as well as impart an extra measure of rigidity to the whole body." The Skylark Gran Sport was the only GM A-body to receive the stiffer convertible frame as standard equipment.

By 1967, Gran Sport buyers could opt for a 340-ci engine (GS-340) rated at 260 hp and 365 ft-lbs of torque or the 400-ci mill (GS-400) pumping out 340 hp and 440 ft-lbs of torque. Even though they were capable cars, only 13,813 GS 400s were sold in 1967, underscoring the fact that the Chevrolet Chevelle Super Sport and the Pontiac GTO were the big guns in the General Motors muscle car arsenal, with 63,006 Super Sports and 81,722 GTOs sold that year.

Buick Gran Sports became some of the most attractive and powerful cars of the era, culminating with the 1970 GSX Stage 1, which boasted 360 hp and a locomotive-like 510 ft-lbs of torque. Up to the introduction of the 1970 GSX, Buick's muscle cars were more conservative in appearance than those of most other manufacturers, which isn't surprising considering the history of the brand. For the 1970 GSX, however, Buick borrowed heavily from cars such as the Pontiac GTO Judge. Bold colors such as Apollo White and the retina-searing Saturn Yellow were accompanied by distinctive stripes on the hood and sides of the car. Front and rear spoilers and a hood-mounted tachometer added to the performance motif.

The Chevrolet Malibu Super Sport, Oldsmobile 4-4-2, and Buick Gran Sport were all impressive machines, and each have stood the test of time quite admirably. Some of these sister-brand models proved to be even faster than comparable GTOs, but Pontiac prevailed in capturing the imagination and desires of the coveted youth market, propelling the GTO to legendary status.

Pontiac introduced the 2+2 in 1964 as an option on the Catalina. In 1965, it became its own model and housed a 338-hp 421-ci mill as standard equipment. This 1965 model features the optional 421 HO engine that produced 376 hp and 461 ft-lbs of torque. Tri-Power induction was part of the 421 HO package.

The 1965 Pontiac GTO hardtop was immensely popular, selling 55,722 units. The clean lines of the hardtop distinguish it from the Sports Coupe version. This Capri Gold example features a black Cordova top, Rally I wheels, and modern radial tires.

the industry. All major makers are offering more models than ever before. All-new styling changes are certainly more evident among certain lines, standing out as 1965 models against competitors' cars with all-new sheet metal but only minor styling changes. In styling, Pontiac shares body shells with other GM cars, but they've maintained, in our opinion, more model identification than their sister divisions. From the Grand Prix to the GTO, anyone can tell they're all Pontiacs." The hard work and vision of John DeLorean and the rest of the team were paying dividends, with Pontiac overcoming stiff competition to retain its position as one of America's top-selling performance brands.

The GTO package for 1965 remained a $295.90 option for the Pontiac LeMans and retained the same sales code of 382. GTO production continued at the same four manufacturing facilities as the 1964 model: Pontiac, Michigan; Kansas City, Missouri; Fremont, California; and Baltimore, Maryland. (Framingham, Massachusetts, was added in 1966.)

The 1965 units were available in the same three configurations as the previous year: hardtop, Sports Coupe, and convertible. Sale figures rose sharply for the hardtop, which sold a staggering 55,722 units, triple the number of the 1964 version (18,422). Convertible sales also increased greatly, resulting in 11,311 drop-tops sold for

For the 1965 GTO, Pontiac continued to produce its two-door sedan known as the Sports Coupe. Not as popular as the other versions, the Sports Coupe sold 8,319 units in 1965. This Mayfair Maize (code Y) example is equipped with a vinyl top, Rally wheels, and redline tires.

Despite being the most expensive model by more than $200, convertible GTO sales soared for 1965, with 11,311 units moved for the year. The convertible now outsold the Sports Coupe and became the second-most popular body style in the GTO lineup.

The fenders and front bumper of the 1965 GTO were redesigned to house the stacked headlights and are one-year-only items. Reproduction fenders for the 1965 model are not presently offered, but the front bumper is available through various restoration suppliers.

For the 1965 A-body lineup, Pontiac retained the same 115-inch wheelbase it employed the previous year, but as a result of styling changes, overall length grew to 206 inches. The 1965 GTO featured many enhancements from the 1964 model, while still retaining the same basic profile and bold, street-tough attitude of its predecessor. A stacked headlight design was employed for the 1965 GTO, similar to what Pontiac had been using in its full-size cars since the 1963 model year. This design brought cohesiveness to the entire Pontiac lineup, as noted in *Motor Trend* magazine's Car of the Year statement. Interestingly, all 1965 and 1966 Pontiacs implemented the stacked headlight feature, making them instantly recognizable.

Owners of 1965–1967 GTOs no doubt love to point out the beautiful front-end design of their beloved Pontiacs, but most enthusiasts do not know where this iconic motif originated. Although the contributions of Pontiac Motor Division innovators such as Bunkie Knudsen and John DeLorean are well documented, designer Jack Humbert is often omitted from Pontiac's success stories. Humbert graduated from the Central Academy of Commercial Art in Cincinnati, Ohio, in 1948 with a degree in automotive design. He was soon working at GM Styling alongside notable stylists Harley Earl and Bill Mitchell, and he was promoted to chief designer in 1959 at the age of 34. The 1961 and 1962 models were already well under development at the time, so Humbert's influence on these cars was minimal, extending mainly to refinement and detail. The stunning 1963 Grand Prix was the first Pontiac designed completely under his leadership

1965 compared to 6,644 for the 1964 model. The Sports Coupe was the least popular body style for 1965, but still managed almost 1,000 more units than 1964, totaling 8,319 for 1965. Total production for the 1965 GTO was 75,352, more than double that of the 1964 models. It was a clear indication that Pontiac was creating exactly what the American public craved. By comparison, sister division Oldsmobile moved just 25,003 4-4-2 models in 1965, while Buick sold a mere 15,780 Gran Sport units. The Oldsmobile 4-4-2 and Buick Gran Sport were both powerful, handsome automobiles, but lacked the relentless advertising campaigns that Jim Wangers and his team delivered for the Pontiac GTO.

Once again, the GTO received a grille treatment distinct from the Tempest models. The GTO's grilles were blacked out, except for a chrome strip around the perimeter, and featured a GTO emblem in the driver-side piece. By contrast, the Tempest unit displayed more brightwork, and while it did have the familiar split-grille theme, it was not as pronounced as on the GTO. Clearly, the Tempest grille is an attractive piece in its own right.

and is considered by many classic car enthusiasts to be one of the most beautiful American cars ever produced. The stacked headlights and restrained use of chrome trim were unique during this time period, bucking the trend of profuse chrome that was in vogue throughout the 1950s and early 1960s. The sleek "Coke-bottle" body lines were revolutionary, and later influenced the 1966 and 1967 GTO's styling cues. Other manufacturers tried to dupli-

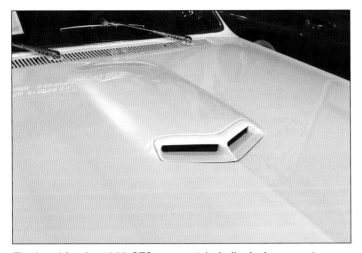

The hood for the 1965 GTO was restyled, displaying a center-mounted, integrated scoop. This piece remained unchanged through the 1967 model year and could be made functional with the optional Ram Air package by opening the hood scoop and installing the supplied metal pan between the carburetors and air cleaners. This allowed the engine to take in cooler outside air that resulted in more power.

cate many of these aspects, but none reached the same level of style and detail as the original Pontiac designs.

To accommodate the new headlight configuration, the fenders for the 1965 GTO used different stampings than those of the 1964 model, and in fact, were a one-year-only design. Likewise, the front bumper was restyled to coordinate with other front-end changes. No reproduction fenders are currently available for the 1965 GTO; the result is premium prices for original pieces in good condition. The "6.5 Litre" fender emblem was identical to the 1964 version and located in the same position, behind the front wheel opening.

Like the 1964 model, the grille area on the 1965 GTO differed from that of the Tempest. The GTO received grilles that were completely blacked out except for trim surrounding the perimeter, which was painted silver and accented by a thin chrome strip. A GTO emblem was placed in the driver-side piece, and the Pontiac crest was moved from the hood to the header panel. In contrast, the Tempest grille was more ornate and featured additional chrome trim, similar to the 1965 Catalina. The combined changes made to the front of the 1965 GTO resulted in a cleaner, more forceful aesthetic than the previous year.

The 1964 hood design, with its twin faux scoops, was supplanted by an entirely new piece for 1965 that displayed a single, integrated, center-positioned hood scoop. Rumors circulated within the industry that the hood for the 1965 model was designed to accommodate a dual-quad carburetor setup, an option that certainly would have elevated the GTO's street machine status into the stratosphere. However, this plan was soon scrapped and a GTO factory issued with two 4-barrel carburetors never came to fruition.

Late in the model year (and much to the delight of both automotive journalists and performance car enthusiasts), the hood scoop for the 1965 GTO could be made functional for Tri-Power-equipped cars with an over-the-counter or dealer-installed Ram Air package. For an additional $49.50 (some sources list $29.65), the Ram Air kit included a metal pan that mounted between the carburetors and air cleaners. A large piece of foam around the perimeter sealed the pan to the hood when it was

The metal Ram Air pan is evident on this Tri-Power–equipped 1965 GTO. The pan replaced the air cleaner bases and was sealed to the bottom of the hood with a thick gasket.

With unique taillight bezels, the 1965 GTO's taillights blended in beautifully with other rear end trim, presenting the car with an almost custom appearance. While similar, the Tempest models featured the same taillights, but did not exhibit the bezels found on the GTO. Both the lenses and bezels are currently being reproduced for the Pontiac hobbyist.

Though not changed dramatically, the 1965 decklid was a different stamping than the 1964 part.

The quarter-panel emblems for the 1965 GTO were the same pieces used on the 1964 models, but they were relocated to better complement the new wraparound taillight design. Note the higher placement on the gold 1964 car compared to the lower positioning on the red 1965 version.

Various shades of gray spatter paint were used inside the trunk area from 1965 onward. Although it is quite durable, it did not provide the same finished appearance as the 1964 models. Interestingly, there have been documented, early production 1965 GTOs that received body color in this area.

closed. A new scoop insert was supplied, but the owner or dealer had to open it to allow for the intake of fresh air. The rush of cooler outside air forced directly into the carburetors allowed the engine to produce more power and provided Pontiac with yet another marketing hook for the GTO. Because of the package's delayed arrival, factory-produced 1965 Ram Air components are extremely rare and valuable.

A quick online search found two original Ram Air pans, both offered at more than $2,000. Through the years, reproductions of varying quality have been produced in fiberglass, steel, and ABS plastic; some high-quality versions are still readily available. As was the case in 1964, Tempest and LeMans models received a flat hood with no scoop; this allows for a simple way to distinguish a Tempest or LeMans from a GTO.

Two different outside rearview mirrors were available in 1965: the standard fixed unit and the remote version. Unlike the 1964 cars, which displayed the remote mirror on the top of the driver's side fender, the 1965 remote mirror (code 444) was located in the same area of the driver's door as the fixed mirror. Moreover, an outside rearview mirror, offered as a dealer-installed item, could be mounted on the driver's or passenger's side of the car.

The doors, roof structure, and quarter panels were unchanged from the previous year, but rear styling changes necessitated a new decklid, taillight panel, and rear bumper, all of which were exclusive to the 1965 model. The "GTO" quarter-panel emblems were the same as the 1964 pieces, but they were positioned far-

ther down on the panel than the previous year. This was done to better complement the 1965's taillights, which had been redesigned to wrap around the quarter panels and blend nicely with the surrounding trim, which contained a Pontiac emblem. The fuel filler was relocated to behind the license plate at the center of the rear bumper. These stylistic changes culminated in a very sleek appearance from the rear, which also tied into the look of Pontiac's full-size cars.

The inside trunk area of the 1965 model received gray spatter paint, which was likely a cost-cutting measure, although it did prove to be more durable than the painted surfaces of the 1964 cars. However, there are known early production 1965 GTOs that received gloss body color in this area, like the 1964 models. A two-piece trunk mat remained standard issue, with a spare tire cover available for an additional fee.

In addition to the mostly restyled body, Pontiac updated much of its color palette to usher in a fresh, new appearance for the 1965 models. There were 15 exterior colors available for the 1965 GTO: Starlight Black (code A), Blue Charcoal (code B), Cameo Ivory (code C), Fontaine Blue (code D), Nightwatch Blue (code E), Palmetto Green (code H), Reef Turquoise (code K), Teal Turquoise (code L), Burgundy Metallic (code N), Iris Mist (code P), Montero Red (code R), Capri Gold (code T), Mission Beige (code V), Bluemist Slate (code W), and Mayfair Maize (code Y). Some hues, such as Iris Mist and Mayfair Maize, were only available for the 1965 model year. Starlight Black and Cameo Ivory were carried over from 1964. (Starlight Black was available on GTOs through the 1974 model year.) Some colors that were introduced in 1965, such as Fontaine Blue and Palmetto Green, were also used for 1966 cars. Hurst Gold and Cadillac Fire Frost, along with other special order GM colors, could be custom ordered for the 1965 GTO. Because of their rarity, cars painted with any of the special-order colors are highly sought after in today's collector car marketplace.

A single painted pinstripe that accented the body line was standard for the 1965 model. The stripe was available in three colors: Starlight Black, Cameo Ivory, or Montero Red. Pinstripe colors were factory designated to each main exterior color to maintain consistency. However, like many other aspects of early GTOs, there are exceptions to the rules, and an article in the December 2000 issue of *High Performance Pontiac* magazine highlights this aspect. The piece, written by Thomas A. DeMauro, featured a Montero Red 1965 hardtop with just a few more than 1,300 original miles and a detailed owner history. The car showcased a Parchment interior

Iris Mist paint was exclusive to the 1965 Pontiac lineup and could be ordered on other models, not just the GTO. A striking color featuring fine metallic shimmer, Iris Mist displayed a predominantly violet hue on the lighter side of the spectrum, resulting in a beautiful, somewhat subdued appearance.

Though the strong sunlight in the photo may fool the eye, this 1965 Chevrolet Malibu Super Sport convertible is painted Evening Orchid, identical to Pontiac's Iris Mist. (Photo Courtesy Derek Knapp)

Montero Red was a bright, solid shade (no metallic) red that was quite similar to 1964's Grenadier Red. Both hues absolutely beam in the sunlight and give the GTO a classic, sports car attitude. Montero Red was used in 1965 and 1966.

A single painted pinstripe accented the crisp lines of the 1965 Pontiac GTO and was available in three colors: Starlight Black, Cameo Ivory, and Montero Red. A Cameo Ivory stripe adorns this 1965 hardtop.

The bright Montero Red paint on this 1965 GTO contrasts nicely with the white convertible top. The cowl data reading for this combination is R 1. This example is shod with whitewall tires, closely resembling the optional tire choice for the 1965 model. (Photo Courtesy Don Keefe)

This detail view shows the correct grain texture, seams, and trim on a Cordova top–equipped 1965 GTO. The fit and finish on this hardtop model are superb. The Cordova top (code 342 for black) was a $75.32 option.

and the original owner opined that a white stripe would be more fitting than the black stripe called for by the factory. It was simple for both the factory and dealer to accommodate this request, and the owner received the stripe color he desired and not the factory default hue. The story also underscores the fact that the car-buying process of the 1960s was a much more personal experience; each car was custom-ordered to the buyer's specific tastes. Today, consumers are generally limited to a few pre-selected option packages on each model with little or no possibility to make special changes.

Convertible tops were available in five colors: white, black, blue, turquoise, and beige. White replaced ivory from the options list of the previous year and turquoise replaced aqua. Saddle was not offered for the 1965 models. As was the case throughout the GTO's entire production life-cycle, all convertible tops were power operated. Tempest convertible models came standard with a manual top but could be ordered with the power top option (code 434).

Cordova vinyl tops were again optional equipment for the hardtop and Sports Coupe bodies in either black or beige, each priced at $75.32. An ivory Cordova top was not available in 1965 but would return for the 1966 model year.

Interior

Although not radically different from the 1964 model, the 1965 GTO's cabin space received some

The interior of the 1964 GTO was thoughtfully fashioned and Pontiac designers did not feel the need to change the 1965 model dramatically, opting instead to make only subtle refinements to upholstery patterns and door panel styling.

tasteful updates and a few welcomed options. Six color choices were available: Black (code 213-30), Dark Turquoise (code 214-36), Gold (code 215-34), Red (code 216-35), Dark Blue (code 217-33), and Parchment (code 218-3E). As in the previous year, bucket seats were standard equipment for the LeMans and GTO; Morrokide upholstery was used once again, but featured a new, diagonal pattern that incorporated a Pontiac arrowhead into each seat.

Pontiac journalist Thomas DeMauro noted in his book, *Pontiac GTO: Collector's Originality Guide 1964–1974*, "A common restoration mistake is to swap the seat-back patterns when restoring the front buckets. The trick is to just use the rear seat-back pattern as a guide." The diagonal design was exclusive to Pontiac's 1965 A-body lineup; the full-size cars equipped with bucket seats displayed a pattern quite similar to that used for the 1964 GTO. The door panels were also updated for the 1965 GTO, with each displaying a GTO emblem much like the ones found on the front fenders.

Power windows were again available for the GTO. An article by Eric Dahlquist in the July 1965 issue of *Hot Rod* magazine made a good case for ordering them. "Electrically-operated window lifts were one accessory that we grew much to admire, not because of any inherent laziness on our part but the fact that with the seat belt fastened, it is well-nigh impossible for the driver to reach across to the opposite door to raise or lower the windows by hand," he wrote. At $102.22, power windows (code 551) were a costly item and many GTO buyers chose to

The diagonal seat pattern was unique to Pontiac's A-body cars and provides an easy way to differentiate the 1965 models from other years. A Pontiac crest was integrated into the seat backs in the four main seating areas.

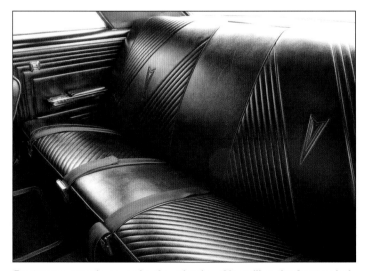

Restorers sometimes make the mistake of installing the front upholstery on the wrong sides. The key is to look at the back seat, as the diagonal ribs should be facing the same direction on the front seats.

From this rear seat view in a 1965 GTO Sports Coupe, the B-pillar, or post, is clearly visible. Even with the quarter window in the down position, the post remains fixed.

The black interior of this 1965 GTO contrasts wonderfully with the Montero Red paint. The four switches toward the front of the panel indicate power windows, a rare and coveted option on early GTOs. The small vent window is not power operated.

Because of the light color, Parchment interiors feature some black components, such as the carpet along the bottom edge of the door panel. The rectangular door panel pattern is exclusive to the 1965 models.

forego such a luxurious option, usually focusing their attention and hard-earned money on more performance-oriented items such as Tri-Power induction and 4-speed manual transmission.

In a 2014 article for *Hemmings Muscle Machines*, Pontiac journalist Thomas A. DeMauro noted, "Muscle-car intentions extend to the spacious interior as well. The four-pod gauge layout is more performance oriented than many of the GTO's contemporary competitors. Careful consideration was afforded to the placement of the gauges and controls and their styling. Although plastic is used for some items, there are still quite a bit of substantial-feeling metal parts employed." One of the highlights of the 1964 GTO interior, the engine-turned dash applique, was replaced by either a real or simulated wood veneer. The basic dash layout was carried over from 1964, retaining the four, circular gauge pods. A welcomed addition was the available Rally gauge option (code 504) that included oil pressure and water temperature gauges, along with a revised tachometer featuring a much larger sweep than the previous year's unit. The attractive and functional design virtually eliminated the need to install aftermarket gauges.

For an extra $16.14, the buyer could receive option 634, comprising a Safeguard speedometer and low-fuel warning lamp. The Safeguard speedometer consisted of an adjustable needle on the face of the gauge. The driver set a predetermined speed and when the vehicle reached the specified setting, a buzzer sounded to alert the driver, encouraging him or her to slow down.

Inspecting the interior space of this 1965 GTO, we discover a well-appointed automobile with Rally gauges, power brakes, and a center console with a vacuum gauge perched on top. Vents in the dashboard indicate this car was equipped with air-conditioning. The steering wheel in this GTO is an aftermarket piece, added by the owner.

The overall dash layout of the 1965 GTO was similar to the 1964 version. The engine-turned dash applique that surrounded the gauges was replaced by either simulated or real wood; both were employed in 1965. This car also features the optional dash pad, considered a safety item in 1965.

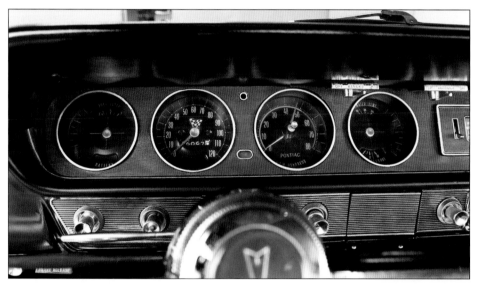

The debut of the Rally gauge option in 1965 (code 504) was stylish and functional. The 1964 models could only receive a tachometer, but the 1965 Rally gauge option included a tachometer as well as gauges pertaining to coolant temperature and oil pressure. The checkered flag is exclusive to the 1965 models equipped with the Rally gauge option.

The tachometer was redesigned for the 1965 models, revealing a much larger sweep than those of the 1964 cars. Most hobbyists agree that the 1965 tachometer is the superior of the two units.

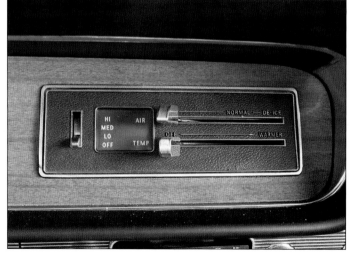

The heater control panel for 1965 was carried over from the 1964 cars with three simple controls for fan speed, air (vent control), and temperature.

The glove box emblem for 1965 differed greatly from the 1964 piece and a grab bar was attached to the dashboard for anxious passengers. A glove box lamp (code 482) could be purchased separately for $2.85 or as part of the 084 Lamp Group.

A revised GTO emblem integrated into a larger applique was placed above the glove box door. New for the 1965 model was a dash-mounted grab bar, which was standard issue and gave the front seat passenger something sturdy to hold on to if the driver suddenly became overly enthusiastic. Tempest and Tempest Custom models did not receive the grab bar; they were issued only on LeMans and GTO models. The 1966 and 1967 models featured similar, but not identical layouts, thereby making the 1965 dash emblem a one-year design.

The standard steering wheel was equivalent to the 1964 piece, but the Custom Sports wheel was redesigned. The 1965 wheel (code 524), like that of the 1964, was a simulated-wood unit, but featured three chrome spokes and a deeper dish, which allowed for less obstructed viewing of the gauges. Unlike the 1964 units, quality aftermarket reproductions are available for the hobbyist or restorer. A padded dash remained a $16.14 safety option.

The optional center console was nearly indistinguishable from the 1964 version, except that black paint was used between the chrome ribs instead of blue. The center console was a popular option for early GTOs, and some enthusiasts mistakenly assume that it was standard equipment with the GTO package. However, there are many documented manual transmission cars without

The standard steering wheel for the 1965 GTO remained unchanged from 1964. Notice the lever for the optional tilt steering column (code 454). This option required the buyer to select power steering (code 501) for a combined price of $139.88. Note: Heater control panel should not display woodgrain vinyl, but rather a textured, dark gray appearance.

The Custom Sports steering wheel (code 524) was redesigned for 1965 but remained a $39.27 option. A beautiful piece, it was one of the more handsome steering wheels of the era. The gearshift knob and radio are not stock components.

The center console was unchanged from the previous year except that it received black paint between the chrome ribs rather than dark blue. Like the 1964 version, it was also equipped with a courtesy lamp at the rear.

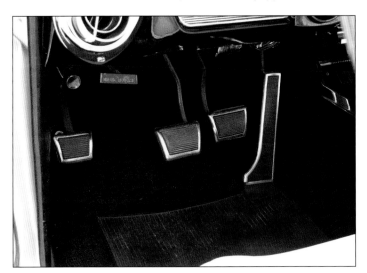

Chrome bezels surrounding the pedals still denoted power brakes in 1965; however, unlike the 1964 models, the parking brake pedal also received the trim.

The AM/FM radio made its debut in 1965 and was only available in push-button form. The slider at the top of the unit displayed the Pontiac name and was used to change from AM to FM.

a console, and even automatic-equipped cars with the shifter mounted on the steering column, as was the case when the 2-speed automatic transmission was ordered and a console was not specified.

Manual and push-button AM radios were still on the 1965 options list, but the big news for 1965 was the availability of an AM/FM radio, which could be ordered with a manual or power antenna just like the AM-only radio. The AM/FM unit was not inexpensive, priced at $136.65 with a manual antenna and a whopping $166.40 with the power antenna, more than 50 percent of the GTO option itself. Rear-mounted Sepra-Phonic or Verbra-Phonic speakers were available for Sports Coupe and hardtop

models, priced at $14.15 and $53.80, respectively. Convertible models continued to employ a narrower rear seat and specific rear side panels to accommodate top hardware. The top mechanisms also limited the space available in the package shelf area and, like the 1964 models, a rear speaker option was not listed for the convertible models.

Driveline

Pontiac took great pride in its automobiles, including entry-level models, with the 1965 sales brochure touting, "And now, for the man who yearns for a Pontiac but

The standard 4-barrel-equipped 389-ci engine fitted in the 1965 GTO produced 335 hp at 5,000 rpm and 431 ft-lbs of torque at 3,200 rpm. This example displays several deviations from stock, but the louvered air cleaner is correct for all 1965 335-hp GTO engines except those sold in California.

Correct air cleaner for a 1965 4-barrel-equipped GTO originally sold in California. Throughout the years, many of these original components have been removed and discarded, and locating a car such as this is quite uncommon. (Photo Courtesy Jim Mott)

This finely detailed 1965 GTO engine displays the correct fuel line routing and single, yellow-painted throttle return spring and factory-spec 500 CFM Carter AFB carburetor. (Photo Courtesy Jim Mott)

thinks he can't afford it, we offer the ultimate induce-ment: the Pontiac Tempest. One look and you see that it's every bit as much Pontiac as every other model . . . that it's every bit as stylish . . . that it carries every bit as much prestige and quality, from its Wide-Track stance to the Pontiac crest up front. But there's more here to like than looks alone. Drive it. Whiz around the block a few times and see how this Tempest responds to the 140-hp six." For 1965, the 215-ci inline-6 engine was unchanged from

the previous year and was retained as the base powerplant for Tempest and LeMans models. Featuring a 1-barrel carburetor and an 8.6:1 compression ratio, the 215-ci 6-cylinder was dependable and had the ability to run on less-expensive regular gas. The 250-hp 326-ci power-plant was also unaltered, although the high-compression, 4-barrel equipped 326-ci engine now rated at 285 hp, an increase of 5 hp from the 1964 version. The various engine options and numerous body configurations for

When searching for the cylinder head casting number on a 1965 GTO, you will not find it in the more traditional location on the center exhaust ports. For the 77 casting number heads, it is located on the front exhaust port on the passenger's side and the rear exhaust port on the driver's side.

the Tempest and LeMans lineup showcased that Pontiac was producing its A-body for a vast array of potential buyers. This ranged from the young family who would likely purchase a four-door Tempest or station wagon powered by the 215-ci 6-cylinder, to the spirited performance devotee who would consider a 285-hp 326-ci LeMans or the now-legendary 335-hp or 360-hp 389-ci GTO.

With the success of the 1964 GTO, other manufacturers soon began producing stylish cars with potent engines, and throughout the muscle car era, Pontiac engineers were constantly striving to enhance every aspect of its popular model. Both the 4-barrel and Tri-Power 389-ci engines received improvements for 1965. Cylinder heads and intake manifolds were revised for superior airflow, increasing horsepower for both powerplants. The cylinder heads were casting number 9778777, commonly referred to as 77 and also used on certain high-performance 421-ci engines in Pontiac's full-size vehicles. Unlike most Pontiac V-8 cylinder heads that display the casting number on the center two exhaust ports, the 77 heads displayed the casting number on the front exhaust port on the passenger's side, and the rear exhaust port on the driver's side. Valves were the same sizes as the previous year: 1.92 inches for the intake and 1.66 inches for the exhaust; compression ratio was advertised at 10.75:1. The bolt pattern mating the intake manifold and cylinder head was changed from 1964, indicating that an intake manifold from 1964 would not bolt onto an engine with 1965 and later cylinder heads, and vice versa.

An interesting anomaly for the 1965 cars was that two different pairs of cylinder heads could be considered correct: the 77 castings and the 093 castings. The *Pontiac GTO Restoration Guide: 1964–1970* by Paul Zazarine and Chuck Roberts states, "There were two heads used in 1965. Originals carried the cast number 77 on the front exhaust port. The part number for this head was 9778777. According to Service Bulletin number 66-12, 093 heads were the correct replacements for 1965 GTO 389 engines. These 093 heads (part number 9784212) were used in 1966 production. A 1965 engine showing a 093 cast number on the cylinder heads would not be incorrect in restoration."

The standard induction system was the familiar Carter AFB 500 cfm 4-barrel carburetor, but it was now mounted on a revised cast iron dual-plane intake manifold with improved flow characteristics. The large, single-snorkel air cleaner of 1964 was supplanted by a low-profile chrome-plated louvered piece, sometimes referred to as a pancake or a pie pan air cleaner.

For the 1964 model, the camshaft was the same design for both 4-barrel- and Tri-Power-equipped cars. Pontiac now had two separate versions for the 1965 GTO, both different from the 1964 unit. The camshaft for 1965 4-barrel engines, part number 9779067 (often referred to as 067), featured an increased valve lift of .410-inch intake and .413-inch exhaust, while duration remained the same at 273 degrees and 289 degrees, respectively. Hydraulic lifters were fitted once again and were reliable until about 5,500 rpm. With these changes, horsepower increased from 325 the previous year to 335, and torque rose from 428 ft-lbs to 431 ft-lbs for cars fitted with the 4-barrel carburetor.

Today, spotting a 1965 GTO with its original 4-barrel carburetor can be a difficult task, as many original 4-barrel cars were converted to Tri-Power induction. Production figures show that, once again, 4-barrel-equipped GTOs far outnumbered their Tri-Power counterparts, with 54,805 4-barrel cars and 20,547 Tri-Power units produced in 1965.

The methodically detailed engine compartment of this 1965 GTO reveals many vital aspects: correct carburetors with foam air filter elements, throttle linkage (for manual transmission), fuel filter, and fuel line routing. Proper valve covers with passenger-side breather and driver-side rubber plug, unpainted hood hinges, and black master cylinder. (Photo Courtesy Jim Mott)

When equipped with air-conditioning (code 582), the engine compartment of the GTO becomes quite crowded. This passenger-side view highlights the detailed A/C compressor and correct upper radiator hose. (Photo Courtesy Jim Mott)

Tri-Power

Like the 4-barrel engines, the Tri-Power versions benefited from a revised intake manifold that increased airflow. The 1965 Tri-Power engines were also fitted with a special camshaft, part number 9779068, commonly referred to as 068. This piece displayed valve lift of .414-inch for the intake and .413-inch for the exhaust. The valve lift was only a marginal increase over the 067 camshaft, but had a noticeably longer duration, with 288 degrees intake and 302 degrees exhaust.

Author Note: 1965 camshaft specifications were sourced from Eric White's book, *The GTO Association of America's Pontiac GTO/GT-37 Illustrated Identification Guide.* Some sources list slightly different numbers for camshaft lift. However, Eric White's research continues to be some of the most trusted within the Pontiac hobby.

These modifications resulted in the 1965 Tri-Power engine pushing out 360 hp and 424 ft-lbs of torque. Curiously, the torque rating was 7 ft-lbs lower than the 4-barrel-equipped GTOs and 4 ft-lbs lower than the 1964 engines. This was likely because the 068 camshaft was designed more for peak horsepower and sacrificed a small amount of low-end grunt. In an increasingly crowded muscle car marketplace, Pontiac needed to extract every last bit of horsepower from the 389-ci engine to remain competitive and uphold its reputation as a performance leader, a challenge that would prove more difficult in following years.

Manual transmission cars now featured mechanical linkage to operate the outboard Rochester 2-barrel carburetors. This was a more precise configuration, and the driver did not have to be concerned about the peculiarities of the vacuum system used on the 1964 models. Automatic cars equipped with Tri-Power induction in 1965 still received the

The 1965 Pontiac GTO was a favorite among drag racers, especially the more rigid Sports Coupe model such as this. Don't let the gorgeous Iris Mist paint deceive you; this car was built with many of the high-performance options available for that year, including the 360-hp Tri-Power 389-ci engine and 4-speed manual transmission.

vacuum-actuated linkage. However, an owner or a dealership often converted it to mechanical linkage later on.

A transistorized ignition (code 671) was again offered and the 1965 GTO sales brochure boasted, "Delco transistorized ignition. No points. No condenser. Next best thing to a magneto. Extra cost."

The March 1965 issue of *Car Craft* magazine featured an in-depth test of a 1965 Tri-Power-equipped GTO conducted by the Chaparels Car Club of Tustin, California. The reviewers stated, "The first time out to San Fernando dragstrip, a good stiff headwind was blowing and the best performances were in the very low 90s (mph) and high 15s (elapsed time [ET]). This was in strictly street condition, a condition we maintained throughout the test: carb cleaners on, ignition normal, suspension untouched, etc.

"Next we went down to the beautiful new Carlsbad strip, where Jim Nelson let us wail away by ourselves one Saturday. After we made a few runs right on 100 with a best ET of 14.86, Nelson couldn't stand it any longer and

came boiling out of the tower to beg a ride. He cranked a best time of 101 mph in 14.65—this still in street trim. We went back to Carlsbad the next weekend after adding Jardine three-port headers installed by Jerry Jardine and some 8.50 M&H cheater slicks. Running 26 pounds of air in the tires uncorked, speed was up to 102 mph and the ET dropped clear to 13.77! Keep in mind that no special tuning had been done on the car, either.

"A couple of pointers on this particular car/engine combination. The hydraulics tend to pump up at about 5,500. If you come off the line at 5 grand, shift to second at 5,100 and the next two gears at 5,200 for the best results. Of course, these figures can change from strip to strip and between individual cars. We point this out to show the car is getting its best performance below the apparent red line. If you pump the lifters, plan on losing at least a half-second."

The reviewers' results were impressive, but not surprising to anyone familiar with a Tri-Power 4-speed-equipped GTO. They also highlighted the fact that a good set of exhaust headers and sticky drag tires could drop the elapsed time by more than one full second, a substantial improvement over stock exhaust manifolds and narrow bias-ply tires. A Royal Bobcat kit would certainly enhance the car's performance even further.

Transmission and Rear End

The Muncie M12 3-speed manual transmission was standard on 1965 models through February 1965. It retained the same gear ratios as the previous year: 2.58:1 in first, 1.48:1 in second, and 1.00:1 in third. This unit featured a cast-iron case and first gear was not synchronized. The input shaft was a 10-spline piece and the output shaft was 27-spline.

For the 1965 model, a fully synchronized 3-speed manual transmission was offered, manufactured by Ford Motor Company (Dearborn). In this unit, all forward gears were synchronized, with ratios of 2.42:1 in first, 1.61:1 in second, and 1.00:1 in third; reverse was 2.33:1. This piece was also constructed of cast-iron and had an input shaft with 10-splines, but an output shaft with 28. The aluminum bellhousing was redesigned to accept the bolt pattern of this transmission.

Like many other aspects of the GTO, there were some inconsistencies with transmission availability, particularly when the Dearborn unit became available. Some sources indicate that this transmission was only available after March 1, 1965. However, there are documented cases of early production 1965 models, some built as early as November 1964 that were positively identified as having the Dearborn 3-speed manual

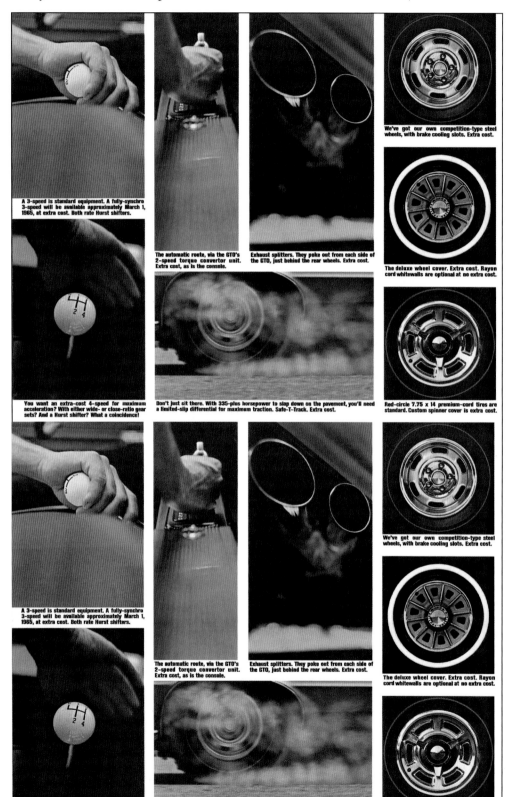

A 3-speed is standard equipment. A fully-synchro 3-speed will be available approximately March 1, 1965, at extra cost. Both rate Hurst shifters.

The automatic route, via the GTO's 2-speed torque convertor unit. Extra cost, as is the console.

Exhaust splitters. They poke out from each side of the GTO, just behind the rear wheels. Extra cost.

We've got our own competition-type steel wheels, with brake cooling slots. Extra cost.

You want an extra-cost 4-speed for maximum acceleration? With either wide- or close-ratio gear sets? And a Hurst shifter? What a coincidence!

Don't just sit there. With 335-plus horsepower to slap down on the pavement, you'll need a limited-slip differential for maximum traction. Safe-T-Track. Extra cost.

The deluxe wheel cover. Extra cost. Rayon cord whitewalls are optional at no extra cost.

Red-circle 7.75 x 14 premium-cord tires are standard. Custom spinner cover is extra cost.

A page from the 1965 GTO/2+2 brochure covers various options of the 1965 GTO, including available transmissions. As noted in the top left photo, the fully synchronized 3-speed manual unit (built by Ford Motor Company) was available beginning March 1, 1965. (Photo Courtesy GM Media Archive)

The Hurst shifters for both the 3-speed and 4-speed manual transmission choices in 1965 proudly bore the Hurst name. Here, a 4-speed stick extends from the optional center console, both popular options for the duration of GTO production.

As in 1964, buyers of automatic transmission GTOs who opted for the center console in 1965 received the floor-mounted shifter. The 1965 shifter was mechanically the same as the 1964 unit, but the shifter plate now displayed a black insert to match the console.

transmission as factory equipment. In addition, in the 1965 Pontiac sales brochure, this transmission was listed as optional equipment for the GTO, as well as for V-8-equipped Tempest and LeMans models.

There were two 4-speed options available to the serious performance fanatic: the M20 wide-ratio and the M21 close-ratio units. The March 1965 issue of *Car Craft* magazine stated, "Probably of most interest to any automotive buff is the 4-speed alloy-cased gearbox. This is available as an option only and consists of two cases, the front holding the four forward gears and the rear case housing the reverse gear. A fully synchronized design, the 4-speed comes with a Hurst floor shifter and two different ratios. (Note: The 3-speed manual transmissions were also equipped with a Hurst shifter.) The wide box has 2.56:1, 1.91:1, 1.48:1, and direct, while the close-ratio transmission (available only with the 3.90 rear axle ratio) has 2.20:1, 1.64:1, 1.28:1, and direct.

"For general driving in city traffic with only an occasional fling at the drags, the wide-ratio gearbox would probably be most satisfactory. This would allow more flexibility in any particular gear. The close-ratio box is for any condition requiring constant engine RPM, such as drag racing, hill climbs, slaloms, etc."

The M21 close-ratio transmission option for 1965 still required the buyer to select the Tri-Power engine option, heavy-duty radiator, metallic brake linings, Safe-T-Track rear end, and the 3.90:1 rear axle ratio. Although it is more common than on 1964 models, 1965 GTOs originally equipped with the M21 close-ratio transmission are quite rare, which makes them a favorite among Pontiac aficionados. Manual transmission sales totaled 56,378 for the 1965 GTO, although further breakdown of specific transmissions is not currently obtainable.

The M31 Super Turbine 300 2-speed featuring a 1.76 first gear and 1.00 second was again the only automatic transmission option available for the 1965 GTO. Likewise, the shifter remained column-mounted unless the center console was specified. Automatic production for the 1965 GTO totaled 18,974 units.

The durable Turbo Hydra-Matic 400 (TH-400) 3-speed automatic transmission, first introduced in the 1965 model year, was available in Pontiac's full-size cars such as the Bonneville and Catalina. Some members within the Pontiac community lamented the fact that it was not available in the 1965 or 1966 GTO, although it was finally offered beginning in 1967 and proved to be a welcome addition to the options list.

Shifters

At the behest of Jim Wangers, beginning in 1965, all GTOs equipped with Hurst shifters wore the Hurst name. In *Glory Days*, Wangers explained, "As a marketer, I wanted to use it in our advertising right away. The problem was that GM had a policy preventing any outside supplier from putting their name on a part or component (except tires) that was built into the car. I had to convince Pete Estes that it really meant more to Pontiac to be able to say their cars came equipped right from the factory with a Hurst shifter by name, than it meant for Hurst to be able to say their shifter was original equipment on every Pontiac built with a manual transmission. Pete listened and, out of respect for my knowledge of the market, allowed us to do it. Beginning with the 1965 models, every Pontiac floor shifter was clearly

Detail of the Hurst logo on the 1965 4-speed shifter. Some early production 1965 GTOs were fitted with the 1964-style shifter without the Hurst logo.

labeled 'Hurst,' and we saw to it that it was in our advertising." As it happened, the partnership between Pontiac and Hurst proved to be mutually beneficial and lasted for several years.

There are documented early production 1965 GTOs that were fitted with the 1964 shifter that did not display the Hurst logo. As was the case in 1964, the Hurst stick in the 1965 GTO was topped with a white shifter ball that displayed a black engraving of the shift pattern.

Rear End

The rear end for the 1965 GTO was equivalent to the previous year's version, which displayed a 10-bolt cover and an 8.2-inch diameter ring gear. Cars equipped with the 4-barrel engine received 3.23 gears as standard issue or 3.08 gears if the car was fitted with air-conditioning and automatic transmission, while Tri-Power GTOs were treated to a 3.55 gear set. For the 1964 model, the gear ratio was stamped directly onto the rear of the passenger-side axle tube; in 1965, a two-letter code was used in the same location.

Suspension and Braking

The 1965 GTO's chassis and suspension was mostly a carryover from the 1964 model. The perimeter frame received a welded rear crossmember that increased structural integrity over the previous year's riveted piece. Various 1965 models from other manufacturers, such as the Ford Mustang and Plymouth Barracuda, still employed unit-body construction, which Pontiac had used on 1961–1963 Tempest and LeMans models. Many classic car aficionados concur that 1960s-era vehicles produced with unit-body chassis are more prone to twisting and flexing under hard driving conditions, which is not ideal for performance applications. The Mustang and GTO did not necessarily compete for the same type of car buyer. However, anyone who has driven both a 1965 Mustang and a 1965 GTO will certainly confirm that the GTO is much more stable and sure-footed; this is due to the vastly different chassis and suspension designs.

Quick-ratio steering (code 612) employed the same 20:1 ratio as the previous year and was a $10.76 option for 1965. It was not available if the buyer selected power steering. Because the tilt steering column required the power steering option, the buyer who desired the quick ratio steering box could not receive the tilt column.

Magazine reviews of the era praised the GTO's firmness and stability. A May 1965 article in *Car Life* magazine reported, "Handling was just as good as the

Even though the suspension on a stock 1965 GTO was well appointed, the owner of this beautiful hardtop chose to upgrade several areas, including suspension, brakes, wheels, and tires.

All 1964 and early production 1965 GTO master cylinders were fitted with a bleeder valve. The valve was discontinued mid-year 1965. (Photo Courtesy Jim Mott)

acceleration. Jesse racked it around a few corners in the Southern Michigan area. There is still plenty of under-steer but the stiff roll bar controls body lean enough so the front end doesn't plow too much. The tires seem to have considerably more casing stability than the average passenger car tire and they're an excellent compromise between ride and handling. And the metallic brakes are great. Pedal pressure with the vacuum booster is reason-able (although more than with organic linings) and there is no noticeable fade under very rough braking condi-tions." It should be noted that while numerous publica-

tions spoke favorably of the GTO's braking components, many enthusiasts lamented the fact that it was essentially the same rudimentary system employed in 6-cylinder Tempest models.

The braking components for the 1965 GTO were the same as offered in 1964: a hydraulic system employing a single-reservoir master cylinder and 9.5-inch diameter drums. Power brakes and metallic linings were once again optional equipment. New for 1965 was the availability of aluminum front drums (code 694). These lighter pieces dissipated heat more efficiently than the iron drums, resulting in better (though still less than stellar) brak-ing ability. These items are currently quite rare and very desirable within the Pontiac hobby, commanding high prices when offered for sale.

Larger drums and disc brakes were still not on the GTO options list, and the 4-wheel drum system was again one of the weakest aspects of the car. By contrast, Ford's popular Mustang model had several different brake sys-tems; some were dictated by engine choice while others were offered as optional equipment. The 6-cylinder Mus-tangs received the standard configuration of front and rear 9-inch diameter four-lug drums. The V-8-powered cars were fitted with 10-inch-diameter drums with five lugs. Each of these systems was available with or with-out power assist. In addition, a disc brake upgrade could be optioned on V-8 models, although this system was not available with power assist. Upgrading the braking components based on engine output was a thoughtful

Unlike the Pontiac GTO, early Ford Mustangs received upgraded brakes on more powerful models, and disc brakes were available as an option for the V-8 versions.

approach on Ford's part; one that many Pontiac aficionados felt would have befitted the GTO.

Wheels and Tires

The 14x6 steel wheels with dog dish hubcaps that were standard in 1964 were once again standard for the 1965 model. Color-keyed wheels were available for cars painted Starlight Black, Teal Turquoise, Fontaine Blue, and Capri Gold. Other exterior colors received Starlight Black wheels, as did cars equipped with any of the optional full wheel covers. Some present-day GTO owners outfit their cars with standard hubcaps and color-matched wheels, even if it was not a factory designated color combination, because they feel this provides a custom appearance while not deviating too far from a factory-issued arrangement.

The Deluxe wheel discs (code 462) were priced at $17.22 and restyled for 1965. These pieces were painted gray with 10 cooling slots accented by 10 chrome spokes and a chrome perimeter topped with a large center cap

The smaller, standard hubcap was the same as the 1964 unit and would be used until the 1972 models. For 1965, cars painted Starlight Black, Capri Gold, Teal Turquoise, and Fontaine Blue received color-keyed wheels when these hubcaps were specified. The Mayfair Maize car shown here is considered incorrect; it should instead showcase black wheels.

The 1965 Deluxe wheel covers were much different from those offered in 1964; while they were affixed to many GTOs when new, they are not commonly seen today.

Many present-day 1965 owners opt for Rally I wheels on their cars, but this Cameo Ivory GTO still proudly wears its original Custom wheel discs (code 521). At $37.12, they were priced slightly higher than the 1964 versions.

that read PONTIAC MOTOR DIVISION. The 1965 Deluxe wheel covers were much sportier than the 1964 versions, and from a distance, could easily be mistaken for aluminum wheels.

The Custom wheel discs (code 521) were a $37.12 option in 1965. Even though they were somewhat revamped (six cooling slots instead of eight and a different center cap), they shared the same overall aesthetic as the previous year's design and were quite attractive. To date, neither the 1965 Deluxe or Custom wheel covers are reproduced, but a quick search of an online auction site revealed a few original sets of each being offered at $200 to $300 per set. They were in varying degrees of condition, with driver-quality pieces that would require only minor refurbishing for use on restored cars.

Wire wheel discs were again available for the GTO and were virtually unchanged from 1964, but the backing received cooling slots to help reduce heat generated by the brakes. These discs (code 411) were a $71.02 option, $18.30 more than the Rally wheel. Several sources indicate that the GTO's wire wheel discs were the same as those offered on other GM cars of the era, with the center caps marking the only difference between brands.

In 1965, Pontiac debuted a styled steel wheel for the GTO, called the Rally wheel (now often referred to as the Rally I wheel). This unit, which measured 14x6 and displayed six cooling slots, was fitted with a center cap and a polished trim ring. The Rally wheels (code 691) were a $52.72 option, and they are quite popular with current owners. Much like the Custom wheel discs for the 1964 model, many enthusiasts consider the Rally wheels the most desirable choice for their GTO, even if their car was not originally so equipped. Produced only in the 14x6 size through the 1968 model year, high-quality aftermarket versions are now available in 14x6, 14x7, 15x7, and 15x8 sizes. The larger sizes allow for the use of wider tires for improved handling.

Redline tires remained standard equipment for the GTO, with whitewall tires again being a no-cost option. Tire size enlarged from 7.50x14 to 7.75x14, which, while not a substantial increase, showed that Pontiac recognized that the 7.50x14 tires issued for the 1964 model

The handsome Rally wheel (now often referred to as Rally I) debuted in 1965 and was a Pontiac exclusive. The wheel was produced through the 1968 model year; however, the 1965 wheels are the only versions to use a chrome center cap.

This GTO also wears the sporty Rally I wheels, but displays black center caps, which are incorrect for 1965. It would be an easy swap should the owner choose to make his car Concours ready.

JIM WANGERS

While John DeLorean, Russell Gee, and Bill Collins are credited with the creation of the GTO, much of the early success of the car can be attributed to famed marketing guru Jim Wangers. His energetic and relentless advertising campaigns convincingly portrayed the Pontiac GTO as the epitome of a high-performance street machine.

In an interview with Lance Lambert for the *Vintage Vehicle Show*, Wangers stated, "In working with the ad agency, we had an opportunity to really get close to the top-level management team at Pontiac. And, in that capacity, both Bunkie Knudsen, who was the general manager earlier on, and John DeLorean, who, at one time was chief engineer, learned in chatting with me that I really did have a pretty good handle on the market, and more specifically on what we were trying to do with Pontiac on the market." It was Wangers's close relationship with Pontiac management, especially John DeLorean, that permitted him and his team to pursue hard-hitting advertisements and promotions that transformed the GTO into a legend.

Wangers explained, "It was, in fact, the perfect time to make a tremendous statement in the consumer marketplace.

That was simply done by employing an old hot rodder's trick; something the hot rod community had been doing for years. Stuff a big engine into a little car. And that's exactly what happened. The 389-ci full-size Pontiac engine was put into the intermediate-size Tempest LeMans chassis, thus, you know, the monster car was created."

It was Wangers's passion for performance and his willingness to continuously push the boundaries of what an American automobile manufacturer could accomplish that led Pontiac to greatness in the 1960s. In a recent phone interview, he said, "No other manufacturer had such a strong image to accompany their product like Pontiac. It really turned into part of popular culture. Pontiac had become the bad boy, always seemed willing to do things that were marginally acceptable."

Wangers was born in Chicago, Illinois, and displayed an enthusiasm for cars at a very young age. Near the peak of World War II, Wangers voluntarily enlisted in the US Navy, where he was a radio operator on the USS *Bunker Hill*. His time in the service was relatively uneventful, as the ship was primarily used to transport American troops back to the United States after the war.

Jim Wangers (left) poses with a 1961 Royal Bobcat Catalina. In addition to being a skilled marketer, Wangers was an accomplished drag racer, piloting a 1960 Catalina to victory in the NHRA's Top Stock Eliminator class that year. (Photo Courtesy Don Keefe)

A few years earlier, Jim Wangers pitched the Pikes Peak hill climb to Kaiser as a way to promote its supercharged flathead 6-cylinder engine. Unfortunately, Kaiser did not have the resources for such a campaign. However, later, at Chevrolet, management loved the idea and Zora Arkus-Duntov handily broke the record in a 1956 Chevrolet.

After World War II, there was a great demand for automobiles in America and Kaiser-Frazer cars sold well from 1946 through 1948. This 1948 Kaiser is part of the Automobile Driving Museum's collection in El Segundo, California. (Photo Courtesy Automobile Driving Museum)

Back home in Chicago, Wangers attended the Illinois Institute of Technology with the hope of becoming an automotive engineer. Struggling, he realized that engineering was not his forte, and he soon enrolled in a liberal arts school, graduating in 1949 with a bachelor's degree in English. He then accepted a position at *Esquire* Magazine, promoting the *Coronet* publication and working alongside a young Hugh Hefner. Wangers turned down an offer to work for Hefner on his new venture, *Playboy* magazine, citing his desire to work in the automotive field.

Bill Weintraub was one of the founders of *Esquire*, and later started his own ad agency, W. H. Weintraub & Company. It was at Weintraub that Wangers landed his dream job of working in the automotive industry for Kaiser Motors. One of his first assignments was to market the Kaiser supercharged, flathead 6-cylinder engine as a superior alternative to the competition's V-8 engines.

Realizing that a supercharged engine performs very well at higher altitudes, Wangers pioneered the concept of using the Kaiser to attempt to break the Pikes Peak hill climb record. Even though it was a brilliant idea, management deemed it too costly. Financially strapped Kaiser eventually became fragmented and produced its last passenger car in 1955, lacking the resources to keep pace with the larger manufacturers.

Upon Kaiser's demise, Wangers soon found a job at Campbell-Ewald, Chevrolet's advertising agency. Wangers was a key figure in changing Chevrolet's advertising strategy from the workaday "Low-cost Motoring" theme to an exciting, performance-based concept. In his book, *Glory Days: When Horsepower and Passion Ruled Detroit*, Wangers said, "I knew from my own experience that the 4-barrel carb, dual-exhaust package would be just the thing Chevrolet needed to get people excited about their 1955 model. I also realized that we needed a way to demonstrate just how capable this new 'Power Pack Chevy,' as they called it, really was." In February 1955, Wangers traveled to Speed Week in Daytona Beach, Florida, where he witnessed firsthand the dominance of the 1955 Chevys equipped with the 180-hp Power Pack option. Wangers informed his superiors about Chevrolet's success at Speed Week, and soon, dealerships were decorated with posters that read, "Chevy Sets Speed Mark at Daytona."

Building upon this momentum, Wangers pitched his unused Pikes Peak hill climb idea to promote the new 1956 models. With Zora Arkus-Duntov behind the wheel, a Chevrolet conquered the mountain, shattering the old record and solidifying Chevrolet as a performance brand.

In 1958, after two years working for Chevrolet, Wangers accepted a position with Pontiac's advertising agency: MacManus, John & Adams. With Bunkie Knudsen at the helm, and the new 1959 models set to debut, it was a very exciting time to be involved with the Pontiac brand. In *Glory Days: When Horsepower and Passion Ruled Detroit*, Jim

JIM WANGERS CONTINUED

Wangers recalled, "The new 1959 car introduced a whole new era, I like to call it the 'Wide-Track Era.' Not only the car, but the entire Division took on a new personality that would lead to an extended period of phenomenal sales growth, not matched in the industry before or since: from that low point of just over 200,000 sales in 1958 to more than 900,000 sales in 1969. Match that! The concept of the 'Wide-Track Pontiac' became the umbrella for this whole new era. It wasn't just about styling or about engineering or about performance. It wasn't just about an old man's car suddenly becoming a teenager's delight. This was about bringing the right car to the right marketplace at the right time, and with the right promotion."

Sensing great opportunity, Wangers pressed Knudsen and his colleagues to educate Pontiac dealers nationwide on the potential profit and publicity that racing and performance could provide. Knudsen agreed and prompted Wangers to pursue a relationship with a Pontiac dealer that could specialize in the sale and installation of high-performance parts and equipment. Royal Pontiac in Royal Oak, Michigan, became the dealer of choice and was vital to the success of Pontiac from the tail end of the 1950s throughout the 1960s.

In 1959, artists Art Fitzpatrick and Van Kaufman, collectively known as Fitz and Van, began their long association with Pontiac, creating countless hand-drawn illustrations for use in advertisements, which became an integral part of the Pontiac brand. Fitzpatrick drew the cars and Kaufman illustrated the backgrounds, portraying each model with a tasteful, elegant

A stunning automobile from all angles, this 1959 Pontiac Bonneville convertible helped usher in the "Wide-Track Era," one of the most prosperous times in the history of Pontiac Motor Division. (Photo Courtesy Don Keefe)

Jim Wangers pushed for the use of action photography to promote the GTO, stating it would better represent the power and features of the car. Pontiac had been using elegant, hand-drawn renderings by artists Art Fitzpatrick and Van Kaufman. Wangers's idea was met with some resistance, but he eventually prevailed.

style. Even though each piece was a true work of art, Jim Wangers felt the need to use photography to successfully promote the new GTO model.

By the mid-1960s, Fitz and Van were still under contract with Pontiac and had built a strong relationship with John DeLorean, so Wangers's idea was initially met with resistance. Wangers was persistent, and a compromise was soon reached; Fitz and Van would focus on illustrating the full-size lineup, while action photography would be used for the GTO. Ultimately, some Fitz and Van renderings did cover the GTO, but research suggests none were created for the 1964 and 1965 models.

Wangers's idea proved to be fortuitous, as the GTO was successfully advertised with exciting action photography strategically placed in enthusiast publications such as *Hot Rod* magazine. When the future of the GTO became more certain, Wangers and his team marketed and promoted the car relentlessly throughout the 1960s as a powerful street machine for the thrill-seeking youth of America.

Later on, John DeLorean selected Wangers to be part of a small team tasked with generating new product ideas in line with Pontiac's performance image. The team included notable names such as Bill Collins, Jack Humbert, Herb Adams, Tom Nell, Dave Wood, Herb Kadau, and Ben Harrison. The Plymouth Road Runner had debuted in 1968 and proved to be very popular thanks to its powerful engine and low cost. Wangers and crew decided to address this competition by developing a stripped-down, low-cost GTO featuring a 350-ci engine. The car was nicknamed the E/T, for "elapsed time," a drag racing reference. To make a bold statement, Carousel Red was chosen for the E/T. When presented with the concept, DeLorean rejected the idea of a 350-ci-powered GTO, claiming it would harm the car's high-performance reputation.

Heeding DeLorean's requests, the team added back many of the options they had removed from the car, including bucket seats and the Endura nose, and offered only Ram Air III and Ram Air IV 400-ci engines as powerplants. DeLorean was impressed with the new approach and decided to name the car "The Judge." It's a bit ironic that what started out as a budget-friendly street car morphed into a high-end muscle car accompanied by a high price tag. Two of the original ideas stayed with the project however: the bright Carousel Red paint and the Rally II wheels, but without trim rings. (Later in the model year, The Judge was available in all Pontiac colors.)

Wangers now had another memorable marketing hook, and made great use of courtroom references including, "All Rise for the Judge," "The Judge Can Be Bought," and "The Judge Will Rule." The Judge ultimately accomplished what DeLorean had intended: create an exciting car to boost the GTO's presence in the marketplace. Wangers fondly recalls one evening in a 1969 Judge, "There was a time I'll never forget. I was with John DeLorean driving a 1969 Judge on Woodward Avenue. It was around eight in the evening and some local car guys were checking out the Judge; guys with Mopars, Chevys, Fords, all of them. Now, the Judge came with the RA III 400 as standard, with the only option being the RA IV, you could not go down from a RA III, so the Judge was a fast car no matter what. You could tell they wanted some action. Remember, DeLorean was general manager of the division so I wasn't sure what he wanted to do, then he casually turns to me and says, 'Jim, if some of these guys want to race you, don't let me stop you.' So that's what we did, we put it on 'em pretty good, too."

In 1971, Wangers purchased Garfield Chevrolet in Milwaukee, Wisconsin, renaming it Jim Wangers Chevrolet. The dealership turned a profit, but employee theft, disputes with labor unions, and government and GM regulations led Wangers to sell the business in early 1974.

The 1969 GTO Judge was initially conceived to be a budget-friendly muscle car to compete with Plymouth's popular Roadrunner model. John DeLorean vetoed a 350-ci GTO, believing that it would tarnish the car's reputation; he opted to use Ram Air III or Ram Air IV 400-ci engines for the 1969 Judge. The first 5,000 GTO Judges were painted Carousel Red, a bold color that appears more orange than red. In fact, Chevrolet used the same color that year with the more familiar name, Hugger Orange.

The same US Royal redline or no-cost option whitewall tires were available for the 1965 GTO, although tire size increased from 7.50x14 inches to 7.75x14 inches. While similar in appearance to the US Royal tires, this 1965 GTO showcases Firestone Wide Oval F-70 redline tires, which were not available until 1967.

were no match for the massive amount of torque generated by the 389-ci engine.

Four distinctive wheel cover options, a styled steel wheel (Rally I), and two different tires offered buyers yet another way to custom order a new GTO to their exact specifications.

Advertising for 1965

Jim Wangers and the rest of Pontiac's advertising team knew that installing a powerful, 389-ci engine into a LeMans and calling it the GTO option was a daring strategy to circumvent GM's internal policy stating that no intermediate-size car could have an engine larger than 330 ci. That, combined with the fact that the 1964 model arrived late in the year, led to a somewhat restrained marketing approach that did not include television commercials for the car's inaugural year.

Early television advertisements for the 1965 GTO were quite moderate, as Wangers explained in *Glory Days*, "When it came to marketing the GTO on television, our initial approach was weak. While we wanted to get more aggressive with our advertising and depict the GTO for what it really was, we restricted that message to print only, and then only in the more sophisticated enthusiast magazines. We knew we'd barely been granted approval for the car, so when we did produce television commercials, we assumed GM management would be more likely to watch TV than read the car magazines so we were very conservative. We had women driving the car, and we

even did one commercial where the voice-over said that GTO stood for 'Girls Take Over,' with a young lady shifting the 4-speed and enjoying the pleasures of driving a convertible."

Another example of the early, restrained ads featured two young ladies casually cruising through the countryside in a 1965 GTO convertible with the narrator simply stating, "The '65 Pontiac GTO, it's the swingingest car . . . 1965, the year of the quick wide-tracks." Jim Wangers is rightfully given credit for portraying the GTO as a powerful and sexy street machine, but he also should be recognized for showing restraint at critical moments where the long-term future of the car was uncertain.

By mid-1965, it was evident that the GTO was a monumental success, and Jim Wangers's fears that General Motors could cancel the car dissolved into a huge cloud of burnt rubber. It was around this time that the Pontiac team realized they could get much more aggressive in their advertising, both in print and on television. Wangers recalled, "It didn't take long for us to assume a posture of confidence, as some of the headlines we used on our early print ads certainly reflected. Consider the ad that simply showed the car with the headline 'Our Thing,' which was a direct play on the then-famous 'Cosa Nostra' concept. Another one read, 'There are few great moments in life. This is one of them,' or still another that read, 'How to tell a real tiger from a pussycat. Drive it!'" For those Pontiac enthusiasts not well versed in organized crime lingo, Cosa Nostra is another name for the Sicilian Mafia, which was very prominent in popular culture in the mid-1960s. The ad went on to list in great detail the standard and optional performance equipment accompanied by an action photo of a GTO rumbling down a dirt road.

A television commercial, which aired in late spring 1965, touted Pontiac's *Motor Trend* Car of the Year award and featured many different Pontiac models, including the GTO, all of which were driven extremely hard during filming. Pontiac was definitely not shy at this point in the game: tires screeching, engines revving, cars racing around a paved track, and even navigating an off-road course. The spot closed with the narrator encouraging viewers to "See and price those wide-track tigers by Pontiac. Winner of the *Motor Trend* Car of the Year award."

Another provocative television advertisement appeared around this time, this one using a live tiger jumping into the engine compartment of a 1965 GTO convertible. The narrator boasts, "Some sporting cars are only pussycats. Pontiac's GTO is all tiger; agile, nimble . . . with plenty of growl and all wide track." Even though

our Thing.

Pontiac Motor Division · General Motors Corporation

Standard equipment: Engine—389 cu. in., 335 bhp, 4BBL; dual exhausts, low-restriction mufflers, lightweight resonators; declutching fan; chromed low-restriction air cleaner, rocker covers, oil filler cap; 3-speed with Hurst shifter; heavy-duty springs, shocks, stabilizer bar; choice of premium 7.75 x 14 red-circle nylon tires or same-size rayon whitewall tires; 14 x 6JK wide-rim wheels; bucket seats; full carpeting; custom pinstriping.

Extra-cost performance equipment: Engine—389 cu. in., 360 bhp, 3-2BBL, with factory-installed mechanical linkage on stick shift jobs (Code 802); all-synchro 3-speed with Hurst shifter (Code 743); wide- and close-ratio 4-speeds with Hurst shifters (Code 744 and 778); Safe-T-Track limited-slip differential (Code 701); axle ratios—3.08, 3.23, 3.36, 3.55, and 3.90:1, factory installed; 4.11 and 4.33:1, dealer installed; metallic brake linings (Code 692); extra-stiff springs and shocks (Code 621); 20:1 quick steering

(Code 612); 17.5:1 power steering (Code 501); tachometer, ammeter, oil pressure and water temp gauges (Code 504); high-performance transistorized ignition (Code 671); competition-type steel wheels (Code 691); exhaust splitters (Code 422); custom sports steering wheel (Code 524); heavy-duty radiator (Code 432); to be continued in our special GTO/2+2 performance catalog, free at any Pontiac dealer's.

Wide-Track Tiger—Pontiac GTO

The now-iconic "Our Thing" 1965 Pontiac GTO advertisement was influenced by the phrase "Cosa Nostra," the name for the Sicilian Mafia that literally translates to "our thing" or "our affair."

The success of the GTO soon led to more aggressive advertising for Pontiac's full-size performance models. This 1965 print advertisement features a 2+2 hardtop and GTO convertible, touting the attributes of both cars.

Action photography was used extensively for the Pontiac GTO, as was the tiger tail. Horsepower figures for both the standard and optional Tri-Power engines were specified. This advertisement for the 1965 model also mentioned the band, The Tigers, promoting their pop single, "GeeTO Tiger."

the car was driven rather modestly, using a live tiger certainly implied that the GTO was a powerful, untamable creature.

The GTO sales brochure was the one marketing tool that was assertive and braggadocious since its inaugural year. In his book, Jim Wangers stated, "Beginning with the 1964 GTO, Pontiac began producing specific brochures for their high-performance models that set the standard for the industry. These brochures included specifications and technical information not listed in other manufacturers' catalogs. I insisted that we include as much technical information as we could to reinforce Pontiac's performance image, for example, cam specs, carburetor jet sizes, all available rear axle ratios, and specific model weights. DeLorean loved it." Indeed, throughout the years, the GTO sales brochures were some of the most informative and well put together in the industry, and original versions are quite collectible.

Pontiac continued to use suggestive print advertisements targeted at the performance enthusiast. One such ad was a full two-page spread, with one half dedicated to the 2+2 and the other to the GTO. Bold text read: "Have new tigers. Need tamer. Apply at any Pontiac dealer." It then listed the performance specifications for both cars, including horsepower ratings and transmission and suspension options. Jim Wangers recalls, "By the middle of 1965 we were committed totally to the Tiger. We were shipping all kinds of merchandising and display items to the dealers for use in their showrooms: tiger skin rugs

that could be draped over a hood; orange and black window trim featuring angry, growling tigers; wall plaques with protruding tiger heads; and thousands of Tiger tails, which could be used anywhere. As Pontiac began to expand its number of performance models in the lineup, these cars became perfect candidates to be called 'Tigers.' The Catalina 2+2 and the 4-barrel 6-cylinder Sprint were good examples. It didn't take long before all of us were thinking the same thing: why not all Pontiacs?"

After witnessing the 1964 hit songs, "G.T.O." by Ronny and the Daytonas, and "My Mighty GTO" by Jan and Dean, Pontiac began to sing its own praises, literally, when Wangers helped assemble the band, The Tigers. The song "GeeTO Tiger," released in May 1965, was not as popular as earlier efforts performed by more established acts, but the album, when the original sleeve is intact, is a collectible piece of Pontiac history. Some versions had the song, "The GeeTO Prowl" on the B-side of the record, while others had what was called "Big Sounds of the GeeTO Tiger" and featured authentic GTO engine sounds accompanied by voices to narrate the experience. Early on, a man warns, "You'd better use your belt. We're gonna do some pretty tough testing." The event was initially to be recorded at the GM Proving Grounds, but according to Jim Wangers, scheduling conflicts forced the project to be recorded at a drag strip in California's San Fernando Valley. Final touches, including additional voices and sound effects, were added later at a studio in Hollywood.

The record was used in a cross-promotion between Pontiac and Hurst; contestants vied for a custom 1965 GTO Tri-Power hardtop, which, like the song, was also named the "GeeTO Tiger." The car was painted Hurst Gold and fitted with gold anodized Hurst wheels, a gold-plated Hurst shifter, and a black Cordova top. Participants would listen to the song and count how many times they heard the word *tiger*. They would then write a short essay on why they would like to own the one-of-a-kind Pontiac, and a winner was chosen from more than 100,000 entries. The contest turned out to be more popular than the song that promoted it, and The Tigers faded away into relative obscurity.

A special 1965 GTO convertible called the GTO Grand Marque V

The grand prize for the Pontiac/Hurst contest was this beautiful 1965 Pontiac GTO painted Hurst Gold and fitted with a black vinyl top. The car also featured the 360-hp Tri-Power engine, gold Hurst wheels, and a gold-plated Hurst shifter. (Photo Courtesy Don Keefe)

How to tell a real tiger from a pussycat:

Pontiac Motor Division · General Motors Corporation

Drive it.

Two seconds behind the wheel of a Pontiac and you know unquestionably you're in tiger country. You realize right away there's more to being a tiger than just bucket seats, carpeting, and sleek upholstery. There's Wide-Track handling, say. And availability of a six or two rambunctious V-8s in the Le Mans. And a snarling 335-hp GTO or its 360-hp, slightly hairier, cousin. Get out and drive a tiger!

Quick Wide-Track Tigers
Pontiac Le Mans & GTO

Advertisements for the Pontiac GTO became provocative, using bold images and text. Jim Wangers has been noted saying that, "The GTO was the right car at the right time," and print ads such as this reinforce that statement.

was built to promote the model on the national show car circuit. The exterior of the car was mostly stock (including the wire wheel discs) but featured a light cream custom paint job and "Grand Marque" fender emblems. The interior displayed seats covered in white leather with genuine tiger skin inserts. The seatbelts were also covered with tiger skin and featured tiger paws covering the buckles. A Custom Sports steering wheel mounted on a tilt column, Rally Gauges, power windows, power antenna, and plush custom carpeting completed this unique GTO.

When recently asked about the dangers and complications that can arise from using live tigers for photos and television commercials, Jim Wangers relates, "I wasn't in charge of those ads but I was always there by request. One particular time, the tiger got upset and completely devoured the car, really tugging away at the steering wheel, like he was attracted to it." According to Wangers, this well-documented instance of a tiger ruining a GTO wasn't the only time one of these jungle cats acted out. "To be honest, we kind of encouraged the

feisty behavior, to make for dramatic photos and TV. Male tigers especially are pretty tough, and they have a certain mystery about them. I like to think that we helped reinvent the tiger; we sort of helped tigers more than they helped us. It was a lot of fun but scary as hell. There's no way people would try to do that kind of thing today with live animals, it could all be done so easily on computers. You could do it and smoke a cigarette at the same time."

Wangers went on to recall how much fun it was to be a part of the Pontiac team in the 1960s, "I was lucky to be working with Pontiac at the time of the GTO's inception, and it was something I really believed in and really enjoyed doing. You could tell we were all having fun in those days, and as a result, our work turned out even better." It is, in fact, clear that the passion and enthusiasm that Wangers, DeLorean, Estes, and others felt had shown through in Pontiac's products and advertising, creating an excitement for the brand that most enthusiasts consider Pontiac's greatest time period.

This Reef Turquoise (code K) 1965 Sports Coupe is outstanding, fitted with Rally I wheels and redline tires. With its chiseled styling and available 360-hp 389-ci Tri-Power engine, it's no wonder that thousands of performance enthusiasts point to the 1965 Pontiac GTO as the ultimate muscle car. (Photo Courtesy Chris Phillip)

CHAPTER FOUR

1966 GTO The Beautifully Restyled GTO Becomes a Stand-Alone Model

The year 1966 was filled with stratospheric highs and devastating lows. The unmanned Soviet spacecraft, *Luna 9*, made a successful landing on the lunar surface and transmitted spectacular images back to Earth. The Beatles released their album, *Revolver*, to critical acclaim and embarked on their last tour, after that choosing to focus on more experimental studio work. The Vietnam War was intensifying; an ever-growing number of American troops were on the ground and protests against the war were increasing dramatically in cities across the United States.

Amid these events, the muscle car phenomenon was surging, and there were plenty of worthy competitors for the Pontiac GTO. The 1966 Ford Fairlane GT and its Mercury counterpart, the Cyclone GT, were handsomely styled, with each employing the stacked headlight design that Pontiac introduced in 1963 and boasting a 390-ci engine pushing 335 hp. Like other manufacturers, Ford was now targeting the GTO specifically in its advertisements. One such piece for the 1966 Fairlane GT read, "Big gun for tiger country, Fairlane GT!" The ad showed a close-up of the Fairlane's fender with four small tiger head stickers applied. This was obviously done to show that the Ford had enough power to "kill" numerous GTOs.

Along with other GM intermediates, the Pontiac GTO was restyled for 1966 and became an immediate success with critics and the general public alike. A record 96,946 GTOs were sold that year, a figure that was never again equaled.

This profile of a stunning Tiger Gold 1966 GTO highlights the semi-fastback roofline and "Coke-bottle" side styling. Hardtop sales totaled an impressive 73,785 units for the model year.

The now-famous Chrysler street Hemi was available in the intermediate chassis and produced an underrated 425 hp. (Many enthusiasts believe the true output to be closer to 500 hp.) *Motor Trend* magazine noted, "The sound of the 425-hp Hemi when fired up is unmistakable; it gives goose pimples to enthusiasts and fits to the competition. It isn't really loud, just powerful and authoritative." Truth be told, in 1966 Pontiac didn't have anything that could compete with the brute power of the street Hemi. Even the hulking, Tri-Power-equipped 421 HO powerplant (with 376 hp) would have been outgunned. Even so, it was never offered for the GTO because of GM's policy limiting engine size to 400 ci in the midsize chassis (a restriction that wasn't lifted until the 1970 model year).

Meanwhile, Pontiac's corporate cousin, Chevrolet, was also hitting its stride with the 1966 Chevelle Super Sport. The 1966 Chevelle SS was only available with a 396-ci big-block, with 325-hp, 360-hp, and 375-hp versions from which to choose, all wrapped in a very handsome package. The automotive press was clearly excited about the car, as Eric Dahlquist wrote in the February 1966 issue of *Hot Rod* magazine, "It's the type of vehicle we hate to part with. It has just the right measures of ride-handling and acceleration that would make it the nuts for all kinds of driving, especially long trips. It's a fun car for today's dull traffic, and if it helps relieve the tedium of travel, you can't ask much more." Even though other period articles echoed Dahlquist's assessment that the Chevelle Super Sport was indeed a hot car, in 1966, Chevrolet was just part of the pack. Pontiac was *leading* the pack.

Once again, the distinct combination of style, performance, and a powerful image distinguished the Pontiac GTO from other muscle cars. Outward changes to the 1966 model were dramatic and significant. In *Glory Days*, Jim Wangers recalled, "Still, 1966 was the year the GTO became a real car. No longer an option on the LeMans, it was now its own model. Along with all the new GM A-body coupes, it featured a new roof styling package introducing the dramatic 'tunneled' back window, or 'backlite' as industry technicians called it. The tunneling effect, along with the severely swept-back C-pillar, gave the car a true fastback profile, while at the same time retaining the positive characteristics and luggage space convenience of a notchback." The smart roof tailoring, which served to enhance the overall "Coke-bottle" styling theme, undoubtedly aided in the model's best-selling year ever, with 96,946 GTOs sold. The advertising campaign was provocative, with one print ad teasing, "To all the other cars from the GTO: 'What's new, pussycats?'"

Body

Pontiac continued to offer the GTO in three body types and sales increased for all variations. The narrator in a promotional film for the 1966 GTO proclaimed, "This GTO is going to take the public by storm," and the sales figures proved the veracity of that claim. The pillared Sports Coupe (style 4207) sold 10,363 units, up from 8,319 in 1965. Convertible models (style 4267) rose from 11,311 in 1965 to 12,798 in 1966. The pillarless hardtop (style 4217) remained the most popular version by far, with an astounding 73,785 hardtops sold in 1966, up from 55,722 for the 1965 model. The 1966 GTO was produced in the same plants as the 1964 and 1965 cars (Pontiac, Michigan; Baltimore, Maryland; Kansas City,

Missouri; Fremont, California), with the addition of the Framingham, Massachusetts, facility.

One major benefit to the GTO being its own model instead of merely an option on the LeMans was the fact that it was assigned its own VIN prefix. The coveted "242" at the beginning of the VIN indicates Pontiac (2) GTO (42); this makes it much easier to identify an authentic 1966 GTO than the 1964 and 1965 models, which displayed LeMans VIN tags. The 242 designation could also be found on the cowl data plate and was used until the 1972 model year, when the GTO once again

became an option on the LeMans. The 1964, 1965, and 1972 Tempest and LeMans models are much more easily cloned into artificial GTOs than the 1966–1971 models, which exhibited the 242 VIN prefix. Sadly, some builders illegally change a car's VIN tag and cowl data plate in search of a large payday.

Although the sheet metal bears little resemblance to the 1964 and 1965 units, the 1966 GTO continued to employ the same 115-inch wheelbase as its predecessors. Overall length extended a fraction of an inch, while overall width grew exactly 1 inch. Weight increased nearly 200 pounds across all body styles but cannot be traced to any one specific change. It was likely a cumulative effect of items such as exhaust resonators, redesigned front seats, the slight increase in the car's width, and now-standard safety items, such as the padded dash and seatbelts.

The artfully redesigned 1966 body displayed a certain elegance and was less angular than its 1964 and 1965 counterparts. Like a Hollywood movie starlet, the 1966 GTO was confident and voluptuous, with curves in all the right places. A slight rise at the front edge of the quarter panels accentuated the car's hourglass profile.

For the 1966 GTO, the cowl data plate was found in the same place as the 1964 and 1965 models: affixed to the firewall near the master cylinder. Inspecting the cowl data plate of this 1966 GTO reveals plenty of useful information: 1966 (66), Pontiac (2), GTO (42), hardtop (17), Pontiac Plant (PON), black interior with Strato Bucket seats (223-B), Blue Charcoal paint lower and upper (B-B), center console (2G), custom front seat belts (5Y). (Photo Courtesy Chris Phillip)

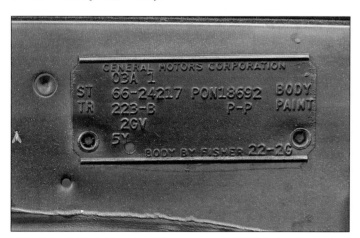

This data plate designates this car as a 1966 (66), Pontiac (2), GTO (42), hardtop (17), Pontiac Plant (PON), black interior with Strato Bucket seats (223-B), Barrier Blue paint lower and upper (P-P), center console with Verbra-Phonic rear speaker (2GV), custom front seat belts (5Y).

The VIN tag for 1966 was again located in the front portion of the driver-side doorjamb area. Now its own model, the GTO carried the prefix 242, indicating Pontiac (2), GTO (42).

The sharp, angular lines of the 1965 model (top) gave way to a sleeker, more streamlined body in 1966 (bottom). Both years are highly coveted by collectors, as they represent some of Pontiac's most enduring body styles. The 1966 GTO retained the 115-inch wheelbase of previous years.

The rear window area of the 1966 GTO (right) was quite different than that of the 1965 model (left). This was a key styling element of both the 1966 and 1967 GTOs. The swept-back roof pillar, combined with the upright glass, resulted in a dramatic appearance, but also created blind spots for the driver.

Hardtop and Sports Coupe versions featured the semi-fastback roofline with recessed rear window that somewhat hindered visibility, while convertible models made do with a more conventional-style folding top.

Pontiac's 1966 promotional film stated, "All series appear slimmer and more graceful. The clean, simple side treatment with the lower beltline suggests a sports car flair. There's nothing boxy about these styles. The windshields of all coupes and convertibles have more rake, or slant, to give a lower silhouette." It's a design that weathered the test of time perfectly, and, decades after it was introduced, the 1966 GTO remains immensely popular among enthusiasts, as proud owner Andre Ray-

man relays, "The 1966 was the first GTO that I had the opportunity to own. The styling was sleek for its day, and its hidden taillights made for an attractive car. The power of the 360-hp Tri-Power engine certainly backed up the car's good looks."

Stacked headlights remained a key styling attribute and were well integrated into the redesigned fenders. The familiar split-grille theme remained, and overall, the look was reminiscent of the base Tempest and LeMans models. Constructed of plastic and quite similar to the 1966 Grand Prix design, the grilles were blacked out and showcased silver-painted edges and a GTO emblem in the driver-side piece. Officially named Kralastic, the use of

Even with the top in the closed position, the appeal of a 1966 GTO convertible is undeniable. Convertible GTOs had their best year in 1966, selling 12,798 units, up from 11,311 in 1965.

The 1966 GTO front end is a favorite among many enthusiasts. The continued use of the stacked headlight theme, along with plastic grilles, echoed the design of Pontiac's full-size cars.

The front-end styling of the 1966 Grand Prix is deliberately similar to the GTO, as Pontiac designers strived for a cohesive appearance throughout their lineup. The plastic grilles, stacked headlight design, parking lamps, and even the placement of the Pontiac arrowhead are nearly identical to the GTO. (Photo Courtesy Ken Nagy)

As in prior years, a GTO emblem was affixed to the driver-side side grille. Parking lamp lenses were clear, but appeared amber when lit.

The hood for the 1966 GTO is the same piece that was used on the 1965 model. The Pontiac crest was moved from the header panel to the hood. The half-moon shaped chrome headlight trim pieces are aftermarket items added by the owner.

plastic for grille material was significant, as it marked the first time Pontiac Motor Division had done so. (Grilles for the 1964 and 1965 models were made from die-cast zinc.) Clear parking lamps (with amber bulbs) were molded into the grilles and adorned by chrome bezels. The front bumper, new for 1966, complemented the headlights and header panel very well. Many reproduction front-end components are available to the restorer from multiple outlets.

The hood panel was one of few that carried over from the 1965 model, with the exception of the Pontiac arrowhead that was now affixed to the hood itself rather than the center of the header panel. Again, the scoop could be made functional with an over-the-counter Ram Air kit, or factory issued with the rare code XS Ram Air engine, which was not available until late in the model year. Factory Ram Air cars came with the Ram Air pan in the trunk and required the dealer to open the hood scoop and install the pan. As in previous years, the hood with integral scoop was an identifying characteristic of the GTO; Tempest and LeMans models received a flat hood with no scoop.

The doors were also re-sculpted for the 1966 GTO. The sharp, square body lines of the previous year gave way to a more free-flowing appearance, contributing to the car's sophisticated aesthetic. A driver-side rearview mirror was now standard equipment, with a remote version (code 394) available for an extra $7.37. Research

The "Coke-bottle" styling is highlighted in this profile of a 1966 convertible; the sculpted body lines of the lower fender, door, and quarter panel are quite pronounced and accentuate the car's curvaceous profile.

suggests that a passenger-side mirror was available as a dealer-installed item.

Quarter panels were new, with pronounced "hips" where the roof panel and quarter panel joined. Though analogous to the 1967 pieces, the 1966 quarter panels were one-year-only components and do not interchange with any other year without modification. Rocker panel trim was expanded to include additional pieces adorning the lower, rear portion of each quarter panel, extending

Additional trim was mounted to the front, lower portion of the fenders. The location of the "GTO 6.5 Litre" fender emblems was unchanged.

from the back portion of the rear wheel opening to the front edge of the rear bumper. Trim was also added to the lower front section of the front fenders to continue the theme. This was a key design element for the 1966 GTO, as it exaggerated the length of the body panels and presented the car with a bit more flair than preceding years. Tempest and LeMans models did not receive the added quarter panel and fender trim.

Taillights were somewhat concealed by decorative louvers unique to the 1966 GTO. (Tempest and LeMans models showcased completely different tail lenses that resembled a kidney shape.) A GTO emblem was placed on the passenger-side rear of the decklid and individual block letters spelled out "Pontiac" between the taillights. The rear bumper accentuated what some hobbyists refer to as the "bow-tie-theme rear styling," as viewing the car directly from the rear reveals a bowtie shape. While both the Tempest and LeMans models featured this styling trait, the distinct taillights of the 1966 GTO make it easily distinguishable from both the 1966 Tempest and LeMans models and the 1967 GTO.

The decklid was redesigned for 1966, but the location of the GTO

The inside trunk area was covered in a gray/blue spatter paint, not the gray/green shade found in the 1965 cars. A spare tire and two-piece trunk floor mat were again standard issue, with a spare tire cover (code 372) available for $2.53 extra. Inside trunk volume was reduced from 23 cubic feet in 1964 and 1965

emblem was unchanged. Polished trim highlighted the trailing edge of the decklid and corresponding trim was added to the rear edge of each quarter panel. This additional brightwork accentuated the car's beautifully sculpted rear end design. Once again, the similarity to the 1966 Grand Prix is apparent.

The 1966 GTO rear end is a favorite of many Pontiac aficionados. The redesigned bumper corresponds well with the contours of the quarter panels, creating a bowtie effect. Backup lamps became standard equipment.

Louvered taillights are similar to those used on the 1966 Grand Prix. Reproduction taillight panels, bezels, and lenses are currently available to the hobbyist.

Tempest and LeMans models did not receive the louvered taillights but rather kidney-shaped units that were well integrated into the rear of the car. The ribbed trim piece containing the Pontiac script was exclusive to the LeMans.

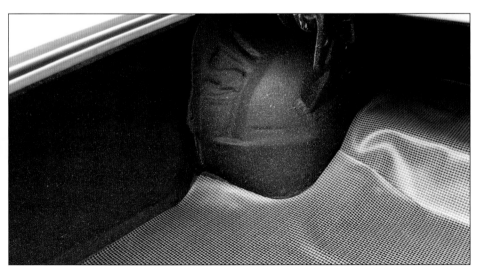

The inside trunk space was painted with a gray/blue spatter paint, slightly different from what was used in 1965. The two-piece mat was standard equipment.

Barrier Blue (code P) was a brilliant metallic hue exclusive to 1966 Pontiac models. A keen eye will notice that this car is missing its lower quarter and fender moldings, as well as some of the window trim.

to slightly more than 21 cubic feet, which still provided more than enough space to haul a pair of drag slicks to the racetrack.

Pontiac again offered 15 regular production paint colors, with some carried over from previous years, while others were new to the GTO's palette. The 15 colors were: Starlight Black (code A), Blue Charcoal (code B), Cameo Ivory (code C), Fontaine Blue (code D), Nightwatch Blue (code E), Palmetto Green (code H), Reef Turquoise (code K), Marina Turquoise (code L), Burgundy (code N), Barrier Blue (code P), Montero Red (code R), Martinique Bronze (code T), Mission Beige (code V), Platinum (code W), and Candlelite Cream (code Y). Cadet Blue (code F), Pinehurst Green (code J), and Sierra Red (code M) were also offered but were not considered regular production colors for 1966. Special-order paint hues such as Tiger Gold, Copper

Montero Red GTOs fitted with a black or red interior featured a Starlight Black pinstripe. A Cameo Ivory pinstripe was suggested for cars painted Montero Red and equipped with a parchment interior. This example displays phenomenal paintwork and was nearly impossible to photograph without any unwanted reflections.

Tiger Gold was a special-order color for 1966 and is coveted by Pontiac collectors. Other visible options on this stunning hardtop include: power antenna, Deluxe wheel covers, redline tires, chrome exhaust extensions, and the highly sought-after red fender liners. To many enthusiasts, this car represents the epitome of the Pontiac GTO.

This 1966 GTO convertible is painted a custom color that is similar to Palmetto Green; it contrasts well with the parchment interior. Driven regularly, this example is shod with modern radial tires for improved handling.

Created under Pontiac materials engineer, Joshua Madden, the red plastic fender liners (code 522) were a $26.33 option in 1966. The liners were not popular when first offered, but they are now coveted by Pontiac collectors.

Because of the intricacies of a folding top, convertible models received more conventional rear window styling that lacked the dramatic effect of the hardtop and Sports Coupe versions.

Convertible owners live for top-down cruising, and the elegant shape of the 1966 GTO enhances this desire. Candlelite Cream (code Y) contrasts beautifully with the black convertible top (code 2) and black interior (code 223).

Blaze, Ramada Bronze, Plum Mist, and Fathom Turquoise were available upon request; these colors are denoted by a number 2 on the cowl data plate. Other GM colors that were not offered by Pontiac could also be specified, and a number 1 is found on the data plate in these instances. A GTO originally painted in any of these special-order colors would be extremely valuable and collectible in today's muscle car marketplace.

As in 1965, a single painted pinstripe was standard on 1966 GTOs, available in Starlight Black, Cameo Ivory, or Montero Red. Pontiac included a list of recommended pinstripe colors, advising the buyer which stripe would best complement the interior and exterior color choices. For example, a black stripe was suggested for a 1966 GTO painted Montero Red and fitted with either medium red (code 222) or black (code 223) interior. However, an ivory stripe was recommended for a car painted Montero Red and equipped with a parchment (code 224) interior. The pinstripe could be deleted if desired, but research suggests that the buyer was not given any monetary credit for choosing to omit it.

An interesting option for 1966 (and 1967) was the red plastic fender liners (code 522) that added a splash of color to the exterior of the car. These liners were designed to protect the inner fenders from road debris and could be cleaned easily. The 1966 GTO/2+2 sales brochure noted, "Extra cost plastic wheelhouse inserts never discolor or fade. They're washable." This was another item that was not yet available at the beginning of 1966 production. At $26.33, it was not an expensive option, but one that few buyers selected, and cars originally so equipped are quite rare and therefore desired by collectors.

It should be noted that, while the red plastic fender liners are mostly associated with the GTO, they were offered on all 1966 and 1967 Pontiac A-body cars. These pieces were notoriously difficult to produce to the exact tolerances needed for correct fitment, as GM historian John Sawruk explained, "I couldn't talk to the product engineer directly on these for fear of causing him to have a nervous breakdown . . . The parts were made of vacuum-formed high-density polyethylene. They were not precise, dimensionally. I can imagine the engineer fitting the design to the ever-changing tolerances of the Pontiac Fisher and Pontiac Assembly Plant cars, and then in addition, having to accommodate all the other assembly plants and body shops!"

Sister division Oldsmobile used comparable pieces on its 4-4-2 W-30 cars from 1967–1971. However, the Oldsmobile versions were complete inner fenders, not just fender liners, which meant the bold, red color could be seen not only from the exterior wheel opening area, but also from inside the engine compartment when the hood was open.

Drop-tops of all makes remained immensely popular during the mid-1960s, as the Ford Mustang sold 73,112 convertibles in 1965 and 72,119 units in 1966. Convertible GTOs had their strongest year ever in 1966, with 12,798 cars produced. While the roofline was a key styling element of the hardtop and Sports Coupe models, a simpler design was employed for convertibles due to the complexities presented by a folding top. Nevertheless, the 1966 body lent itself beautifully to the convertible, especially with the top down.

Current 1966 GTO owner Tim Perry recalls, "I remember when I was about 10 years old, a friend of mine had

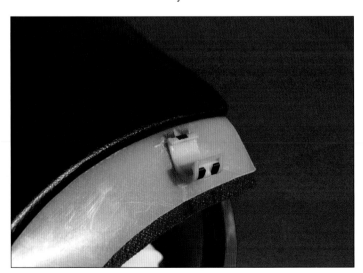

Several plastic clips attach the convertible boot to the stainless-steel trim. The boot provides a clean, finished appearance when the top is in the down position.

This interior view of the convertible frame assembly shows the rear side panels, which are unique to convertible models; they accommodate the folding top and associated components. The reconfigured side panels and narrower rear seat reduced rear passenger hip and shoulder room.

an older brother that had a 1966 GTO. Seeing that car for the first time stopped me in my tracks. I distinctly remember the front grille and stacked headlights. Years later, when I was searching for a classic car, I instantly gravitated to the GTO." Perry further elaborated on the highlights of owning such a vehicle, "I wanted a convertible as they were not as common as the hardtop models, and, living in Florida, there is nothing better than driving with the top down and letting in the sky during the winter months." Indeed, convertibles have their own enthusiast following, with a strong camaraderie shared among fellow owners.

Convertible tops for the 1966 GTO remained power operated (optional for Tempest and LeMans models) and were available in ivory, black, blue, turquoise, and beige. As in previous years, the convertible frame assembly was painted gloss black. A plastic rear window was still used until a glass window debuted on the redesigned 1968 model.

Cordova tops endured as a fashionable choice and the roofline of the 1966 GTO gives the impression that it was designed with the Cordova top in mind. Now priced at $84.26, the buyer could select from three colors: ivory, black, or beige. Black appears to have been the most common Cordova top color, as it readily complemented any exterior color choice. Again, any prospective buyer looking to purchase a classic GTO should inspect the roof thoroughly for any signs of rust, which usually shows as bubbles under the top. It should be noted that even small areas of corrosion can lead to costly repairs, as proper restoration would require metal patches, paint and bodywork, and a new Cordova top.

Interior

Like the exterior, the interior of the GTO was beautifully restyled for 1966. The dashboard retained

its four-pod layout but eliminated the two-tier design of 1964 and 1965 in favor of a single, large, walnut veneer panel face. It was handsome but the new dashboard no longer tied in with the chrome-ribbed center console as it had in 1965. The passenger-side grab handle remained but did not protrude as far and no longer displayed the small ridges of the 1965 bar. A GTO emblem remained to

The interior space was thoughtfully restyled for the 1966 GTO. A large walnut veneer dash surrounded the gauges, replacing the two-tier designs of 1964 and 1965. For improved safety, the dash pad was made larger and became standard issue.

The black interior of this 1966 GTO presents very well. The passenger grab bar was changed slightly for 1966 and the ignition switch was moved to the right of the steering column. Stylistically unchanged from 1965, the optional center console became code 472 and cost $47.13.

Gauges were redesigned for 1966, and they were not as bold as the 1965 versions. The tachometer, part of the Rally Gauge package (code 448), displayed a redline of 5,100 rpm. The turn signal and high-beam indicators were located between the center of the four dash pods.

Coolant temperature and oil pressure gauges occupied the far-right dash pod. Readings on the temperature gauge were 100–180–245 (Fahrenheit); oil pressure readings were 0–30–60 (PSI).

The owner of this 1966 GTO chose to install a Rally tachometer in the far-right dash pod to complement the standard instrumentation. The difference in appearance between the standard gauges and the Rally versions are evident.

the left of the grab bar as it had the previous year. The dash pad, now standard equipment, was larger than prior years and displayed a deep overhang above the gauges. The ignition switch, still located in the dash, was now to the right of the steering column.

Rally gauges (code 448) returned as an $84.26 option but differed in appearance from the 1965 components. Whereas the 1965 Rally gauges sported a bold look, with large font and a checkered flag on the speedometer, the 1966 versions were somewhat subdued, featuring smaller font and no longer displaying the checkered flag. The faces of the Rally gauges were now a blue-green color. Standard gauges retained the look of previous years, with larger numbers and gray-blue appearance.

The two-spoke standard steering wheel was restyled for 1966, with the horn button revised to activate when pressing the chrome arms on either side. This presented the 1966 standard steering wheel with a rather spartan appearance, unbefitting of the GTO's sports car aesthetic. The optional Custom Sports steering wheel (code 471) was identical to the 1965 version, available for an additional $38.44. The 1966 GTO/2+2 sales brochure brilliantly described the Custom Sports steering wheel, "Only a hungry termite will know it's not wood." Like the 1964 and 1965 models, many 1966 GTO owners choose to fit their car with the Custom Sports steering wheel, even if not originally equipped. A tilt steering wheel (code 504) was offered at $43.13 and required the buyer to also order power steering. The tilt steering wheel was not compatible with the column-shifted manual transmission.

The bucket seats were completely revamped for 1966, incorporating painted steel backs and a more supportive

The standard steering wheel for the 1966 GTO was a simple, two-spoke design. This car is also equipped with the Rally gauge option, push-button AM radio, and center console.

The optional Custom Sports steering wheel is much more elegant than the standard two-spoke version. The wheel coordinates well with the large walnut veneer dash surrounding the gauge cluster.

Detail of the 1966 optional Custom Sports steering wheel horn button. Complete reproduction Custom Sports steering wheels, including the detailed Lucite emblems, are available through multiple restoration parts suppliers.

seating position than previous years. The new seats also displayed an updated upholstery pattern: a clean, straightforward design showcasing several horizontal pleats broken up by two vertical pleats. Headrests (code 571) were made available for the first time on the GTO and were a $52.66 option. Headrests are an important safety feature but are not commonly found on 1966–1968 GTOs; however, partway through the 1969 model year, they became standard equipment. Seat belts could still be deleted in 1966, if requested (code 434).

With a vast array of muscle cars crowding the marketplace, Pontiac Motor Division was offering additional luxury options, which sought to maintain a competitive edge for the GTO. Jim Wangers noted, "A mature performance market emerged as a significant factor, and we felt that perhaps some people might be turned off by the Grand Prix or the Bonneville as being just too big. We thought they may be looking for some kind of personal sophistication in a little smaller package." A front bench seat, called the Strato Bench Seat (code 568), was a special-order item carrying a hefty price tag of $92.22, just under $700 when adjusted for inflation. GTOs equipped with the Strato Bench option and automatic transmission necessitated a column-mounted shifter.

While the Strato Bucket Seats (code 562) were standard issue on the 1966 GTO, another somewhat unusual comfort option (for a muscle car) were the Strato Bucket Seats with headrests and a reclining passenger seat (code 574). By adding a power driver's seat (code 564) for $69.51 and power windows (code 551) for an extra $100.05, a buyer could make his interior quite lavish, if desired.

The door panels were restyled to coordinate with the seat upholstery and featured a padded armrest and a GTO emblem. Rear side panels were correspondingly redesigned. Resilient Morrokide vinyl was again used extensively for the GTO's upholstery, while base model Tempests used a combination of fabric and Morrokide.

As in previous years, bucket seats were standard equipment in the Pontiac GTO. The seats, redesigned for 1966, featured more support than earlier versions and displayed a clean, simple horizontally ribbed upholstery pattern.

The new seat design in 1966 included hard-shell seat backs. Constructed of steel, they were painted to match the other interior components.

Door panels were new for 1966, and they incorporated a simple vertical ribbed pattern that harmonized well with the rest of the interior space. A GTO emblem was placed in the center, just above the armrest.

Rear seat area of a 1966 GTO hardtop equipped with the bronze (code 221) interior. Ashtrays were integrated into the rear seat armrests. Notice the blind spot created by the swept-back roof pillar.

The interior of this Tiger Gold 1966 GTO is nicely appointed. Visible options include: Custom Sports steering wheel, Rally gauge package, power brakes, center console, walnut shift knob, AM/FM radio with power antenna, and floor mats.

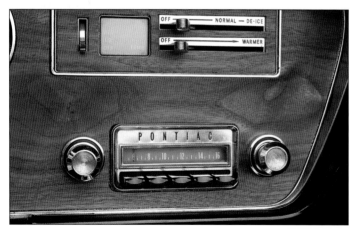

The AM push-button radio with fixed (fender-mounted) antenna was a $61.09 option. AM radios featured black buttons, while AM/FM versions used chrome buttons. If no radio was specified, a block-off plate was fitted. Enthusiasts sometimes mistakenly refer to a car ordered without a radio as "radio-delete"; however, that term only applies if a radio was standard equipment, not an extra-cost option.

The push-button AM/FM radio with power antenna (code 345) was the costliest radio option available, at $162.88. That translates to approximately $1,231 in 2017, adjusting for inflation. The heater controls for this non-A/C-equipped car are also clearly visible. A three-speed fan switch was accompanied by air (vent) and temperature controls.

The optional center console was unchanged from 1965 and was available with either an automatic or manual transmission. There has been at least one documented case of a column-shifted 1966 GTO equipped with a center console. A block-off plate was used where the shifter would normally have been.

Loop carpeting remained standard, but a redesigned heel pad was implemented. The accelerator pedal was new and no longer attached to the floor at its base; instead, it was suspended from the accelerator rod. Floor mats were optional factory pieces, (code 631 front and code 632 rear) and differed slightly from previous years to better contour to the shape of the floor. Floor mats were also available as dealer-installed items and were priced slightly higher than if factory equipped.

As in 1965, numerous radio options were offered to the potential buyer in 1966. AM units were available in various configurations with manual or push-button control and manual (fixed) or electric antennas. AM/FM radios were available with push-button control only, but they were available with a manual or electric antenna. Sepra-Phonic and Verbra-Phonic rear speakers were extra-cost items, but they could not be ordered together and were not available on convertible models. A radio was an extremely popular option and could be ordered separately or as part of the 061 option group, which included a push-button radio with manual antenna (code 342) and electric clock (code 444) for an extra $80.05.

Driveline

Some minor mechanical changes did occur, but the 1966 GTO was very similar to the 1965 model. Horsepower ratings stagnated for the first time in the car's brief history, with the 4-barrel version still rated at 335 hp and 360 hp for the Tri-Power-equipped cars. Changes were more noticeable for the lower-level Tempest and LeMans models, which were now fitted with the new 165-hp 230-ci overhead-camshaft 6-cylinder engine as standard equipment, superseding the more conventional 215-ci 6-cylinder used in 1964 and 1965. The optional Sprint package used a higher compression ratio and a Rochester Quadrajet 4-barrel carburetor to produce 207 hp. Tying into the success of the GTO, a print advertisement for the LeMans Sprint was titled, "GTO Jr."

Engine block identification, as in previous years, could be found stamped on the passenger-side front of the block, just below the deck surface. The six-digit number was simply the block serial number and does not correspond to the VIN of the car. The two-letter code just below the serial number can be decoded as follows: YS (335 hp with automatic transmission), XE (335 hp with automatic transmission and the air injector reactor [A.I.R.] system), WT (335 hp with manual transmission), WW (335 hp with manual transmission and A.I.R. system), YH (360 hp with automatic transmission),

Code WT on this 1966 389-ci block indicates 335 hp (4-barrel) and manual transmission. The six-digit number above the block code is a serial number and does not relate to the car's VIN. The 389 in this case is purely coincidental and does not represent 389 ci.

Output for the optional Tri-Power engine remained at 360 hp and 424 ft-lbs of torque. Even though the Tri-Power arrangement is more commonly seen on present-day GTOs, the 335-hp 4-barrel engines were much more popular in 1966, with 77,698 units produced, compared to only 19,063 Tri-Power-equipped cars (excluding the 185–190 Ram Air Tri-Power engines).

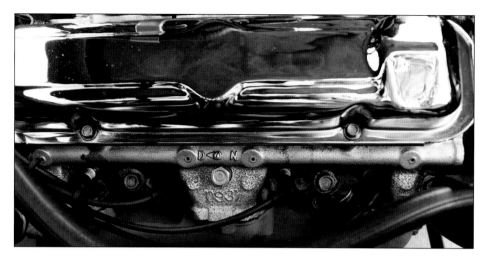

Casting number 093 cylinder heads were used on the 1966 GTO. The bulge in the heads just below the valve cover facilitated the use of the air injector reactor (A.I.R.) system, a mandatory pollution control device implemented for cars sold in California. A special head bolt was required for the center exhaust ports to allow clearance for a socket to fit.

YR (360 hp with automatic transmission and A.I.R. system), WS (360 hp with manual transmission), WV (360 hp with manual transmission and A.I.R. system), and XS (360 hp Ram Air with manual transmission).

The GTO's 389-ci cylinder head castings changed to the 093 units but retained the same 1.92-inch intake and

The 093 casting number is clearly visible on the center exhaust ports of the cylinder heads for the 1966 GTO. These ports share a common wall and a pronounced D-shape is evident. As with many other Pontiac heads sharing this attribute (such as the 1964 716 and 1965 77 castings) these heads are commonly referred to as D-ports. (Photo Courtesy Robert Bennett)

Closed combustion chambers, 1.92-inch intake, and 1.66-inch exhaust valves were used in the 1966 093 cylinder heads. Compression ratio was rated at 10.75:1. (Photo Courtesy Robert Bennett)

1.66-inch exhaust valve sizes found in the 77 heads used on the 1965 cars. The casting number is easily found on the center exhaust ports. The familiar Carter 500-cfm carburetor returned for 4-barrel 335-hp engines, as did the low-profile pie pan air cleaner. Camshaft profiles also remained unchanged, with 335-hp engines receiving the 067 camshaft, while 360-hp Tri-Power mills were fitted with the 068 grind.

The Tri-Power induction system was upgraded for 1966; the center carburetor was enlarged for improved airflow and a revised intake manifold was implemented. As there were no factory-equipped Tri-Power GTOs after 1966, this setup was a one-year-only design. The horsepower rating was the same as the previous year. However, many enthusiasts deem the 1966 Tri-Power system superior to the 1964 and 1965 units because of the increased airflow provided by the larger center carburetor and redesigned intake manifold.

The 1966 Tri-Power intake manifold, casting number 9782898, was redesigned to accept the larger center Rochester 2-barrel carburetor. Although these two revisions improved airflow, the engine remained factory rated at 360 hp, the same as the 1965 models.

The A.I.R. system used a belt-driven pump located between the A/C compressor and alternator to recirculate unspent gases back into the cylinder heads for further combustion. This arrangement also required additional plumbing and an air cleaner specific to the A.I.R. system. (Photo Courtesy Ken Nagy)

This 1966 GTO was heavily optioned from the factory, resulting in a crowded engine compartment, even by modern car standards. The A.I.R. pump (mandatory on vehicles sold in California) shares the space with an A/C compressor, alternator, and power steering pump. (Photo Courtesy Ken Nagy)

By 1966, air quality concerns mandated certain emissions-control equipment on automobiles produced for sale in California. To comply with California's strict regulations, Pontiac implemented the use of the A.I.R. system, which added $44.76 to the price of a new GTO. Cars equipped with A.I.R. used a belt-driven pump that forced pressurized air into the exhaust ports, facilitating a more complete burning of exhaust gases. Specifically, jetted carburetor(s) and ignition timing further helped to reduce emissions. The 093 cylinder heads were designed to work in concert with the A.I.R. system and displayed small ports on the front of the heads, along with a pronounced bulge that ran the length of the head located just above the exhaust ports. The ports on the cylinder heads of 1966 GTOs for sale outside of California were simply blocked off.

Although GTOs sold in California were required to be fitted with A.I.R., many enthusiasts removed the cumbersome, power-robbing components shortly after purchase. These pieces were often not stored away for future use; they were discarded altogether. Today, a GTO equipped with an original, functioning A.I.R. system is a rare and collectible piece of Pontiac history.

Ram Air Engine

While the 4-barrel and Tri-Power engines remained mostly unchanged, a Ram Air engine was offered later in the model year as a factory option. It is generally believed that just 190 of these engines carrying the code XS were produced in 1966 and they exemplify a significant piece of the GTO's legacy. The Ram Air scoop package was only part of this option, as the 1966 XS Ram Air engine included stiffer valve springs and a special camshaft (PN 9779744,

Even though the carburetors are fitted with later-style replacement paper elements, and not the original-style foam pieces, this 1966 GTO is a Pontiac Historical Services (PHS) documented XS Code Ram Air car. (Photo Courtesy Chris Phillip)

commonly referred to as 744) that featured increased intake and exhaust duration. These components were different from the pieces used on both the 4-barrel and non–Ram Air Tri-Power-equipped cars. Curiously, the XS Ram Air engines were rated at the same 360 hp as the non–Ram Air Tri-Power versions.

In the March 2014 issue of *High Performance Pontiac* magazine, well-known Pontiac author Don Keefe related,

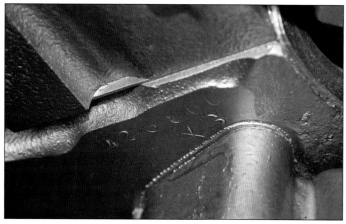

At first glance, the block stamp on this 1966 Ram Air block appears to be XG (there was no such stamping), but a closer look reveals that it is, in fact, the coveted XS. Documentation has been found indicating that 190 of the XS Code Ram Air engines were produced in 1966. The number of factory-built 1966 Ram Air GTOs is thought to be around 185, with five engines perhaps available as service replacement components. (Photo Courtesy Chris Phillip)

"Why weren't any of the 1966 Tri-Power engines re-rated from 1965, especially the XS engine? It was a matter of getting around corporate edicts. After the delightfully sneaky moves that put a 389 in the 1964 GTO engine bay, everyone else at GM had big-inch engines in their intermediates. In order to keep some sort of control over the divisions, GM's new edict stated that cars could not weigh fewer than 10 pounds for every horsepower. To prevent that from happening, Pontiac and other divisions began downrating their engines in order to comply with the rulings." If the 1965 Tri-Power engine was rated accurately at 360 hp, it's safe to assume that the 1966 version, with its revised center carburetor and intake manifold would have produced 365 to 370 hp. In addition, one could speculate that the XS engine would have gained about 20 to 25 hp more than the 1966 Tri-Power engine, pushing the output closer to 400 hp. With such limited production, XS code Ram Air 1966 GTOs are highly sought after by serious Pontiac collectors.

Research suggests that certain options were mandatory with the 1966 XS engine option, including M21 close-ratio 4-speed transmission, Safe-T-Track differential, 4.33:1 rear end ratio, heavy-duty fan, and metallic brake linings. This was indeed a potent combination, and it would likely have been the quickest 1964–1966 GTO available. The buyer would have been wise to also invest in a set of drag slicks, as the brute force of the XS Ram Air engine and the steep 4.33:1 rear gears would have instantly overcome the narrow 7.75-inch-wide factory-issued tires.

The March 1966 issue of *Car and Driver* magazine featured a six-way test between the Oldsmobile 4-4-2, Chevrolet Chevelle Super Sport, Buick Skylark Gran Sport, Ford Fairlane GT/A, Mercury Comet Cyclone GT, and Pontiac GTO. The object of the test was to determine the best overall performer (acceleration, braking, handling) and "usefulness as high-performance, over-the-road vehicles, and not as potential racing machines." The rules stipulated that the cars must be in a stock configuration, or at most, tuned with parts that were easily available to the consumer. Participating manufacturers interpreted this rule in different ways:

A Tiger Gold 1966 GTO fitted with Hurst wheels, similar to the car used in the March 1966 Car and Driver *tests. Participants were thoroughly evaluated to see which machine exhibited the best all-around street performance. (Photo Courtesy Andre Rayman)*

the Chevelle, 4-4-2, and Skylark Gran Sport were virtually showroom stock, while the Fairlane, Comet, and GTO were treated to various levels of tuning and performance enhancements. When the Comet arrived at the test on the back of NASCAR great Bud Moore's transporter, with Moore himself present at the test sessions, the *Car and Driver* staff knew that the Comet Cyclone GT was going to be the most highly modified car of the group. In an effort to maintain consistent test results, all cars were fitted with Firestone Super Sports 500 7.75 x 14 street tires, and Hurst forged-aluminum wheels were offered to all competitors. However, an inspection of the photos showed that both the Skylark Gran Sport and Fairlane GT/A retained their factory-issued wheels for the test sessions.

The GTO was painted "eye-popping" Tiger Gold, which the Hurst wheels complemented beautifully. The car's appearance made a strong impression on the writers at *Car and Driver*, "This is the car that started it all, and in some ways the GTO still has a year's jump on the competition. It is certainly the sportiest looking and feeling car of the six, and it indicates an awareness on the part of its builders about what this market demands."

The piece did not specify if the GTO was fitted with an XS Ram Air engine; nevertheless, with Pontiac's history of issuing specially prepped test cars to the press, it was plausible. Ram Air engine or not, the 389-ci Tri-Power mill was treated to a thorough Royal Bobcat conversion: carburetor re-jetting, thinner head gaskets to raise compression, blocked heat risers, and special ignition timing. The article mentioned, "This left us somewhat less than ecstatic because the Royal kit is available only through a single Royal Oak, Michigan, dealer and can therefore

hardly be described as universally available. However, Pontiac was perfectly candid about the alterations, which did involve stock parts and could be made by any GTO owner in his own garage, so we decided to let them run." The GTO was also equipped with a 4-speed manual transmission and 3.55:1 rear end gearing.

The staff wrote, "The GTO sounded almost as fierce as the Fairlane and the Comet while it turned the second-fastest ET of the day. Much of the noise was traceable to the blocked heat risers, which caused a deep resonance in the exhaust, and the optional cold air box, which amplified the sound of air being sucked into the carburetors. The car turned the fastest trap time, at 105.14, while clocking an ET of 14.05 seconds." It should be noted that the quarter-mile tests were also performed with the Firestone street tires and traction was an issue for all test cars. Drag slicks would likely have dropped the times into the mid-13 second range.

Test driver Masten Gregory commented, "The GTO had more horsepower than the rest of the cars. It certainly made more engine noise, and this sucking sound from the carburetors tends to give you the impression of power. It felt *very* strong." Even though Gregory was unimpressed with the GTO's handling and braking capability, his comments about the engine's power and its "impression of power" seemed to reinforce the high-performance image and attitude that Pontiac engineers and marketers had been cultivating since the car's debut in late 1963.

Exhaust

As in previous years, the 1966 GTO employed a true dual exhaust system. Cast-iron manifolds flowed into

ROYAL PONTIAC

In 1959, with Pontiac rapidly gaining a reputation as a performance brand, Jim Wangers had the idea to assemble a traveling seminar to educate dealers on the benefits of marketing, selling, and installing performance hardware. He presented the concept to Bunkie Knudsen, Pete Estes, and Frank Bridge. Knudsen and Estes were quiet during the proposal while Bridge was openly opposed, stating that the dealers should focus on selling "regular cars." Wangers felt defeated, but later received a call from Knudsen, who encouraged him to find a dealer that would like to participate in this high-performance venture. Wangers contacted Bill Packer Jr. of Packer Pontiac, who had dealerships in Detroit and Flint, Michigan, as well as Miami, Florida. Packer was hesitant about the idea of becoming a performance-based dealer, and he wanted some time to consider the proposition.

Meanwhile, Wangers visited with Asa "Ace" Wilson Jr. at Royal Pontiac in Royal Oak, Michigan. According to Wangers, Ace Wilson was more than receptive to the notion. In fact, "He was so enthusiastic about it, he went ballistic and would not let me out of his office until he signed a contract." Located just 15 miles outside of Detroit, it was the perfect place to conduct a race-inspired business, and ultimately proved to be beneficial for both Pontiac Motor Division and the Royal Pontiac dealership.

Asa Wilson Jr. was born into a wealthy family that made its money with a dairy farm. Asa Wilson Sr. recognized his son's lack of enthusiasm for the family business and purchased Royal Pontiac, which Ace managed. Ace's freewheeling attitude played a key role in his zeal for Jim Wangers and his performance dealership idea. Before the GTO's arrival, Royal Pontiac focused on full-size cars, such as the Catalina, with great success. When the GTO debuted in late 1963, Royal Pontiac played a key role in its history, improving the car's performance through special "Bobcat Packages" and furthering the belief that a Pontiac GTO was the ultimate street car.

A red 1959 Tri-Power Catalina driven by Bill Sidwell became the first Royal Pontiac race car and boasted a 389-ci engine with 345 hp and 425 ft-lbs of torque. The 389 was treated to an array of performance upgrades and ran quite well, but the column-shifted 3-speed manual transmission proved to be cumbersome and the crew eventually installed a 4.88:1 rear end, enabling Sidwell to launch the car in second gear and make just one shift in the quarter-mile.

After an accident on the street involving Sidwell and the 1959 Catalina race car, Jim Wangers assumed driving duties for the Royal racing team. Wangers piloted a 1960 Catalina (with a floor-mounted, 4-speed manual transmis-

Royal Pontiac in Royal Oak, Michigan, was the premier performance dealership throughout the 1960s. Its legacy is far reaching, and enthusiasts continue to adorn their cars with Royal Pontiac livery.

For 1960, Royal Pontiac campaigned two 1960 Catalinas: a red one, which Jim Wangers drove to the NHRA Top Stock Eliminator title that year, and this white car that Dick Jesse usually drove. This car remains in excellent condition and can be seen at Pontiac national events. (Photo Courtesy Don Keefe)

Driven by Jim Wangers, this 1962 Catalina was a highly successful Royal Pontiac race car. It featured aluminum front fenders and hood to reduce weight; a keen eye will also notice the Grand Prix grilles, which were lighter than the standard Catalina pieces and used for further weight reduction. (Photo Courtesy Don Keefe)

and became an integral contributor to the Royal Bobcat team. In Keith J. MacDonald's book, *Milt Schornack and the Royal Bobcat GTOs,* Schornack recalls, "The first project they put me on at Royal was the Royal Bobcat Tempest, which was actually a station wagon with a 421 Super Duty engine." Milt performed a complete teardown and rebuild of the engine and was soon working with senior Royal Bobcat mechanics Bud Conrad and Chuck Brumfield.

Royal Bobcat performance tunes were becoming very popular with non-professional street racers who wanted to dominate the boulevards of the Motor City and its surrounding areas. Eventually, a Bobcat kit could be mail-ordered and a competent car owner could have it installed over the course of a weekend. Schornack states, "I want everyone to know that I didn't introduce the Bobcat package. That claim belongs to people like Frank Rediker, Wynn Brown, Dick Jesse, and another salesman at Royal Pontiac, John Martin." The Royal Bobcat kit included various fine-tuning components such as a distributor re-curve kit, which came with new points, a condenser, and lighter weights and springs. The buyer also received thinner cylinder head gaskets to raise the compression ratio, locking rocker arm nuts, and new valve cover gaskets. New carburetor jets and an intake manifold gasket to block the heat riser for a cooler air/fuel mixture completed the package.

sion) to victory in the Top Stock Eliminator class at the U.S. Nationals in 1960. He is credited with the idea of using the name "Bobcat," formed by re-arranging the letters from the Bonneville and Catalina models. A white 1961 Catalina served as the first official Royal race car to use that moniker and came equipped with the 348-hp 389 engine with Tri-Power induction. Royal Pontiac soon became the unofficial test dealership for Pontiac Motor Division, gaining a solid reputation for extracting the most power out of the 389, and later, the 421 and 428 engines.

Milt Schornack was a talented young mechanic from Detroit who began working at Royal Pontiac in October 1963

While the mail-order kit was a huge success, in-house packages, which were more thorough and custom tailored to each vehicle, remained popular with serious performance enthusiasts. Schornack stated, "Those Pontiac engines just loved compression, so when you combined the shaved heads with the thinner head gaskets, you'd decrease head-to-block clearance about .035 inch. This would increase the compression ratio to a true 11:1." At its peak in 1966, Royal Pontiac sold approximately 1,000 Bobcat conversions.

With the GTO now a huge triumph for both Pontiac Motor Division and Royal Pontiac, Royal decided to build two GTO

ROYAL PONTIAC *CONTINUED*

drag cars that would be raced at numerous drag strips in the Midwest to further hype the GTO's race image and promote the Royal Bobcat performance package. Mechanically, the two cars were nearly identical, with the obvious difference being the color schemes; one was painted Cameo Ivory, the other was Iris Mist with a black vinyl top.

In the book, *Milt Schornack and the Royal Bobcat GTOs*, Schornack relayed, "In 1965, Royal Pontiac decided to test the market by running two GTOs at drag strips in the Detroit area. I'm sure everyone has heard about these match races. The cars were called the *GeeTO Tigers*. Many people have been told that these cars arrived in 1966, but they actually debuted in 1965. They were Bobcat cars with Tri-Powered 389 engines: the very first *GeeTO Tigers*.

"These two *GeeTO Tiger* cars had a complete Bobcat package installed. Cylinder heads were milled .030 and the thin [.028–.032] head gaskets were used to increase compression. We blocked the heat riser with Pontiac-issued gaskets, re-curved the distributor, re-jetted the carburetors, and installed the rocker arm lock nuts. While the cylinder heads were off, we gave them a performance valve job and shimmed the stock valve springs by .060. For the show, I would deliberately retard the timing and overinflate the tires in an attempt to slow them down. In this state of tune, they would run 13.50 quarter-mile times at 101–104 mph.

"We played around with off-the-shelf cams. We tried Isky, Crane, and Crower and all three performed well, but for some reason the white GTO performed better than the Iris Mist car. These cars could run the quarter-mile in the high 12-second range with a good set of tires."

Commonly, Dave Landrith or John Politzer would drive one of the cars and assume the role of the Tiger. Clad from head to toe in a tiger costume, the drivers were challenged by poor visibility and summer heat. Tickets were drawn out of a hat to determine who would be chosen to race against the Tiger. Milt Schornack recalled, "It was a pretty tough deal to put a per-

Many of Royal Bobcat's modifications could not be seen by just peering into the engine compartment. Carburetor jetting, thinner head gaskets, and distributor recurving are all undetectable with the engine completely assembled. Unlike Tri-Power-equipped GTOs, Pontiac's full-size cars (such as this 1961 Bonneville) employed a more traditional-style air cleaner assembly. (Photo Courtesy Don Keefe)

It's no surprise that 1966 was the year Royal Bobcat sold more than 1,000 Bobcat packages; that was the peak of GTO production, with 96,946 cars sold. This Barrier Blue hardtop would have been a perfect candidate for the Royal Bobcat treatment.

The GeeTO Tiger, a race-ready 1966 GTO, pays tribute to the two popular drag cars from 1966. It's painted white and gold on the driver's side; black and gold on the passenger's side. This represents the two paint schemes used on the original cars. (Photo Courtesy Don Keefe)

Driver Dave Anderson poses next to the GeeTO Tiger 1966 GTO replica owned by Jim Wangers. It remains a crowd favorite at Pontiac events across the United States. (Photo Courtesy Don Keefe)

son into a 12-second car that they weren't used to. Anyone who was lucky enough to have their name drawn had to be interviewed by me and I had to decide whether they were qualified to drive one of our cars. They also had to possess a driver's license. Before I forget, I must say that the participant always got to choose which car they wanted to drive. Once in a while, we let some of the participants win, but usually the tiger would win. At the end of the day, we would issue a challenge to anyone with a B/stock race car. After re-tuning the *GeeTO Tiger*, I would drive the car against a worthy opponent. There was a rumor that these cars had blueprinted 421 HO engines. Those rumors were false. They had 360-hp 389-ci WS engines with Ram Air and the Bobcat package."

ROYAL PONTIAC *CONTINUED*

For 1966, Jim Wangers and Royal Pontiac upped the ante, and the *GeeTO Tiger* campaign employed four 1966 Tiger Gold GTOs: two tow vehicles and two race cars. One race car had white accents down its body, while the other had black. The cars were immensely popular, and drag strip promoters kept the Royal crew busy throughout the racing season. While Milt Schornack insisted that the 1966 cars retained their 389-ci engines, in his book, *Glory Days: When Horsepower and Passion Ruled Detroit*, Jim Wangers stated, "The two cars were named the *GeeTO Tiger*s and were set up to run like absolute twins. They both featured blueprinted 421 HO engines, Tri-Power, a close-ratio 4-speed transmission, 3.90:1 Safe-T-Track rear ends, and 'cheater slicks,' as we used to call them." One could make the argument for both scenarios: Milt Schornack, as one of the lead mechanics at Royal Bobcat at this time, worked extensively with the *GeeTO Tiger* cars and would have intimate knowledge about every performance modification performed on them. However, there was also motive to build the absolute most powerful GTOs possible, even if this meant installing the larger 421 HO engine that was never available in a showroom GTO, adding to the legend and mystique of the model.

Even though the 1967 GTO, with its 400-ci engine and available TH-400 3-speed automatic transmission, was a

With the new 400-ci engine and available TH-400 3-speed automatic transmission, the 1967 GTOs would have been fantastic as GeeTO Tiger drag race cars. This modified 1967 model currently sees regular drag strip use and runs the quarter-mile in the high 11-second range with a modest 3.23:1 rear gear ratio.

solid performer, the *GeeTO Tiger* campaign was dissolved after the 1966 season, primarily because of insurance costs and the time-consuming nature of the project. Jim Wangers sought to maintain the momentum and brought in two new 1967 Firebirds approximately halfway through the model year (the 1967 Firebird debuted well after the 1967 Camaro). These cars were given the same Bobcat treatment as the *GeeTO Tiger* cars and ran consistent 12.30 second quarter-mile times at about 116 mph.

Pontiac debuted the 428-ci engine in 1967, but never offered it in the GTO or Firebird models. Again, Royal Pontiac seized this opportunity by offering a Bobcat version of the 428-ci engine for $650 with an exchange for the stock 400-ci mill. Of the 428-ci powered GTOs, Milt Schornack stated, "When combined with a Bobcat Package, the car was absolutely untouchable." In the February 1968 issue of *Car and Driver* magazine, a road test noted a 13.8 second quarter-mile time at 104 mph on street tires; the reviewers were thoroughly impressed with the all-around performance of the car, remarking, "Our 428 GTO was a fine, exciting car for either fast touring or tootling around in traffic. Not overly fussy. Not difficult to drive, up to a point. And that point could be reached and exceeded in a flash with a casual downward movement of the right foot. In the hands of an inexperienced or irresponsible driver, the 428 GTO would be as dangerous as a basket of hair-trigger hand grenades." The article further noted, "The 428 GTO will rumble along like a leashed tiger even for granny, but if granny puts her foot down, she's in for the ride of her life. The GTO delivers everything on demand and no expertise asked; only expertise required." It's evident that the *Car and Driver* staff enjoyed the 428 GTO, but they were also very clear about the potential hazards regarding the brute force of the car.

By the late 1960s, the daily responsibilities of running an automotive dealership began to take their toll on Asa Wilson Jr. He became frustrated by internal dealership politics and eventually sold Royal Pontiac in 1970 to John DeLorean's brother, George.

Cast-iron exhaust manifolds were again used for the 1966 GTO. They were restrictive when compared to long-branch manifolds or tubular headers but were quite common for the era.

Pontiac engineers paid special attention to the exhaust tone emanating from the GTO, as this contributed substantially to the car's image, and the sound clearly had Kelly's attention. He noted, "If anyone should ever steal a GTO, its owner could advise the local authorities to stand near stop signs and keep an ear out for 'that low-octave B note.'"

Transmission

Transmission choices for 1966 differed slightly from the previous year. If no transmission option was specified, the Saginaw M11 3-speed manual unit was installed and the shifter was mounted on the steering column. Because Pontiac produced the

2-inch pipes and dual mufflers. Separate resonators were used and mounted at the very end of the system, just aft of the tailpipes. These resonators were specifically designed to generate the most desirable exhaust note possible. Chrome tailpipe extensions (code 482) were a $30.23 option. The 1966 extensions were a trumpet-style, and therefore, the term 'splitters' would no longer apply as it had in 1964 and 1965.

In the May 1966 issue of *Motor Trend* magazine, writer Steve Kelly noted, "When driving either of the cars around town, we turned quite a few heads, especially at stoplights; while waiting for them, not leaving them. Resonators on the exhaust pipes emit a 'pock-pock' sound with every engine revolution. This gives a very distinctive air, as well as sound, to the car." It is well known that

Trumpet-style chrome exhaust extensions replaced the splitter-style of 1964 and 1965. If the extensions were not specified, the tailpipes terminated just before the rear bumper at an angle of approximately 45 degrees.

A Hurst 4-speed shifter protrudes proudly from the optional center console of a 1966 GTO. A black knob with the shift pattern engraved in white was the standard piece for manual transmission GTOs in 1966. Original knobs simply had threads cut directly into the plastic, while most reproductions have a metal insert. (Photo Courtesy Andre Rayman)

ARNIE BESWICK

Hailing from the small town of Morrison, Illinois, Arnie "the Farmer" Beswick is perhaps the most recognizable name in Pontiac drag-racing history. Beswick boasts a resilient blue-collar background and epitomizes the hard-working American spirit that helped him become a legend in both the drag racing and Pontiac communities.

In an interview with Steve Magnante for *Car Craft* magazine, Beswick recalled, "When the Mopars let me down in 1957, I didn't want a Chevy since they were like belly buttons, even then. So, I looked at Pontiac and liked the 1957 Tri-Power 347. When it grew to 370 cubes for 1958, I bought one." His 1958 Pontiac performed quite well, but the column-shifter of the 3-speed manual transmission could not withstand repetitive gear slamming, so it was replaced with a BorgWarner T-10 4-speed and a floor-mounted shifter for 1959.

Shortly after purchasing a brand-new 1960 Ventura hardtop from Morrison Pontiac in Clinton, Iowa, Beswick drove it the entire 1,200-mile journey from Illinois to the first-ever NHRA/NASCAR Winternationals in Daytona, Florida. His new Ventura, which packed the punch of a 389 Tri-Power engine and a floor-shifted 4-speed manual transmission, had enough muscle to secure the win in the Stock Eliminator class.

When Beswick began making his mark at drag strips in the southeastern United States where the payouts were biggest, complaints from local racers resulted in many time-consuming engine teardowns. He recalls, "Pontiac had everything going for it in the early 1960s, and the Chevrolet guys were so damn jealous."

One of Beswick's more noteworthy cars was his famous 1964 Pontiac GTO named the *Mystery Tornado*. The GTO began life as a 389 Tri-Power car and Beswick removed the stock engine in favor of a 421 Super Duty, even though the 389 had accrued a mere 16 miles. The 421-ci powerplant was the same engine used in Beswick's successful *Grocery Getter*, a 1963 Tempest wagon.

A large GMC supercharger was soon added, and the *Mystery Tornado* competed in the Supercharged/Factory Experimental class. The car also showcased a lightweight, dealer-installed aluminum front-end. Beswick stated, "Pontiac had intentions of selling more of those front ends, but

The 1964 GTO Mystery Tornado *was one of Arnie Beswick's most popular cars. Powered by a supercharged 421-ci engine, it was a crowd favorite at a time when Pontiac officially withdrew from racing. This car is a meticulously detailed replica of Beswick's famed machine. (Photo Courtesy Don Keefe)*

upper management went berserk and stopped it immediately. They sent at least 30 to the crusher and had top-level executives present as witnesses to make sure they got destroyed. That was a direct result of GM's 1963 racing ban, it definitely killed that for us."

With Pontiac (and the rest of General Motors) officially out of racing, the sport was overflowing with Ford and Mopar racers, and drag strip promoters across the nation wanted a piece of Beswick's one-of-a-kind *Mystery Tornado*. Despite zero factory support, Beswick's GTO ran with the best of them, including a long-standing rivalry with Mr. Norm and his Hemi-powered machines and Dyno Don Nicholson in his factory-backed Mercury Comet Cyclone.

Back in Illinois, one of Beswick's neighbors had purchased his son a brand-new 1964 GTO as a graduation present, and Beswick would occasionally lend his expertise. He recalls, "I would help him tune it, and it ran great; he wasn't supposed to be racing it, but he was. That car became known as the 'Little Farmer' and was even lettered for a little while, until the kid's dad found out and put a stop to it." One can only imagine how wild it must have been to have the Farmer in your neighborhood, wrenching on your brand-new GTO.

After nearly two years devoted to racing Pontiacs with no manufacturer help, Beswick decided to accept an offer from Mercury, and was soon behind the wheel of a new SOHC 427 Comet Cyclone. The Mercury deal was short lived, however, as the 427 needed constant adjustments and maintenance; in addition, track promoters and crowds were still clamoring to see Beswick piloting one of his legendary Pontiacs.

Weighing close to 3,500 pounds, the *Mystery Tornado* was too heavy to remain competitive against the lightweight Ford and Mopars of the day. Never one to disappoint his fans, Beswick soon focused his attention on morphing his 1963 Super Duty Tempest into an altered wheelbase monster called the *Tameless Tiger*. Moving both the front and rear axles forward allowed for better weight transfer and increased traction on hard launches. While the *Mystery Tornado* was on a full frame platform, the *Tameless Tiger* was unibody construction; this, combined with other weight-saving measures, dropped the heft all the way down to approximately 2,800 pounds.

Powered by a supercharged fuel-injected 421 Super Duty Pontiac, the *Tameless Tiger* was running mid-8 second passes in the quarter-mile at nearly 170 mph and proved to be wildly popular at drag strips across the nation. Throughout the rest of the 1960s and the first two years of the

Arnie Beswick's "Star of the Circuit" 1966 GTO race car is currently owned and driven by John Holmes. The car was immensely popular in the 1960s, and today, remains a spectator favorite at Pontiac events. (Photo Courtesy Don Keefe)

ARNIE BESWICK CONTINUED

Arnie Beswick's 1964 pro-mod GTO does a burnout in preparation for a quarter-mile exhibition pass. Beswick remains a fan favorite, taking time for photos and signing autographs for fans. (Photo Courtesy Don Keefe)

1970s, Beswick campaigned numerous Pontiacs in various classes, and in most cases, was highly competitive.

In 1966, with the competition using full tube chassis and flip-top fiberglass bodies, Beswick decided that he needed to employ a similar strategy to remain competitive and built his "Star of the Circuit" 1966 GTO match racer. Unlike most other funny cars of the era, Beswick's car used a 1964 GTO frame with a full roll cage added for strength and safety. He altered the wheelbase by moving the front wheels 10 inches forward and lengthening the fenders and hood. A supercharged 421 Super Duty mated to a modified TH-400 automatic transmission enabled the GTO to make consistent mid-8 second passes at more than 170 mph. Later, powered by a 428-ci Pontiac topped with 1963 Super Duty cylinder heads, the car proved to be very competitive. As the nickname implies, Beswick's 1966 GTO was immensely popular with drag strip promoters and the general public alike.

In April 1972, a terrible fire ravaged Beswick's shop, destroying nearly all of his race cars, engines, and tools, along with most of his farm equipment. He steadily restored

his livelihood and returned to racing in 1986, participating in the *Blast from the Past* nostalgia series with a 455-powered 1963 Pontiac Tempest. Piloting this car fueled his desire to resurrect his own 1963 Tempest, the *Tameless Tiger*. With renewed enthusiasm, Beswick was once again burning up the pavement for young fans and fans young at heart.

Beswick's continued success led him to develop the *Tameless Tiger II,* an outrageous pro-mod race car based on a 1964 GTO. Painted in the familiar orange and black tiger theme, the *Tameless Tiger II* features a fierce 572-ci Pro Stock engine and approaches a speed of nearly 200 mph in the quarter-mile.

With innumerable victories spanning more than six decades, Arnie "the Farmer" Beswick is one of the most admired drivers in the history of drag racing. He is the recipient of numerous awards, including 1996 Driver of the Year, and has been inducted to the NHRA Division 3 Hall of Fame. Beswick remains immensely popular within the hobby and continues to participate in Pontiac-related events throughout the Midwest United States.

The walnut shift knob (code 524) was available only for the 4-speed manual transmission. Consoles differed for manual and automatic transmissions; manual versions featured a pronounced bulge to accommodate the shifter and its movement.

The shifter for the Super Turbine 300 2-speed automatic transmission featured a chrome shaft, a large black plastic handle, and chrome push-button. The available center console was identical to the 1965 version.

column shifter rather than Hurst, it implied that the 1966 GTO represented one of few instances when a Hurst shifter was not standard equipment. The Saginaw M11 employed a cast-iron case and used ratios of 2.54:1 in first, 1.50:1 in second, 1.00:1 in third, and 2.63:1 in reverse. All forward gears were synchronized.

The heavy-duty, Ford-built M13 (code 785) 3-speed manual transmission was an $84.26 option and received a Hurst floor-mounted shifter. Gear ratios remained the same as in 1965: 2.42:1 in first, 1.61:1 in second, 1.00:1 in third, and 2.33:1 in reverse. The Muncie M20 wide-ratio 4-speed manual transmission was again a popular option, as was the Muncie M21 close-ratio 4-speed. Gear ratios for the M20 differed slightly from the 1964–1965 units and now featured 2.52:1 in first, 1.88:1 in second, 1.46:1 in third, and 1.00:1 in fourth. Reverse gear was changed from 2.64:1 to 2.59:1.

The M21 transmission option still necessitated the Safe-T-Track rear end with 3.90:1 or numerically higher gears, heavy-duty fan and clutch assembly, and metallic brake linings. Both the M20 and M21 4-speeds are popular with restorers, and many convert original 3-speed cars to a 4-speed configuration. With the exception of the column-shifted M11 3-speed, all manual transmissions received a Hurst floor-mounted shifter as standard issue. A stylish walnut shift knob was a $3.69 option for 4-speed cars. Interestingly, the buyer could order a floor-shifted manual transmission in conjunction with the Strato Bench Seat. This was accommodated by using a shift lever with a sharper bend than the levers used for cars equipped with bucket seats. Total manual transmission

production reached 61,279 units for the 1966 model year.

Author note: Most sources agree that the Saginaw M11 3-speed manual transmission was standard equipment on the 1966 GTO. However, because of the scarcity of these cars, some members of the Pontiac community believe that the majority of GTOs equipped with a 3-speed manual transmission were fitted with the heavy-duty Ford-built M13 unit. This likely reflects what Pontiac dealers held in stock, and the fact that buyers were well informed and simply did not desire a column-shifted manual transmission in a GTO.

As in 1964 and 1965, the M31 Super Turbine 300 2-speed transmission remained the only automatic transmission available for the GTO (the 3-speed TH-400 replaced the Super Turbine 300 in 1967). The shifter was mounted on the steering column unless the center console was selected. Automatic transmission–equipped GTOs totaled 35,667 in 1966, nearly doubling 1965 output.

In the October 1966 issue of *Speed and Supercar* magazine, the staff tested a 1966 GTO equipped with the 360 hp Tri-Power engine and Super Turbine 300 2-speed automatic transmission. "When it comes to acceleration, a four-speed box is the undisputed king, unless it comes up against a 3-speed automatic like the Chrysler Torque-Flite, which can hold its own with any manual box in the quarter. But the Chrysler and GM boxes are horses of different colors. The GM 2-speed will never make it with the strip side bunch." This was not necessarily new information to savvy gearheads; most enthusiasts already knew that the Super Turbine 300 was not a race-ready transmission. Nevertheless, the staff did make some dragstrip passes with their test GTO, and noted, "Our quarter-mile runs, however, pointed clearly against the slush box. We did get a few minus-16-second and plus-90 mph runs, but almost any long-ratio stick Tiger will find it easy to match and better this mark."

The Super Turbine 300 was better suited to leisurely driving, and the staff at *Speed and Supercar* magazine praised the unit's smoothness, stating that it was "great on the street" and "just the thing for the lazy GTO lover."

The suspension of the 1966 GTO was largely a carryover from the 1965 models, and it was a competent road car, impressing automotive critics and the buying public.

Rear End

Pontiac continued to use the 10-bolt rear end in 1966, which contained an 8.2-inch diameter ring gear, with ratios available from 3.08:1 to 4.33:1. In 1966, rear ends fitted with 3.90:1 or 4.33:1 gears used a heavy-duty, four-pinion, limited slip unit. Axle ratios of 3.08:1 to 3.55:1 continued to employ the two-pinion design.

As in 1965, a two-letter code was stamped on the rear of the RH axle tube to identify the gear ratio and whether the car was fitted with either the open differential or the optional Safe-T-Track unit. The *GTO Restoration Guide: 1964–1970* by Paul Zazarine and Chuck Roberts added, "However, due to a stamping machine breakdown, the code stamp was moved to the top of the LH axle tube (refer to Service Bulletin 66-73). This malfunction occurred toward the end of the 1966 production year, so the change should appear on GTOs dated 07C and later. It is not known if this malfunction affected any early-production 1967 GTOs." While this may be an inconsequential detail to some devotees, those wishing to restore their 1966 GTO to original condition will likely find value in such minutiae.

Suspension and Braking

The underpinnings of the 1966 GTO were nearly identical to the 1965 versions. Full-perimeter frames were painted semi-gloss black and the heavy-duty frame option (code 661) was offered for hardtops and Sports Coupes at $29.69.

The steering gearbox was the same as in 1964 and 1965, with the 20:1 quick ratio (code 511) offered for an extra $10.53. The quick-ratio steering option was not

Once again, Saginaw steering boxes were used for the GTO. The standard steering gearbox (shown) featured a ratio of 24:1, with available quick ratio (20:1) or power ratio (17.5:1).

available with power steering. Power steering, now called Wonder Touch (code 501), was $94.79 in 1966.

Most aficionados were pleased with the handling characteristics of the GTO, as an article penned by Steve Kelly that appeared in the May 1966 issue of *Motor Trend* magazine confirms, "This car was equipped with heavy-duty suspension, so we put it through a few curves to find out how good it is. It's good—no doubt about that. You don't have to go fast to find it out, either. A slow-rolling curve shows off the heavy-duty suspension's penchant for keeping the car nearly flat to the road." There were, however, a few tradeoffs for having a firm suspension, as Kelly went on to note, "It does make the GTO ride stiff for normal driving, and exaggerates seams in cement roads, but we're sure that anyone who orders it could make good use of it on winding roads or a drag strip." As Kelly alluded, the prospective GTO buyer was more likely concerned with performance than comfort, and would view the tauter ride as an asset, not a liability.

A noteworthy option for 1966 was the availability of Soft Ride Springs and Shocks (code 628), which used the softer Tempest springs and shocks instead of the GTO's firmer components. This was a no-cost option and likely done to broaden the appeal of the GTO to those consumers who desired the looks and performance of the car but wanted a more comfortable ride.

Brakes

Much to the chagrin of many in the automotive press, the braking system for the 1966 GTO was largely a carryover from the 1964 and 1965 cars. In the May 1966 issue of *Motor Trend* magazine, Steve Kelly lamented, "While performance is one of the GTO's main claims to fame, its brakes certainly are not. With 9.5-inch diameter drums all the way around, the GTO with standard brakes has the same binders as the economy-priced 6-cylinder Tempest. This falls short of effective braking action that is most certainly needed on a car capable of 100 mph in a standing quarter-mile." Kelly went on to recommend one of the few brake upgrades for the GTO, "Metallic linings are available as an option, which we wouldn't hesitate to order if we were buying the car, but they are still fitted to the 9.5-inch drum. Discs would be a welcome addition to the options list."

The October 1966 issue of *Speed and Supercar* magazine echoed this sentiment, "Stopping with the 9.5-inch metallic-lined and power-assisted drum brakes was ade-quate, but not really up to the performance potential of the car. We encountered fade after two panic stops. A car like the GTO really needs discs—at least in the front—and it looks like GM will have something to beat the drums in the near future for all of its supercars." Pontiac Motor Division finally responded to these requests by offering a disc brake option for the 1967 models.

A single-reservoir master cylinder remained standard issue and was superseded by a much safer dual-reservoir design in 1967. Power brakes, now called Wonder Touch (code 502), were offered for an additional $41.60. Brake drums were painted red when Rally I wheels were specified, and red-painted aluminum front drums were separate, optional components. Aluminum dissipates heat more quickly than cast iron, thereby reducing brake temperatures and heat-related brake issues.

Wheels and Tires

Wheel and tire choices were plentiful for 1966 and included restyled Deluxe and Custom wheel covers. Stamped steel wheels in 14x6 sizes were used for all applications unless the Rally I wheel was specified. With the GTO's emphasis on performance, it's interesting to note that a wheel larger than 14x6 was not offered until the 1971 model, when both 15x7 Rally II and 15x7 Honeycomb wheels became available. Dog dish hubcaps were the default units if no wheel or wheel cover option was selected. These were the same as used in previous years and came standard with color-keyed wheels on cars painted Starlight Black, Fontaine Blue, Marina Turquoise, and Martinique Bronze. All other exterior colors received Starlight Black wheels.

With many current owners opting for the Rally I wheel, it's refreshing to see GTOs with their original wheel covers. At $16.85, the Deluxe wheel covers were an inexpensive upgrade over the standard dog dish versions.

Custom wheel covers (code 458) were an all-new design, breaking away from the "spinner styles" of 1964 and 1965.

The posh standard interior. Blue, turquoise, bronze, red, black, or parchment.

Standard engine: 335-hp 4-barrel 389. Chromed air cleaner, rocker covers.

Our famous 360-hp Tri-Power. Mechanical throttle linkage with stick. Extra cost.

Heavy-duty all-synchro 3-speed with Hurst floor shifter. Extra cost.

All-synchro 4-speed with Hurst shifter. Extra cost. So is the special shift knob.

The custom sports wheel. Only a hungry termite will know it's not wood. Extra cost.

What the 2-speed automatic looks like with console. Both extra cost.

Full instrumentation. Fuel, ammeter, tach, water temp, oil pressure. Extra cost.

Reclining passenger seat. Headrests. Extra cost. But worth it on long hauls.

Rally wheels with cooling slots. Extra cost, but you also get red brake drums.

Cast-iron brake drum with integral hub.* Extra cost. Red-line nylon tires standard.

Custom wheel disc. Extra cost. Special brake cooling slots are functional.

Extra cost plastic wheelhouse inserts* never discolor or fade. They're washable.

Heavy-duty shocks, springs, stabilizer bar standard. Stiffer shocks are extra cost.

Deluxe wheel disc. Extra cost. Rayon cord whitewalls are optional at no extra cost.

Safe-T-Track limited-slip differential. A must for maximum traction. Extra cost.

Delco transistorized ignition. It's the next best thing to a magneto. Extra cost.

Finned aluminum brake drum for front wheels, seen from inside. Extra cost.
*Not available at start of production—See dealer for availability.

The Deluxe (code 461) wheel covers were quite similar to the 1965 pieces, but did not display the "Pontiac Motor Division" script on the center cap. The 1966 Deluxe wheel covers also featured black paint around each of the 10 cooling slots, resulting in a sporty and attractive appearance. Curiously, the 1966 GTO and 2+2 sales brochure showed the Deluxe wheel cover with script on the center cap. Anomalies such as this did occur occasionally. The literature needed to be printed before the release of the cars and their optional components, which were sometimes changed before production began.

By comparison, the Custom wheel covers (code 458) of 1966 looked nothing like their 1965 counterparts. Six cooling slots and the lack of a spinner center cap gave the Custom wheel covers a racy aesthetic. At $36.33, they complemented the car beautifully, providing an inexpensive way to simulate the look of pricey mag wheels. With many current 1966 GTO owners opting for Rally I wheels, spotting cars equipped with the Deluxe or Custom wheel covers is quite rare, even if the car was originally ordered with them.

The 14x6 Rally I wheel was again offered as the only wheel option for the 1966 GTO. Similar to the 1965 unit, the main difference was the use of a black center cap, instead of chrome. Priced at $56.87, they were actually less expensive than the wire wheel covers, which were a costly

The eight-lug wheels were to be offered on Pontiac's 1966 A-body cars and were included in the sales brochure. They were to be constructed from cast iron and feature 24 cooling fins. Pontiac ultimately canceled the option because of excessive cost and weight.

The handsome Rally I wheel returned as a $56.87 option. Black center caps replaced the chrome units of 1965 and brake drums were painted red when the Rally wheel was specified.

$69.51.

In addition to the four different wheel cover choices and the Rally I wheel, a special version of Pontiac's popular eight-lug wheel manufactured by Kelsey-Hayes was seriously considered for the A-body cars, including the GTO. They were similar to the eight-lug wheels found on Pontiac's full-size cars but there were some noticeable differences between the two. The traditional eight-lug wheels featured aluminum drums with 16 fins while the A-body units were designed to use cast iron and display 24 fins.

In Paul Zazarine's book, *Muscle Car Color History 1964–1967 GTO*, he wrote, "This wheel was constructed of cast iron, used the same hub and drum assembly, and was retained by eight chrome-plated socket-head Allen bolts threaded into the brake drum. It was to be offered on all Tempest, LeMans, and GTO models in an attempt to improve the series' woeful braking system. By using 24 radial cooling fins, the gain in heat dissipation over the separate iron drum would provide better braking characteristics and longer brake-lining life. It was canceled just prior to production because the wheel was too heavy and costly to produce." Although they certainly looked great, it's difficult to determine if the eight-lug wheel and drum combination would have noticeably improved braking performance, especially compared to the aluminum front drum option. The wheel was so close to production that it was included in the 1966 GTO/2+2 sales brochure and looked dazzling wrapped in a redline tire. It noted,

"Cast-iron brake drum with integral hub. Extra cost. Redline nylon tires standard." A small note at the bottom of the page informed potential buyers, "Not available at start of production. See dealer for availability."

Furthermore, the 1966 full-line brochure showcased both a LeMans two-door hardtop and a LeMans four-door hardtop, each equipped with eight-lug wheels, revealing that Pontiac was quite intent on promoting the new wheel design for its A-body lineup. Again, one of the notes in the catalog declared, "The integral wheels shown on the LeMans hardtop coupe are not available at start of production. Check with your dealer for availability." In addition to tying into Pontiac's full-size models, the A-body eight-lug wheels would have provided the Pontiac intermediates with a second styled wheel option, as the Rally II wheel would not debut until 1967.

The now-iconic five-spoke Hurst wheel was also given serious consideration as a factory option in 1966. There were two major problems with this idea: The wheels were extremely heavy and very expensive to produce. Despite several attempts by Pontiac to persuade George Hurst to reduce both wheel weight and cost, a deal was never reached. The wheels proved to be popular as aftermarket items and could be spotted on various muscle cars of the era, including GTOs.

Tires were the same as offered in 1965: 7.75x14 redlines featuring a nylon cord, or the no-cost optional 7.75x14 whitewalls, which had a rayon cord. Redline

At one time, the gorgeous 5-spoke Hurst wheels were considered as an option for the GTO. Cost and weight were the two mitigating factors in bringing this concept to fruition. Today, Hurst wheels remain popular with many present-day GTO owners, adding a "day two" appearance to their beloved machines.

Redline tires measuring 7.75x14 were again standard issue on the GTO, with whitewall versions available at no charge. This restored example is fitted with BFGoodrich radial redlines, which are similar in appearance to the original tires while providing the added performance of radial technology. Note the correct black center cap on the Rally I wheel and the red-painted brake drum.

versions are commonly installed by current owners, even if not originally equipped.

Advertising for 1966

Thanks in large part to Jim Wangers and his marketing team's relentless approach in print advertisements, radio, television, and live events across the nation, the GTO recorded its best-selling year in 1966. The GTO's image and sales were extremely robust, and competitors began targeting the GTO directly in their own advertising campaigns. Ford released a print ad displaying a tiger tail poking out from under the hood of its Fairlane GT/A with the heading, "How to Cook a Tiger." It was a clever strategy on Ford's part, and even though the Fairlane GT and Fairlane GT/A (automatic) were potent machines, these models never reached the same level of popularity that the GTO enjoyed.

As other manufacturers attempted to exploit the use of the tiger theme to their advantage, Pontiac remained unfazed, and continued to create fun, imaginative advertisements for the 1966 GTO employing the tiger motif. The colorful 1966 GTO/2+2 sales brochure featured four photos on the cover: a GTO, a 2+2, an OHC 6-cylinder

An ocean-side setting is idyllic for this Montero Red GTO convertible. (Artists Art Fitzpatrick and Van Kaufman employed a similar scene for a 1966 Tempest rendering.) Even though this car is fitted with Rally II wheels, which debuted in 1967, the similarity between the 1966 and 1967 body styles present this car with a factory-like appearance.

What does it take to make a new improved GTO?   Pontiac.

Who else could but Pontiac? After all, little things like 335 or 360 hp, stick-like-glue handling and fantastically plush interiors just don't come from anybody. Or drive a GTO. Best way in the world to tell a real tiger from a would-be. The tiger scores again!

Wide-Track Pontiac/'66
Pontiac Motor Division · General Motors Corporation

The use of tiger-themed imagery remained strong in 1966, as this GTO print advertisement illustrates. Captivating photography and prominently displayed horsepower figures were constant in Pontiac marketing from this period.

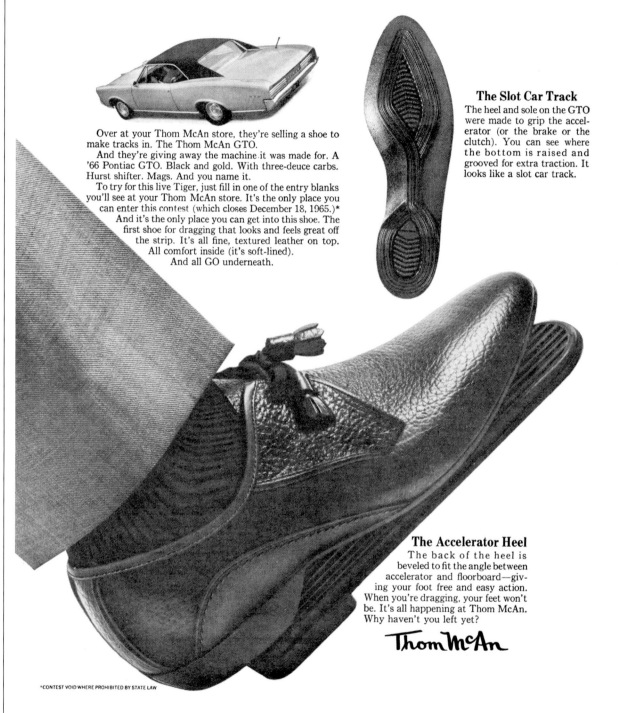

Made to fit the Tiger.
The Thom McAn GTO.

Over at your Thom McAn store, they're selling a shoe to make tracks in. The Thom McAn GTO.

And they're giving away the machine it was made for. A '66 Pontiac GTO. Black and gold. With three-deuce carbs. Hurst shifter. Mags. And you name it.

To try for this live Tiger, just fill in one of the entry blanks you'll see at your Thom McAn store. It's the only place you can enter this contest (which closes December 18, 1965.)*

And it's the only place you can get into this shoe. The first shoe for dragging that looks and feels great off the strip. It's all fine, textured leather on top. All comfort inside (it's soft-lined). And all GO underneath.

The Slot Car Track
The heel and sole on the GTO were made to grip the accelerator (or the brake or the clutch). You can see where the bottom is raised and grooved for extra traction. It looks like a slot car track.

The Accelerator Heel
The back of the heel is beveled to fit the angle between accelerator and floorboard—giving your foot free and easy action. When you're dragging, your feet won't be. It's all happening at Thom McAn. Why haven't you left yet?

Thom McAn

*CONTEST VOID WHERE PROHIBITED BY STATE LAW

Marketed as "America's first high-performance shoe," the Thom McAn GTO was specifically designed with the driver in mind. Pontiac lent the use of the GTO name and created a successful cross-promotion; Thom McAn stores across the nation were filled with Pontiac GTO displays.

equipped Tempest, and a running tiger. Inside, the text bragged, "There is only one GTO. Never forget that. There are a lot of pretenders around. There always are in the wake of a winner. But it takes more than a big-bore V-8 on a little chassis to make a GTO. The genius of the GTO is that it's the world's greatest compromise. In its proletarian version, it's a very manageable machine to drive. With its 4-barrel, standard cam, and firm but civilized suspension, your grandmother can even pick up her sauerkraut juice in it. But if you want to start grubbing around the parts bin, you can turn your GTO into the famous GeeTO Tiger in nothing flat. The parts bin is down a few pages. Go get 'em, tiger." It was a brash proclamation, but Pontiac's confident attitude was ultimately justified, with a record 831,331 total Pontiacs sold for the 1966 model year, including 96,946 GTOs.

The tiger imagery continued with print advertisements placed in enthusiast publications including *Hot Rod* and *Car and Driver* magazines. One piece depicted a large photo of a tiger-skin clad model leaning against the roof of a GTO accompanied by two smaller photos: one highlighting the Rally I wheel and redline tire; the other showcasing the dash and steering wheel, with a real tiger peering in the windshield. The ad claimed that driving a GTO was the "Best way in the world to tell a real tiger from a would-be."

To promote the use of the plastic material in the 1966 GTO's grille components, Pontiac created a special print ad featuring a full tiger skin draped over the car's hood with the grilles removed and displaying within the text, "The tiger's teeth are made of Kralastic: the engineering plastic." It was a dramatic statement, which also underscored the fact that the new plastic grilles were 35 pounds lighter than the previous die-cast zinc units installed in the 1964 and 1965 models.

The tiger theme continued in television commercials, one of which opened with jungle sounds and the narrator stating bluntly, "The tiger scores again. Pontiac GTO for '66. Six point five litres of young tiger." The ad portrayed two young women in a 1966 GTO convertible equipped with a manual transmission driving on back roads through a remote, wooded area. It then touted the availability of the 360-hp engine and the "sumptuous interior." The commercial closed with the hood springing open, a live tiger growling angrily from the engine compartment, and the narrator urging, "See it in captivity, at your Pontiac dealer. Everything's new in tiger country."

Pontiac provided 50 Tiger Gold 1966 GTO hardtops as contest prizes as part of the Thom McAn GTO shoe promotion. The campaign proved to be a success for both Pontiac Motor Division and Melville Shoe Corporation, makers of the Thom McAn GTO shoe.

MONKEEMOBILE

The Monkees were a group of young actors/musicians formed in 1965 by Bob Rafelson and Bert Schneider in Los Angeles, California. Rafelson and Schneider developed the concept for the television show in 1962, but they had trouble selling the idea to network executives. In the summer of 1964, Rafelson and Schneider's desire to get their show on the air was renewed with the success of the Beatles' film, *A Hard Day's Night*. *The Monkees*, which ran from 1966 to 1968, was to be scripted as lighthearted and fun, and the producers wanted a custom car for the Monkees to cruise around in, believing it would add to the show's quirky appeal.

Some enthusiasts believe that the Monkeemobile was the handiwork of George Barris, but it was Southern California–based builder Dean Jeffries who created, not one, but two of these radically customized machines. Using the 1966 Pontiac GTO as its foundation, the Monkeemobile is instantly identifiable more than 50 years after its debut. (Photo Courtesy Don Keefe)

Universal Studios chose car customizer Dean Jeffries to build the custom car for the Monkees television program. Pontiac marketing guru and "Godfather of the GTO," Jim Wangers, had heard about the concept through a mutual friend, George Toteff. Two cars would be needed: one for use on the show, the other for promotional events across America. Wangers struck a deal with the show's producers and ordered two brand-new 1966 GTO convertibles, each equipped with a 4-barrel 389-ci engine backed by a floor-shifted 2-speed automatic transmission, painted Martinique Bronze with Fawn interior. The only difference was that the car used for promotional purposes was equipped with an air conditioner.

Jeffries did not receive approval for the two-car project until one month before both cars needed to be completed. Jeffries and his crew worked tirelessly to get the cars finished within the extremely tight time frame. An article written by Don Keefe *Pontiac Enthusiast* magazine explains, "Wangers knew the cars were to be customized pretty heavily and that GM management might not be pleased with what Hollywood would want to do with the cars. The last thing they wanted was a car that would be the object of ridicule.

"What Jeffries came up with was much more radical than anyone at Pontiac had anticipated. While the front end was easily recognizable as a GTO, the rest of the car was heavily customized."

A T-bucket–type convertible top was used, along with a tall, split windshield that added to the hot rod appearance (all other windows were eliminated). The hood was reshaped extensively with a large cutout exposing the 389-ci engine. The car was originally fitted with a 6-71 supercharger, but it proved to be too temperamental for television use, so a

The 389-ci Pontiac engine was initially modified with a 6-71 supercharger but was quickly deemed too radical for television purposes. This photo shows the dummy system that was installed over the original 4-barrel intake and carburetor. (Photo Courtesy Don Keefe)

replica version was installed to retain the outrageous appearance. The fenders and nose area of the GTO were also heavily modified and it was fitted with Cibie rectangular headlights. The grilles remained stock Pontiac pieces. Four trumpet-style exhaust tips exited just behind both front wheels (two on each side were functional), providing a unique sound. The quarter panels were lengthened and flared, with custom taillights and a parachute added to the rear. Chrome wheels and bright red paint with graphics featuring The Monkees logo added to the wild appearance of the GTO.

The interior of the GTO was also heavily customized. An aftermarket tachometer sat atop the stock Pontiac dash and a Grant walnut steering

Today, it's difficult to imagine someone taking the beautiful lines of a 1966 GTO and altering them almost beyond recognition, but that's exactly what Dean Jeffries and his crew did to create the now-iconic Monkeemobile. An astute observer will notice this 1966 convertible is fitted with Rally II wheels, an option not made available until 1967.

wheel was added. The car was transformed to accommodate three rows of seats: the first and second row contained bucket seats and a custom bench seat was fitted to what was formerly the trunk area. Custom tuck-and-roll upholstery was added throughout the interior space. Inspecting the car now, it's astounding that Jeffries and his team were able to finish not just one, but two of these radical GTOs in a single month.

Jeffries had taken many of the GTO's beautifully sculpted

lines and either exaggerated or eliminated them, and the car was initially not well received by Pontiac management. Jim Wangers recalled in a 2014 interview for *RodWriters*, "We thought it was pretty bad, to be honest with you. The only thing that was acceptable was the front end. The car itself was almost a put-down. In fact, to the people at Pontiac, since I was behind that and sold it to them, the idea of putting a car on *The Monkees* television show, the car became kind of a joke. They called it 'Wangers' Folly' at Pontiac." Later in the interview, however, Wangers agreed with the assessment that over time, the Monkeemobile gained acceptance as one of Hollywood's most memorable automobiles.

The car was shown during the opening theme for each show and also featured prominently in several episodes; perhaps most notably in "The Monkees Race Again" (also known as "Leave the Driving to Us"), in which singer Davy Jones pilots the Monkeemobile in a race against the show's villain, who is behind the wheel of a Shelby Daytona coupe.

One of the two original cars was sold at the 2008 Barrett-Jackson auction in Scottsdale, Arizona, for an astounding $396,000. The Monkeemobile is perhaps the world's most iconic GTO, but because of its wild, extensive customization, some people do not recognize the car as a GTO. Nevertheless, the car remains a legend within the custom car and television communities, showcasing the creativity possessed by both Dean Jeffries, for building such a distinctive machine, and Jim Wangers for pursuing yet another avenue to further promote the Pontiac brand.

Even though the steering wheel, tachometer, and radio are not factory stock, the dash area remains recognizable as factory-spec GTO. The remainder of the interior space was heavily customized, including tuck-and-roll upholstery and three rows of seating. (Photo Courtesy Don Keefe)

One of the more unusual marketing campaigns was a cross-promotion with shoemaker, The Melville Shoe Corporation. One of their brands, Thom McAn, was advertised heavily on Top 40 radio stations and Jim Wangers recognized the powerful influence it held over America's youth. In *Glory Days*, Wangers recalled, "So I approached Thom McAn with the idea of taking the image of our GTO and applying it to one of their shoes. The idea was to relate the image of the new shoe to the exciting image of the existing car. The Melville people were very receptive, and they showed real interest in working out a program. We let them name the shoe 'The GTO' and refer to it as 'America's first high-performance shoe.'" Constructed of black grained-leather and displaying a pointed toe design, the Thom McAn GTO also featured the "Accelerator Heel." As the ad pointed out, "The back of the heel is beveled to fit the angle between accelerator

and floorboard—giving your foot free and easy action."

As part of the promotion, Pontiac agreed to provide 50 Tiger Gold GTO hardtops as contest prizes. To become eligible, interested persons simply went to any of the 1,500 nationwide Thom McAn stores and filled out an entry form. The campaign, viewed by some GM executives as a juvenile concept, ultimately proved to be beneficial to both parties. Shoe sales increased for Thom McAn and Pontiac received additional advertising through radio play, print publications, and large in-store displays at all 1,500 Thom McAn locations. Thom McAn GTO shoes represent another unique and collectible piece of Pontiac history.

Another fun publicity campaign (and clever cross-promotion) was an idea from George Toteff of Model Products Corporation (MPC) to create a functioning 1/25-scale dragstrip for use at Autorama Custom Car Shows

The success of the GTO led some competitors to attempt to emulate the design characteristics of Pontiac's trend-setting automobile. This pristine example of a 1966 hardtop clearly demonstrates why Pontiac was leading the muscle car movement, sending other manufacturers scrambling to keep up. This GTO is an ultra-rare Ram Air car and represents the pinnacle of GTO performance for 1966. (Photo Courtesy Chris Phillip)

across the United States. Sponsored by Pontiac, Hurst, and Thom McAn, the display featured a 60-foot-long track, two 1/25-scale GeeTO Tiger slot cars, and a Christmas tree at the starting line. To simulate a real drag race experience, two full-size GTO cockpits were used, each with a bucket seat, steering wheel, and Hurst shifter. The accelerator pedals in the cockpits were connected to the model cars and the goal was to shift at predetermined times while keeping the cars running as straight as possible. The program was extremely popular, with some participants waiting hours for a turn behind the wheel, and through it many younger enthusiasts were exposed to the GTO for the first time. In just one year's time, the 1/25-scale dragstrip traveled to 32 cities and reached more than 150,000 fans. It was an innovative and exciting way to promote the GTO, while using a limited amount of resources.

The tiger theme was employed extensively (and successfully) for most of 1966, but by year's end, GM's Board Chairman James Roche expressed his disapproval with the concept, citing that it was a reckless, and therefore inappropriate, tactic for selling cars. By late 1966, Roche had effectively persuaded Pontiac management to cease the tiger campaign. What was originally perceived by many within the division as a huge setback, not only to the GTO but also to Pontiac's other performance models such as the full-size 2+2, forced Jim Wangers and his team to reinvent the GTO's image. It kept the car fresh and exciting in the minds of consumers and enthusiasts alike.

In hindsight, 1966 was a banner year for Pontiac, particularly the GTO, which sold an exceptional 96,946 units, the highest production in the car's history. By 1967, new mandates set forth by General Motors, such as the elimination of multiple carburetion on all cars except the Chevrolet Corvette, and heightened competition from other manufacturers, posed new challenges to the GTO and its position as the reigning king of the muscle car.

Imposing from any angle, this 1966 GTO in Blue Charcoal fitted with standard hubcaps and redline tires appears race ready. The factory recommended stripe color for Blue Charcoal was Cameo Ivory, but this GTO was issued with a Montero Red stripe, which adds to the aggressive, understated appearance of the car. (Photo Courtesy Chris Phillip)

CHAPTER FIVE

1967 GTO The Great One Gets Better and Faster

By 1967, muscle car fever had swept the nation, and nearly every American automotive manufacturer was producing stylish, powerful machines, vying for the coveted youth demographic and the accompanying improved sales figures. The GTO would have to compete not only with its familiar GM rivals (the Chevrolet Chevelle SS 396, Oldsmobile 4-4-2, and Buick Skylark Gran Sport) but also with increasingly competent entries from Dodge/Plymouth, Ford/Mercury, and even AMC. The 1967 Plymouth GTX 426 Hemi was a serious contender; with an astonishing 425 hp and 490 ft-lbs of torque housed in a handsome exterior design, it could easily out-muscle a GTO. The 1966 and 1967 Fairlane 427 was Ford's impressive muscle car entry, with a 427-ci FE series engine doling out 425 hp and 480 ft-lbs of torque. However, unlike the 390-ci-equipped Fairlane GT and GT/A, Fairlane 427 production was extremely limited, and the cars carried a very high price tag, putting them out of reach for most consumers.

General Motors, rather than rival manufacturers, presented some of the GTO's challenges. Upper management had deemed the tiger marketing campaign and its associated imagery as careless and irresponsible, forcing Pontiac's advertising team, McManus, John & Adams, to reinvent the GTO's persona. "The Great One," a simple play on the car's name, developed into a highly successful campaign that rejuvenated the model. In addition, General Motors had banned multiple carburetion on all cars except the Chevrolet Corvette, denying Pontiac one of its signature features. Once again, Pontiac engineers were able to overcome numerous obstacles to ensure that the GTO remained a viable performance car.

While some of the GTO's competitors may have outgunned it, Pontiac was still enjoying its high-performance, youth-oriented image, which enabled the GTO to remain relevant in the increasingly crowded muscle car market. For the 1967 GTO, styling changes

The Pontiac GTO faced formidable competition from rival manufacturers in 1967 but was able to retain substantial market share thanks to its sleek styling and various engine options. This fabulous Burgundy hardtop is a pristine example of what became known as "The Great One," a play on the GTO's initials.

were relegated to minor revisions of the 1966 model. Mechanically, however, changes were both drastic and numerous. A new 400-ci engine replaced the tried and true 389-ci powerplant, the durable TH-400 3-speed automatic transmission was available for the first time in the GTO, and front disc brakes were now a welcomed safety option. Even though sales dropped for the first time in the car's history (81,722 in 1967, down from 96,946 in 1966) the 1967 GTO endures as a favorite of both diehard Pontiac enthusiasts and more casual muscle car fans.

Body

The Pontiac GTO remained a separate series in 1967 and retained its 242 VIN prefix designation, as it did until the 1972 model, when it reverted back to being an option on the LeMans. The GTO was offered in three familiar configurations. The Sports Coupe (style 4207),

still most often referred to as a "post car," sold 7,029 copies in 1967, down from 10,363 in 1966. Convertible models (style 4267) sold 9,517, down from 12,798 the previous year. The hardtop remained the most popular body (style 4217) and moved 65,176 units in 1967, roughly 8,500 fewer than 1966 production. Total Pontiac A-body production (Tempest/LeMans/GTO) for 1967 was 301,639 cars.

The wheelbase remained at 115 inches and overall weight was within 10 to 30 pounds of the 1966 cars. A 1967 manual transmission–equipped Sports Coupe weighed 3,593 pounds and a manual-equipped hardtop tipped the scales at 3,598 pounds. An automatic transmission added 50 pounds and air-conditioning added approximately 125 pounds. External dimensions were nearly identical to the 1966 models. The most noticeable change was an increase of about .5-inch in overall height to 53.7 inches for Sports Coupe and hardtop versions, up from 53.1 inches in 1966.

At a glance, the 1967 GTO appears quite similar to the 1966 model; only minor changes were made to the previous year's design. The overall profile was equal to the 1966 cars, including the swept-back roofline and

The Sports Coupe was the least popular body style in 1967, with 7,029 units produced. Today, those low production numbers often translate into higher collectability, especially when combined with rare options. Inset: Passenger-door window frame on a 1967 Sports Coupe model. The door frame, combined with the B-pillar, resulted in superb structural rigidity. Convertible and hardtop GTOs do not display these features.

Pontiac moved 9,517 convertible GTOs in 1967, the second-most produced body style that year. Convertibles remained the heaviest of the three available configurations, weighing 3,733 pounds when equipped with an automatic transmission.

recessed rear window. Stacked headlights remained a key styling trait (1968 would see the return of horizontal headlights). The plastic grilles of the 1966 model were replaced with wire-mesh units that enhanced the car's muscular appearance. These new grilles were exclusive to the 1967 GTO, differentiating it from both the 1966 GTO and 1967 Tempest and LeMans models. A new header panel was employed to accept the new grilles, and the parking lamps were now separate pieces, not molded in like the 1966 versions. The front bumper and doors were identical to the previous year's components; the new, rev-olutionary Endura bumper would be introduced in 1968. The fenders had only very minor differences and could be interchanged with minimal modifications. Externally, the hood was equal to the 1966 version, but employed a different attachment method. The 1966 models used studs that clipped into the hood, passing through the hinges, with nuts securing it to the hinges. The 1967 cars used cage nuts mounted into the hood; standard bolts were used to fasten the hood to the hinges.

The rear styling of the 1967 GTO was noticeably more refined than the previous year and simple, straight

A distinguishing feature of the 1967 GTO was the revised grille and header panel design. The wire-mesh grilles presented the car with a more aggressive appearance than the 1966 model. The hood scoop was a carryover from 1965 and 1966. As in previous years, a GTO emblem was affixed to the driver-side grille. Parking lamps were now separate pieces, not molded into the grille itself like the 1966 versions.

lines replaced the somewhat busy bowtie theme. The quarter panels differed slightly from the 1966 units at the rear, and the taillights were now flush-mounted into the rear body panel; both contributed to the clean, classy aesthetic. Interestingly, the 1967 LeMans received simulated quarter-panel vents, much like those used on the 1967 Firebird. The LeMans was the only Pontiac A-body to display this feature; neither the Tempest nor the GTO received this design element.

Today, numerous aftermarket restoration suppliers offer new, reproduction sheet metal for the 1967 GTO, virtually eliminating the need to search for used and often damaged or rusted original replacement parts.

Ames Performance Engineering, Year One, and Original Parts Group are some of the leading names in the Pontiac restoration business. Hoods, fenders, quarter panels, complete floor sections, and many other components are readily available for the serious Pontiac enthusiast.

Decklid and quarter-panel GTO emblems were affixed in their familiar locations, but the Pontiac letters that graced the rear body panel of the 1966 car were eliminated for 1967. A redesigned rear bumper was used (much straighter than the previous year's unit), complementing the tidy rear end treatment. Rectangular backup lights were employed, replacing the circular lamps of 1966, and were mounted more toward the center of the

The rear-end treatment of the 1967 GTO was decidedly clean and simple. The slotted taillights were similar to those employed on Firebird and Gran Prix models and presented the three Pontiacs with a cohesive aesthetic.

A side-by-side comparison highlights the changes made from the 1966 to 1967 model years. The bowtie theme and louvered taillights gave way to clean, straight lines. Removal of the Pontiac letters and a redesigned bumper with rectangular backup lights completed the rear styling revisions.

In 1967, both the Pontiac Tempest and LeMans models received distinctive taillight lenses, each of which differed from the GTO. The 1967 LeMans taillights (shown) were unique to the model and display integrated back-up lamps.

Blue/gray spatter paint was used for the inside trunk area on 1967 models. The two-piece rear mat from the previous year was replaced by a single version, which was simply the rear section from the 1966 model.

bumper. Again, Pontiac engineers strived for a cohesive design across the entire lineup, and the rear end styling of the 1967 GTO is almost identical to the 1967 Gran Prix. The only major difference was that the GTO displayed four taillight lenses on each side, and the Grand Prix had two.

Rocker panel trim was much larger for the 1967 GTO, which necessitated corresponding trim along the bottom edge of each door, and presented the car with a more formal, upscale appearance. Previously affixed higher on the fender, the familiar GTO 6.5 Litre crest was now located farther down, on the rocker trim itself, drawing the eye to the expanse of brightwork. This 1967 GTO's larger side trim is a notable feature; it distinguishes the car from the 1966 cars. In addition, the 1967 Tempest

and LeMans models did not receive the large rocker trim; it was exclusive to the GTO.

The inside trunk area was covered in dark blue/gray spatter paint with the spare tire and jack mounted on the passenger's side. The trunk mat was no longer a two-piece set; it now consisted of only the larger rear section. A spare tire cover (code 372) was optional. While remote trunk releases had been offered since 1964, they were either cable or vacuum operated. That changed for the 1967 model with the introduction of the electrically operated trunk release (code 492). The switch to activate the remote release was located in the glove box.

Fifteen exterior colors were available for the 1967 GTO, with some carrying over from the previous year. Three colors offered for the first time were Montreux

The large rocker trim presented the GTO with an upscale appearance and was not available on other Pontiac A-body cars. The GTO fender emblem was relocated and placed within the trim.

Tempest and LeMans models did not receive the large rocker panel trim. This 1967 LeMans Sprint highlights the difference between the standard trim and the dramatic pieces employed for the GTO.

Montreux Blue (code D) was introduced in 1967 and was available for one year only, making it a desirable hue among collectors. This clean hardtop also showcases the optional hood-mounted tachometer, Rally II wheels, and redline tires. (Photo Courtesy Andre Rayman)

Plum Mist (code M) was a one-year color and a favorite among GTO enthusiasts. Parchment interior, painted top, and period correct Hurst wheels complement this 1967 model wonderfully. (Photo Courtesy Mark Cronk)

Not commonly seen today, two-tone paint was quite popular in the mid-1960s. The Cameo Ivory roof (code C) on this 1967 GTO contrasts well with the main color, Plum Mist (code M).

Another beautiful two-tone combination, this Signet Gold 1967 model displays a Starlight Black–painted roof. In this instance, the cowl data plate would read: G A. (Photo Courtesy Mark Best)

Blue, Plum Mist, and Montego Cream. The 15 colors and codes are as follows: Starlight Black (code A), Cameo Ivory (code C), Montreux Blue (code D), Fathom Blue (code E), Tyrol Blue (code F), Signet Gold (code G), Linden Green (code H), Gulf Turquoise (code K), Mariner Turquoise (code L), Plum Mist (code M), Burgundy (code N), Silverglaze (code P), Regimental Red (code R), Champagne (code S), and Montego Cream (code T). Starlight Black (code A) was available for every year of 1964–1974 GTO production.

Two-tone paint remained an option, costing an additional $31.07 if a standard paint color was selected, and $114.27 for one of the special color choices. Two-tone paint is indicated on the cowl data plate. For example: H H indicated Linden Green, for both the main and accent (roof) color, while H A denoted Linden Green with a Starlight Black roof color. Throughout the years, many factory two-tone GTOs were repainted a single color, and some owners may not realize they possess such a car. Again, a hobbyist can glean useful information pertaining to his or her GTO by inspecting the cowl data plate closely.

A dual painted pinstripe replaced the single line of the 1965 and 1966 cars, and was available in Starlight Black, Cameo Ivory, or Regimental Red. The pinstripe was standard issue on all 1967 GTOs, and the only year for a dual stripe version. As in previous years, Pontiac had a list of recommended pinstripe colors that best complemented both the interior and exterior colors. For example, Fathom Blue was available only with a Cameo Ivory pinstripe, and Montego Cream could only be had with a Starlight Black stripe, regardless of interior color. By contrast, Silverglaze was the only exterior hue that offered all three stripe colors. Starlight Black was chosen if the car was equipped with black interior (code 223 for bucket seats and 235 for bench seat). Cameo Ivory was selected for cars with dark blue (code 219), dark turquoise (code 220), and parchment interiors (code 224 for bucket seats and 236 for bench seat). Regimental Red was used for Silverglaze GTOs fitted with a red interior (code 225). Deleting the stripes was again a no-cost option (code 491). Like many other aspects of the GTO, the stripe color could have been special ordered to create a unique color combination not listed in the Pontiac literature (see example in chapter 4).

A dual painted stripe was introduced for the 1967 GTO. This Plum Mist model displays the correct Cameo Ivory stripe color, which corresponds well with the parchment interior and Cameo Ivory roof.

Red plastic fender liners (code 522) were again offered at $26.33, and much like the 1966 cars, 1967 GTOs originally equipped with this option are highly coveted by collectors. The red plastic fender liners were only available in 1966 and 1967, adding to the value and rarity of these components.

Cordova and convertible tops were offered in the same colors as the 1966 models: ivory (code 1), black (code 2), and beige (code 6) for Cordova tops, and ivory (code 1), black (code 2), blue (code 4), turquoise (code 5), and beige (code 6) for convertible tops. As in previous years, the code for the Cordova or convertible top was located just to the right of the paint code on the cowl data plate. A data plate reading A 2 indicated Starlight Black paint with a black top. Likewise, a data plate reading R 1 denoted Regimental Red paint with an ivory top.

As was the case in previous years, tinted glass called Soft Ray was available for an additional charge. It could be ordered for the windshield only (code 532) for $21.06, or for all windows (code 531) for $30.54. Factory-tinted glass is much subtler than what we have come to recognize in today's aftermarket; the casual observer may not realize that a car has tinted glass. Nevertheless, it did help reduce the sun's penetrating rays and keep the interior of the car slightly cooler in the summer months.

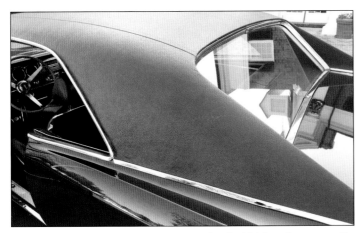

Cordova tops remained a popular option in 1967 and were available in ivory, black, or beige. As in prior years, the 1967 model employed additional trim around the perimeter for a finished appearance.

A common misconception among Pontiac enthusiasts is that tinted windows (code 531) were a mandatory option when air-conditioning was ordered. This Pontiac Historical Services (PHS) document clearly shows this 1967 model as factory-equipped with air-conditioning and tinted windshield only (code 532), not all windows (code 531). Research suggests that tinted windows may have been suggested by the salesperson, but they were not actually required for the air-conditioning option.

Interior

Stricter federal safety standards, along with GM's own renewed focus on safety, led to many improvements in the GTO's cabin. The 1967 Pontiac brochure proclaimed, "We've never worked harder on designing, engineering, and styling our Pontiacs than we have this year. And we think our 1967 Wide-Tracks prove it. You not only get a sleeker car with an infinitely superior engineering concept, but you get more car than ever before. For example, standard on all 1967 Pontiacs is a host of safety features designed to help make your driving as reassuring and safe as modern technology allows." The brochure touted such items as padded sun visors, push-button seat belt buckles, and passenger guard door locks, all of which seem quite rudimentary by today's standards. One truly notable safety improvement was the energy-absorbing steering column. This component was designed to compress, somewhat like a shock absorber, in the event of a collision, reducing the chance of serious injury to the driver. The passage from the brochure ended with, "Naturally, the best way to enjoy your new Pontiac is on the road. Enjoy it—but please observe the good rules of safe driving. We've long made your safety our business. Won't you make it yours, too?"

Although not dramatically different from the 1966 model, the interior space of the GTO received numerous

For 1967, the interior space of the GTO underwent several changes while retaining a similar overall appearance to the 1966 models. Seat and door panel patterns were again revised, and the optional center console now displayed a woodgrain vinyl overlay in place of the chrome-ribbed design of previous years. Pedal trim and kick panel speakers are owner additions.

Even though the dashboard of the 1967 GTO was similar to the 1966 model, there were a few subtle differences. The padded portion did not extend to the defroster vents and a simulated woodgrain vinyl insert replaced the wood veneer. The interior space of this Regimental Red convertible has been restored to mostly stock specifications; the aftermarket steering wheel is a notable exception.

updates for 1967. The dash pad was smaller than the previous year's design and did not extend to the defroster vents. The dash face was now covered with a vinyl woodgrain insert instead of the real wood veneer used in 1966. The turn-signal indicator was now divided in the middle, whereas the 1966 version was not. Gauge layout was unchanged, and the Rally gauge package (code 444) returned, with slight changes in the numbers on the oil pressure and coolant temperature gauges. The oil pressure gauge reading changed from 0–30–60 to 0–40–80 and the coolant temperature gauge changed from 100–180–245 to 100–210–250.

Notable for 1967 was the introduction of the hood-mounted tachometer as a dealer-installed item. The 1967 GTO/Sprint/2+2 brochure proclaimed, "Our hood-mounted tach option. You don't know what shifting is unless you have one." The unit was difficult to see at night (early units were illuminated with only one bulb), but it did present the car with a race-inspired attitude and it attracted a lot of attention from curious gear heads. The 1967 gauge was slightly taller than the versions that followed, and the gauge face was unique to 1967, making it a one-year-only design. Other issues with the hood-mounted tachometer included continual opening and closing of the hood, which could damage internal parts, and the propensity for the lens to fog up. Beginning in 1970, Pontiac added a vacuum line from the heater box to the tachometer, thereby eliminating the issue of the lens fogging over. Reproduction hood tachometers (and tach vent line kits) are currently available from various restoration supply companies. Today, hood tachometers are synonymous with 1967–1972 GTOs and many

The Safeguard Speedometer (code 442) was a $15.80 option and could not be ordered with Rally gauges. Turning the chrome knob at the center of the speedometer sets the adjustable needle. Once the car reached the predetermined speed, a buzzer would sound, notifying the driver to slow down. This unit is set at approximately 85 mph.

Pontiac's famed hood tachometer debuted for the 1967 model year as a dealer-installed item and is quite popular among today's enthusiasts. In 1968, the tachometer was redesigned with a lower profile in an effort to improve the driver's view of the road. The taller, 1967 version is shown here.

Rally gauges (code 444) remained an $84.26 option for the GTO. The high-beam indicator is located near the top of the dash face between the speedometer and tachometer.

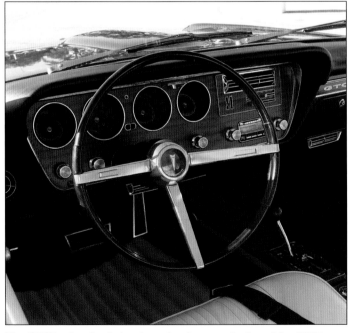

The GTO's standard steering wheel was redesigned for 1967. Now a three-spoke unit, it was color-keyed to the other interior components. This car is equipped with parchment interior (code 224) and therefore received the black wheel.

For 1967, the optional Custom Sports steering wheel differed slightly from the previous year's version. Brushed trim in place of chrome was the most noticeable change. Today, many GTO owners opt to install a Custom Sports wheel in their GTO, even if not originally so equipped. The underdash air-conditioning and radio are aftermarket items. The white shift knob is considered incorrect for 1967.

Durable Morrokide upholstery was again used for many interior components of the 1967 Pontiac GTO. Seat patterns changed every year; the 1967 models displayed a stylish, vertical ribbed design.

As in 1966, front seat headrests (code 571) were available in 1967 for an additional $52.66. Seat-back locks were a new feature for 1967, as was the larger diameter, impact-absorbing steering column.

present-day owners add them to their cars, even if they were not originally so equipped.

A three-spoke standard steering wheel replaced the uninspired two-spoke 1966 unit. The Custom Sports simulated wood steering wheel returned as a $30.02 option. At a glance, the 1967 Custom Sports unit looked similar to the 1966 wheel, but there are several differences between the two. The spokes on the 1967 version feature brushed trim, not chrome as found on the 1966 wheel. The horn buttons also varied slightly, but each contained the same Lucite Pontiac Motor Division emblem. The collar of the 1967 wheel was a larger diameter to accommodate the new, energy-absorbing steering column.

Cruise control (code 441) was first made available for the GTO in 1967. Only offered with the automatic

transmission, it was activated by a small button at the tip of the turn signal lever. The system could be deactivated by either again pressing the button or by applying the brake. The cruise control option was an additional $52.66 and is rarely seen today.

Seat upholstery was updated for 1967, incorporating a simple vertical ribbed pattern. The seats also featured locking backs, which could be unlocked by pushing a chrome button located near the top of each seat back. Front seat headrests (code 571) remained optional equip-

Like the seat patterns, the door panels were redesigned for every year throughout the GTO's production. Parchment door panels received black carpet along the bottom edge. This car is also equipped with the remote mirror (code 394). Inset: Soft window crank knobs debuted in 1967 as a safety feature. In the event of an impact, the soft knobs would, theoretically, inflict less harm on vehicle occupants compared with the metal knobs of earlier years.

ment, as did the reclining passenger seat (code 578). The reclining passenger seat option included the front seat headrests and was priced at $84.26. The Strato Bench front bench seat, with its center folding armrest, (available only in black and parchment) was now a no-charge option, with 759 1967 GTOs so equipped.

The door panel design changed from vertical to horizontal pleats, with a GTO crest mounted above the armrest, higher on the door than in 1966. Each window crank now featured a soft knob, which was considered a safety improvement over the metal knobs used from 1964–1966. Power windows (code 551) remained a $100.05 option and added approximately 21 pounds to the weight of the car.

The center console no longer displayed the chrome-ribbed design of 1964–1966 and for the first time was listed separately for the automatic and manual transmission versions. The manual transmission console (code 472) was a $52.66 option; the automatic (code 472) was $68.46. The automatic console was mandatory with the tilt steering option. Each version now featured a wood-grain vinyl insert, complementing the insert that surrounded the gauges.

Roof-rail reading lamps (code 404) were available on hardtop and Sports Coupe models for $13.59 or as part of the Lamp Group (code 074). The Lamp Group for hardtops and Sports Coupes included luggage lamp (code 401), glove box lamp (code 402, standard on GTO models), roof-rail reading lamps (code 404), courtesy lamps (code 411), ashtray and lighter lamp (code 412, standard on GTO models), under-hood lamp (code 421), and an ignition switch lamp (code 422). Price for the hardtop and Sports Coupe Lamp Group was $22.61.

Even though the convertible Lamp Group was still designated (code 074), because of the folding top, it did not feature the roof-rail reading lamps (code 404). Convertible models did not display a dome light; therefore, interior courtesy lamps (code 411) were standard issue. All other lamps that were included in the hardtop and Sports Coupe Lamp Group were also offered for convertible models.

Radio choices were the same as in 1966, but the Sepra-Phonic or Verbra-Phonic rear speaker options were now available on convertible models. A small enclosure was used and mounted behind the passenger's side of the rear seat. The addition of the stereo tape player (code 354) was also new for 1967. More commonly referred to as an 8-track player, it was a $128.49 option, a considerable sum in 1967. Developed by Bill Lear of the Lear Jet Corporation (with contributions from various audio

The optional center console (automatic transmission version shown) now displayed a simulated wood-grain insert, which corresponded with the dash trim. A manual transmission console added $52.66 to the price of a 1967 GTO, while the console for an automatic transmission raised the price by $68.46.

Radio and speaker options were plentiful for the 1967 Pontiac GTO. This model features an AM/FM pushbutton unit with manual antenna (code 344), a $133.76 option.

and automotive manufacturers), it was officially named Stereo 8. Lear had a working relationship with Motorola, which provided most of Ford Motor Company's electronics, and consequently, Ford had introduced the 8-track player as an option on its 1966 models. Other manufacturers followed suit, and by 1967, 8-track tape players were offered in most American-made automobiles.

The 8-track player for the 1967 GTO was affixed to the underside of the dash, just below the radio. Although it was quite large, it integrated well with the rest of the interior space; it featured a plastic housing, woodgrain vinyl insert, and chrome trim. Four knobs (select, volume, tone, balance) mimicked the style of the radio

A new option for the GTO was the stereo tape player (code 354), commonly referred to as an 8-track player or simply 8-track. At $128.49, roughly $950.00 when adjusted for inflation, it was not an inexpensive option. (Photo Courtesy Don Keefe)

The stereo tape player mounted under the dash, just below the radio. Knobs for select, volume, tone, and balance were employed. A Y-shaped heater outlet (shown) was needed, as the tape player would obstruct the standard outlet. (Photo Courtesy Alan Swearingen)

1967 FIREBIRD

The genesis of the Pontiac Firebird can be traced back to John DeLorean's desire to design and produce a two-seat sports car under the Pontiac marquee. Work commenced on this project in August 1963 and became known as the XP-833 and later, the Pontiac Banshee. Four full-scale, non-functioning mockups were produced and, eventually, two fully operational cars were built: the SP-5, an OHC-6-powered coupe; and the SP-6, a 326-HO–powered roadster. The cars were beautifully executed, displaying a strong resemblance to what Chevrolet eventually used for its 1968–1981 Corvette models.

At the time, General Motors was attempting to develop a renewed focus on safety, and GM chairman James Roche felt that the designs were too aggressive; he and DeLorean were constantly at odds with each other over the XP-833. The conflict between the two men, along with the XP-833 program, ended in March 1966. Roche's decision to not display the SP-5 or SP-6 at the International Auto Show in New York the following month was the final nail in the coffin for DeLorean's two-seat sports car.

With the Banshee off the table, DeLorean and the Pontiac team focused on bringing a version of the Chevrolet Camaro to market. It was eventually named the Pontiac Firebird and employed the new F-body platform. Unlike the GTO, the Firebird used unit body construction with a separate front subframe that bolted to the body. Because of DeLo-

rean's reluctance to accept a Pontiac based on the F-body, the Chevrolet Camaro had debuted five months before the Firebird. However, this delay benefited the engineers, giving them time to refine and upgrade the car and present it with a noticeable Pontiac identity. The simulated quarter-panel vents were akin to those used on the 1967 LeMans, while the taillights echoed those used on the 1967 GTO and Grand Prix. The familiar split-grille was prominent, and the hood (Firebird 400 only) bears a strong resemblance to the 1968–1970 GTO units. Together, these styling cues helped to distinguish the Firebird from the Camaro and imbued the car with its own personality.

The Firebird was also given numerous suspension upgrades, resulting in handling that was superior to Chevrolet's Camaro. Altering the rear suspension geometry and adding a single radius rod on all Firebirds rectified wheel hop that afflicted the Camaro. The 6-cylinder cars equipped with an automatic transmission received none, while cars fitted with the Sprint-6 or V-8 engine and manual transmission received two radius rods. Stiffer springs and shocks were installed, and the 6-inch-wide wheels (standard on all Firebird models) increased the track width.

Pontiac created five distinct versions of the 1967 Firebird and branded them as "The Magnificent Five." The base Firebird was fitted with a 230-ci OHC-6 engine producing 165 hp. The Firebird Sprint was a step above the

Even though Pontiac introduced the Firebird partway through the 1967 model year, sales were strong, with 82,560 Firebirds sold. The Firebird HO (shown) was fitted with a 285-hp 326-ci engine, dual exhaust, and special stripes. The wire wheel covers were an extra cost option. (Photo Courtesy Rocky Rotella)

base model, also employing the 230-ci OHC-6 engine but topped with a 4-barrel carburetor that upped the output to 215 hp. Situated in the middle of the Firebird pack was the 326-ci 2-barrel that pushed out 250 hp. Things began to get serious with the Firebird HO, a 4-barrel version of the 326-ci producing 285 hp and 359 ft-lbs of torque. The Firebird HO also had a dual exhaust and heavy-duty suspension. The most magnificent of The Magnificent Five was the Firebird 400, doling out 325 hp and 410 ft-lbs of torque from its 400-ci mill.

The Firebird 400 employed the same strategy as the GTO: install a large-displacement, high-performance engine in a compact package. Even though the 1967 GTO was indeed a fine road car, the Firebird capitalized on its lighter weight and shorter 108-inch wheelbase, compared to the GTO's 115-inch length, which resulted in more-nimble performance. The Firebird 400 used the same engine as the GTO, but was rated at 325 hp, GM's self-imposed limit for the smaller, lighter Firebird. In the December 2009 issue of *Hemmings Muscle Machines*, writer Daniel Strohl stated, "Faced with a shortened development cycle for the 1967 introduction, Pontiac engineers simply nabbed the L78 335-hp 400-ci from the GTO and renamed it the W66." Strohl

went on to explain how Pontiac did more than just reduce the Firebird 400's output on paper, "The only difference, according to Jim Mattison of Pontiac Historical Services, was a slightly different throttle linkage that prevented the Rochester Quadrajet's secondaries from opening more than 90 percent. With the new throttle linkage, Pontiac could officially rate the Firebird 400's engine at 325 hp at 4,800 rpm and 410 ft-lbs of torque at 3,600 rpm."

To further hype the 1967 Firebird, a special color, Verdoro Green, was formulated and used exclusively for the Firebird lineup, although at least one documented example of a Verdoro Green 1967 GTO does exist. In 1968, the hue was available on all Pontiac models and became extremely popular on the GTO. It was not shared with any other GM divisions.

Despite its mid-year introduction, the Firebird sold 82,560 units in 1967, edging out the GTO, which sold 81,722 copies. It's difficult to say how many GTO sales were lost to Pontiac's new F-body, as the Firebird was just one of many increasingly potent offerings available to the performance enthusiast in 1967. This forced the GTO to compete with other manufacturers as well as other models produced by the Pontiac division.

controls and contributed to the cohesive appearance. A print advertisement for the 1967 GTO boasted, "Our 8-track stereo tape player. It sounds unbelievable even in an open convertible. Extra cost." To give a true stereo effect, the 8-track option also included the Sepra-Phonic rear speaker. Because the 8-track player plugged into the back of the radio, a radio option was required. In addition, the Verbra-Phonic rear speaker was not available because it used the same plug as the stereo tape player on the radio. Eric White's comprehensive book, *The GTO Association of America's Pontiac GTO/GT-37 Illustrated Identification Guide*, noted that the stereo tape player was not available with the heater delete option (code 584). Research suggests that this is because the rear support strap for the tape player attached to the heater box.

One can easily imagine a newly minted 1967 GTO owner cruising the boulevard with a rumbling 400-ci engine, Hurst-shifted manual transmission, and the Rolling Stones blasting from the Stereo 8. The epitome of cool. There are no breakdowns as to how many 1967 GTOs were equipped with the 8-track player, but today it is considered a rare and coveted option. A quick search of a popular online auction website revealed a reconditioned 1967 8-track player with housing offered at $799.99 and another, minus the housing, available for $425.00.

Driveline

The exterior of the 1967 Pontiac GTO was limited to minor styling revisions but, mechanically, the car was vastly different than the 1966 model. The venerable 389-ci was supplanted by the new 400-ci engine that displayed a bore size of 4.12 inches (compared to 4.0625 inches for the 389-ci). Many Pontiac enthusiasts wrongly assume that the 400-ci was simply an overbored 389-ci, but an all-new block was cast to maintain sufficient cylinder wall thickness. The new block also received an additional freeze plug on each side, but it retained the two-bolt main configuration (some high-performance 400-ci blocks featured four-bolt mains). The 400-ci displayed the same 3.75-inch stroke and 10.75:1 compression ratio as the 389-ci mill. Four different camshaft profiles were used, depending on which version of the 400-ci was selected. The A.I.R. pollution control system was again installed on all engines in cars to be sold in California, except the 255-hp 2-barrel, which employed the Controlled Combustion System to reduce greenhouse gases.

335-hp

The standard engine for the 1967 GTO was the L78 400-ci that produced 335 hp at 5,000 rpm and 441 ft-lbs of torque at 3,200 rpm. New cylinder heads, casting number 670, were employed, and flow was far superior to the 1964–1966 units. The valve angle was changed from 20 degrees to 14 degrees, and valve spacing was altered to accommodate the larger 2.11-inch intake and 1.77-inch exhaust valves. Redesigned, high-flowing ports exploited the big valves, and closed, fully machined combustion chambers were used. Screw-in rocker arm studs (more reliable than the pressed-in rocker studs of previous years) and pushrod guide plates were also included in the 670 cylinder head design. The 335-hp engine received

A 400-ci engine producing 335 hp and 441 ft-lbs of torque was standard issue for the 1967 Pontiac GTO. The chrome-plated, louvered air cleaner is a simple way to identify the base engine from the HO and Ram Air versions. (Photo Courtesy Don Keefe)

This Signet Gold 1967 hardtop has won numerous national awards. The attention to detail inside the engine compartment was a key element to its success. Note the transition of body color to black paint on the firewall, and, while not all GTOs are identical, this closely matches the factory process. (Photo Courtesy Don Keefe)

An all-new cylinder head design, casting number 670, was used for the 1967 GTO. These units performed considerably better than the 1964–1966 heads. The casting number is located on the center exhaust ports.

The 670 cylinder heads employed larger valves than those fitted on 1964–1966 GTOs, with 2.11-inch intake (right) and 1.77-inch exhaust (left). The heads also featured screw-in rocker arm studs and fully machined, closed combustion chambers. (Photo Courtesy Rocky Rotella)

the 067 camshaft with 273/289 advertised duration and .410-inch lift on both the intake and exhaust valves.

The new 670 cylinder heads were intriguing to many in the Pontiac performance community, and in the February 1967 issue of *Hi-Performance Cars* magazine, writer Alex Walordy teamed up with Royal Pontiac's Milt Schornack and Sid Warren to cover the in-depth process of retrofitting 670 castings onto an earlier 389-ci engine. Walordy extolled, "The secret weapon in getting all this power out is a new set of heads with bigger valves and

Intake manifold casting number 9786286 was employed on all 4-barrel-equipped 1967 GTOs. This cast-iron intake is based off the Super-Duty versions of the early 1960s and is still considered a great choice for many performance applications. (Photo Courtesy Rocky Rotella)

revised combustion chambers." Later in the piece, Walordy touted the redesigned ports, stating, "While the mating surfaces of the cylinder heads at the intake and exhaust manifolds have not changed, the port shapes have been improved to cope with the increased gas flow. For instance, the ledges in the exhaust ports have gone, and the roof of the intake port is contoured differently." This was not a simple cylinder head swap that could have been carried out by the novice mechanic; it involved a near-complete engine overhaul with specialized tools and skills. It did, however, underscore the enthusiasm and expected horsepower potential of the 670 cylinder heads.

The January 1967 issue of *Motor Trend* magazine echoed this sentiment. "You'll be glad to know that parts from the new 400-cubic-inch engine will bolt onto the old 389-cubic-inch engines, so '67 heads will probably find themselves on many 389 blocks. They have larger valves, relocated valve positioning, improved combustion chambers and larger ports."

All 4-barrel-equipped engines (standard 335-hp, 360-hp HO, and 360-hp Ram Air) featured a new intake manifold based on the 4-barrel NASCAR units from the early 1960s. This dual-plane, cast-iron manifold was a high-flowing design, and is still recommended by numerous Pontiac high-performance engine specialists. In his book, *How to Rebuild Pontiac V-8s*, renowned Pontiac engine expert Rocky Rotella explained, "General Motors

The Rochester Quadrajet was used in all 1967 GTO applications except the 255-hp 2-barrel-equipped version. Combined with the new intake manifold and redesigned cylinder heads, it was a potent combination that ushered in a new era of Pontiac performance.

Bottom view of the Rochester Quadrajet carburetor. The 1.38-inch primary throttle bores and large, 2.25-inch secondary bores offered a combination of economy and performance. (Photo Courtesy Rocky Rotella)

banned the use of multiple carburetion on all 1967 vehicles, except the Corvette. Pontiac developed a beautiful cast-aluminum single 4-barrel intake manifold for the early-1960s Super Duty, and it featured long, smoothly contoured runners. It offered an excellent combination of low-speed torque and high-speed horsepower. A modified version of this intake manifold was used with the new Rochester Quadrajet to produce an induction package that performed as well as, and quite possibly better than, the Tri-Power it replaced in 1967."

Pontiac first used the Rochester Quadrajet 4-barrel carburetor on the 1966 Sprint OHC 6-cylinder engine, followed by the GTO for all 4-barrel applications in 1967. Displaying small 1.38-inch primary throttle bores and massive 2.25-inch secondary bores, it provided respectable fuel economy in typical driving conditions and copious amounts of power when the large secondaries opened. Research suggests that these early Quadrajet carburetors flowed

The A.I.R. system was again used on all GTOs to be sold in the state of California. It added $44.76 to the price of the car. Inset: Cars equipped with the A.I.R. system required specific ignition timing and carburetor adjustments to achieve maximum efficiency. This decal notified service technicians to consult the service or owner's manual for correct settings.

The Capacitor Discharge Ignition (CDI) system included an ignition control unit/amplifier located in the driver-side front of the engine compartment, along with a red distributor cap and ignition coil. The transistorized voltage regulator (shown) was included with this system on cars equipped with air-conditioning and was optional on cars without. (Photo Courtesy Alan Swearingen)

approximately 750 cfm. Although not nearly as visually impressive as the Tri-Power induction systems of previous years, the new 4-barrel intake and Quadrajet carburetor performed wonderfully.

In the Summer 2011 issue of *Motor Trend Classic* magazine, author and muscle car guru Steve Magnante stated, "Compared with the Tri-Power, the combination served up superior low-end throttle response, better wide-open breathing, and smoother transitions between these extremes of operation. Truth be told, the audible surge in engine noise caused by the Tri-Power's end carbs snapping open was actually a slight acceleration-hampering bog. Still, many mourn the Tri-Power's passing to this day." Interestingly, Pontiac used both Rochester and Carter 4-barrel carburetors in its 1967 lineup, but no Carter units were installed in 1967 GTOs. Chrome valve covers and a louvered chrome air cleaner were standard issue on the 335-hp engine.

As in 1966, the A.I.R system was employed for 1967 GTOs sold in California. The 670 cylinder heads were produced with the same passages as the previous year's 093 heads to accommodate the A.I.R. components. This pollution control system was used in 1966 and 1967 only; the 1968 and later cylinder heads burned the air/fuel mixture more efficiently and decreased emissions without the assistance of A.I.R.

A Capacitor Discharge Ignition system (code 671) was available for $114.80 if equipped with an air conditioner, and $104.26 if not. The 1967 GTO/Sprint/2+2

brochure touted, "Our new Capacitor Discharge Ignition system is available on all premium fuel engines (except cars with AM/FM radios). The higher the RPM, the hotter the spark." A red distributor cap and ignition coil were included with this option. An excerpt from *Pontiac GTO Restoration Guide 1964–1970* by Paul Zazarine and Chuck Roberts detailed, "The 1967 GTO transistorized ignition was completely redesigned. The system used a capacitive discharge (CD) control unit (part number 1115010). It was mounted on the LH splash shield (part number 9787753) and was protected by a cover (part number 9787094). The control unit wire harness ran through a grommet (part number 9786871), along the LH upper fender skirt—retained by the headlamp harness clips—and to the distributor and coil. The harness rested along the firewall harness clips.

"The ignition coil (part number 1115248, Delco part number D516) was bright red. The natural-metal-appearing coil bracket (part number 1968034) was mounted to the rear of the RH cylinder head. The distributor cap (part number 1968018) was also bright red. The 1967 CD system was not available with GTOs equipped AM/FM radios.

"The transistorized voltage regulator (RPO 664) was available on both the 1966 and 1967 GTO not equipped with air-conditioning. It was available only as a factory-installed option. The replacement part number was 1116378, Delco part number D-639. The transistorized voltage regulator could be ordered with or without transistorized ignition, and no modifications had to be made to the existing harness." Even though it was costly, the Capacitor Discharge Ignition system eliminated the points and condenser and provided a more reliable spark at high RPM.

360-hp

The L74 400 HO (code 802) engine was a $76.89 option for the 1967 Pontiac GTO. Rated at 360 hp at 5,100 rpm and 438 ft-lbs of torque at 3,600 rpm, it was a competent performer that could easily keep pace with the previous year's 389-ci Tri-Power engine. The 400 HO used the same 670 cylinder heads as the standard 335-hp version but was fitted with the hotter 068 camshaft, boasting 288/302 advertised duration and .410-inch valve lift. The 400 HO also featured new high-flowing exhaust manifolds that were much less restrictive than those installed on the 335-hp engine. The new manifolds (also used in Ram Air applications) featured four individual runners and allowed the exhaust gases to escape more efficiently. This not only improved horsepower,

The 1967 400 HO engine is easily identified by its open-element air cleaner and special exhaust manifolds. Factory rated output was 360 hp and 438 ft-lbs of torque. (Photo Courtesy Rocky Rotella)

The 1967 Ram Air engine was rated at 360 hp, but most knowledgeable enthusiasts estimate the true output at or greater than 400 hp. A hotter camshaft with 301/313 duration, modified cylinder heads, HO/Ram Air exhaust manifolds, and a functional Ram Air induction system were part of the package. (Photo Courtesy Rocky Rotella)

but also provided slightly better fuel economy over the standard manifolds. Some present-day 1964–1967 GTO owners opt for these pieces because they deliver almost the same level of performance offered by tubular headers, but without the clearance and installation issues. A chrome-plated, open-element air cleaner, which was unique to the 400 HO (Ram Air engines used a different base), completed the package.

The 1967 GTO/Sprint/2+2 brochure referred to the 360-hp engine as the Quadra-Power 400 and stated, "New heads. New combustion chamber design. Bigger intake and exhaust valves. New valve location. Enlarged ports. New intake manifold with smoother, more efficient runners. New free-flow header-type exhaust manifold. New Quadrajet 4-barrel carburetor." Clearly, Pontiac was attempting to convey that even though the Tri-Power induction system had been discontinued, horsepower had not declined. Pontiac Motor Division produced 13,827 (some sources list this figure at 13,310) HO-equipped GTOs in 1967.

Ram Air

The 360-hp Ram Air engine was the top engine option for the 1967 GTO. At $263.30, roughly $1,935 in 2017 dollars, the L67 Ram Air engine option required buyers to order the heavy-duty radiator (code 681), Safe-T-Track differential (code 731) housing a mandatory 4.33:1 gear set, and either the M21 close-ratio 4-speed manual transmission (code 778) or the TH-400 3-speed automatic (code 781). A functional Ram Air system was shipped in the trunk from the factory to be installed at the dealer, which included a Ram Air pan and an open hood scoop

insert to allow the intake of cooler, fresh air. A special camshaft, commonly referred to as the 744 cam, was fitted with an advertised 301/313 duration and .410-inch intake and exhaust lift. The high-flowing exhaust manifolds found on the HO engine were also employed on the Ram Air version.

A topic of debate within the Pontiac community involves which cylinder head castings were employed for 1967 Ram Air applications. Research suggests that early production Ram Air engines used 670 cylinder heads machined to accommodate stiffer (single) valve springs required for use with the 744 camshaft. A small "x" was stamped on the circular pad on the center exhaust port to denote that the heads were upgraded to Ram Air specifications. The single, heavy-duty valve springs proved to be unreliable, forcing Pontiac to implement further changes to the Ram Air cylinder head later in the 1967 model year. The 670 castings were still employed, but were machined even further, now to accommodate a stiffer, dual valve spring arrangement. The heads were re-stamped as 97. The 6 and 0 were ground down, and a number 9 was stamped in front of the number 7. The 97 versions are believed to be the rarest of the three 1967 Ram Air cylinder heads.

Well-known Pontiac engine expert and author Rocky Rotella explains, "Most Pontiac hobbyists are unaware that the 1967 400 Ram Air used a single valve spring package, part number 9785720—an assembly composed of the single valve spring and an internal metal damper—was introduced in midyear 1966 with the XS-code 389-ci

A small "x" was stamped on one of the pads near the center exhaust ports on 670 cylinder heads that were modified for use on Ram Air engines. Stronger valves produced from 8440 alloy and stiffer, single valve springs were used. (Photo Courtesy Alan Swearingen)

Even with the modified 670 X cylinder heads, the aggressive camshaft profile of the 1967 Ram Air engine led to valvetrain instability at high RPM. A second attempt was made to correct this issue: 670 heads were further modified and fitted with stiff, dual valve springs. To indicate the machining and hardware employed for these units, the 6 and 0 were ground down and a 9 was stamped near the 7, creating the 97 head. (Photo Courtesy Rocky Rotella)

Casting number 997 cylinder heads were used late in the model year for Ram Air applications and are highly valued by enthusiasts. Like the 97 units, the 997 heads featured stiff, dual valve springs and polished valves constructed from 8440 alloy. This photo also provides a detailed perspective of the HO/Ram Air exhaust manifolds. (Photo Courtesy Alan Swearingen)

Tri Power. It was then carried over into 1967 for the 400 Ram Air. The single valve spring boasted increased pressure to complement the aggressive lobe profile of the newly developed 744 camshaft, but because there wasn't an inner valve spring to positively locate it around the valve guide boss, or a separate locator cup, the valve spring was susceptible to uncontrolled oscillation at high RPM and failure was common. Pontiac recognized this and in midyear 1967 replaced the 400 Ram Air's single high-rate valve spring package with a dual high-rate spring package. It coincided with the introduction of the number-97 cylinder head, which ultimately resulted in the 997 casting."

Toward the end of the model year, 997 cylinder head castings were employed for Ram Air engines. These were considered functionally identical to the 97 cylinder heads but displayed the 997 casting number at the base of the head to the right of the center exhaust ports.

Valves constructed of 8440 alloy, along with heavy-duty valve springs (single in 670 X, double in 97 and 997) were used in all 1967 Ram Air applications. Polished valves were used in 97 and 997 heads, but not the

On April 24, 1967, Pontiac produced a limited number of four-bolt main blocks for use in Ram Air applications. Although they were assigned part number 9792506, they appear to display the number 9792510. Today, they are most commonly referred to as 9792510 and are extremely collectible. (Photo Courtesy Alan Swearingen)

The block casting date was cast into the block near the distributor hole. The four-bolt 1967 Ram Air block was dated D247: April (D), 24th day (24), 1967 (7). (Photo Courtesy Alan Swearingen)

670 X versions. Air-conditioning was not available with the Ram Air engine. Block codes for the 1967 Ram Air engines were: XS (manual transmission), XP (automatic transmission), XP over-stamped as XF (California A.I.R.–equipped with automatic transmission, and YR (California A.I.R.–equipped with manual transmission).

On April 24, 1967, Pontiac produced a limited run of four-bolt main blocks for use in Ram Air applications, assigned part number 9792506. The blocks are cast with what appears to be number 9792510; however, the "0" is virtually illegible and thought to be an error by the foundry. Because they were manufactured for just one day, these 1967 four-bolt main blocks are extremely rare and desirable within the Pontiac community. The casting number for the standard, two-bolt main 400-ci block was 9786133.

In the August 1967 issue of *Popular Hot Rodding* magazine, the staff thoroughly tested a 1967 360-hp Ram Air GTO at Irwindale Raceway in San Gabriel, California. The car was equipped with a TH-400 automatic transmission with Hurst Dual Gate shifter, heavy-duty suspension, power front disc brakes, power steering, Firestone Wide Oval tires, and 4.33:1 rear gear ratio with a Safe-T-Track differential. Writer Forrest Bond noted, "We tested the car 'as delivered' so the times indicate performance that can be expected right off the showroom floor. After trying various techniques, we settled on one that seemed to suit the chassis-tire-horsepower combination. After staging, we locked the brakes, brought the RPM up to 1,400, let off the brake, and floored the throttle." The *Popular Hot Rodding* staff made 11 passes, with a best ET of 14.26 seconds at 100.11 mph. The relatively high trap speed indicates that traction was a contributing factor, which is not surprising considering the Firestone Wide Ovals measured 7.75 inches wide and were mounted on the factory-issued 14x6 wheels. They had concluded that with some tuning and drag slicks, consistent high-12 second times would likely be realized.

The staff at *Car Life* magazine experienced similar results when they thoroughly tested a 1967 Ram Air-equipped GTO (1 of just 20 fitted with the California A.I.R system and automatic transmission) in the October 1967 issue. At the dragstrip, *Car Life* reported mid-14 second passes with driver, passenger, and test equipment. With driver only, the GTO blistered the quarter-mile in 13.9 seconds at 102.8 mph. It should be noted that the car was in stock trim, including the factory-issued Firestone Wide Ovals. The article noted, "Dragstrip potential is sure to be in the bottom 13-sec. bracket with slicks, open tuned headers, and all power and emissions control equipment removed."

While the 1967 Ram Air engine was officially rated at 360 hp at 5,400 rpm and 438 ft-lbs of torque at 3,800 rpm, many Pontiac enthusiasts believe the actual output to be at or above 400 hp. Equipped with the large-profile 744 camshaft, mandatory 4.33:1 gear ratio, and no available air conditioner, the 1967 Ram Air GTO was high-revving and somewhat uncomfortable for any sort of highway excursion, and the *Car Life* article confirmed, "The Ram Air GTO definitely is not pleasant for normal city traffic operation. The test car surged, loped, and generally ran miserably at part throttle up to 60 mph (3,000 rpm). Part of this was no doubt due to California emissions-control apparatus on the test car, but part must be blamed on the high state of tune of the Ram Air engine."

The article went on to assert, "With a 4.33:1 axle ratio, 70 mph requires approximately 3,500 rpm, an engine speed unpleasant to the ears and undesirable for engine wear." However, both Pontiac Motor Division and knowledgeable enthusiasts recognized that this car was designed more for quarter-mile passes than lengthy, sightseeing road trips. By 1967, Pontiac sales departments were well educated in high-performance, and it is unlikely that a 1967 GTO fitted with the 360 hp Ram Air engine would have been sold to someone who desired anything less.

Author note: Although both the *Popular Hot Rodding* and *Car Life* articles were printed using black and white photography, it appears that the same car was used for both publications (Cordova top, Ram Air engine fitted with A.I.R. emissions system, TH-400 automatic transmission, Rally I wheels, power brakes, and power windows).

With a scant 751 Ram Air–equipped GTOs produced in 1967, they are highly collectible in today's classic car marketplace. Of those 751 Ram Air GTOs, 532 were code XS manual transmission cars, 136 were XP automatics, 63 were YR manual transmission A.I.R. (California market), and a mere 20 were XP (over-stamped XF) automatic A.I.R. (California market) units.

2-Barrel

A new engine option for the GTO was the low-compression 400-ci equipped with a 2-barrel carburetor (code 803). Available only with the automatic transmission, it generally appealed to the more relaxed buyer who desired GTO styling without having to worry about the higher cost associated with premium fuel. Rated at 255 hp at 4,400 rpm and 397 ft-lbs of torque at 2,400 rpm, it featured many components not shared with the other GTO powerplants. To achieve its 8.6:1 compression ratio, the 142 cylinder heads were used, which displayed

In an effort to appeal to the more casual GTO buyer, a low-compression, 2-barrel-equipped version of the 400 ci was offered. Available only with the automatic transmission, the L65 400-ci (code 803) engine developed 255 hp and 397 ft-lbs of torque; it did not require premium fuel. (Photo Courtesy Eric Foehr)

With the air cleaner removed from the L65 400-ci engine, the Rochester 2GC 2-barrel carburetor is revealed. The 2-barrel option for the GTO was offered from 1967 to 1969. (Photo Courtesy Eric Foehr)

The 255-hp 2-barrel-equipped 400-ci engine available in the 1967 GTO was fitted with 142 cylinder heads that yielded an 8.6:1 compression ratio. Even though 2,967 1967 GTOs were produced with this engine, they are seldom seen today. (Photo Courtesy Eric Foehr)

smaller 1.92-inch intake and 1.66-inch exhaust valves. In addition, a much milder camshaft was used for the 255-hp mill. Known as the 254 camshaft, it featured an advertised duration of 269/277, and a valve lift of .375-inch intake and .410-inch exhaust.

With these combined changes, the 255-hp engine would have made an ideal cruiser, with very smooth idle characteristics and ease of operation suited for first-time muscle car buyers. In 1967, Pontiac was able to lure 2,967 customers with this no-cost engine option, many of whom may not have previously considered a GTO. The 2-barrel engine option was no longer offered after the 1969 model year. The availability of both the 255-hp 2-barrel and the 360-hp Ram Air engines in 1967 highlighted the fact that Pontiac Motor Division was catering to both the casual enthusiast and the serious, performance-minded racer.

Exhaust

The 335-hp cars employed a dual, 2-inch exhaust system mated to the standard exhaust manifolds with a two-bolt flange. Automatic-transmission GTOs continued to employ exhaust resonators, while manual transmission versions did not. HO and Ram Air cars used a larger 2.25-inch exhaust connected to the HO/Ram Air manifolds via a three-bolt flange. Trumpet-style exhaust extensions (code 482) remained a $30.23 option.

Chrome-plated exhaust extensions (code 482) were a $30.23 option for the 1967 GTO and complement the tasteful rear-end styling of the car.

Transmission

Manual transmission options remained the same as the previous year, with the column-shifted Saginaw M11 3-speed as standard issue. The heavy-duty M13 3-speed, M20 wide-ratio 4-speed, and M21 close-ratio 4-speed units were all optional equipment and each was fitted with a Hurst shifter. The M20 wide-ratio 4-speed retained the same gear ratios as the 1966 version: 2.52:1 in first, 1.88:1 in second, 1.46:1 in third, 1.00:1 in fourth, and 2.59:1 in reverse.

The much stronger Turbo Hydra-Matic 400 (TH-400) 3-speed finally replaced the dismal Super Turbine 300 2-speed automatic transmission. It should be noted that the GTO was the only 1967 Pontiac A-body to receive the TH-400; Tempest and LeMans models continued to employ the lesser Super Turbine 300. The TH-400 featured gear ratios of 2.48:1 in first, 1.48:1 in second, 1.00:1 in third, and 2.08:1 in reverse gear. Full-throttle shifts were set at 5,000 rpm. The TH-400 transmission added approximately 50 pounds of weight to the car, when compared to a manual transmission–equipped GTO. Even today, the TH-400 transmission is considered one of GM's most durable designs and has been installed in countless performance and heavy-duty applications.

Cars fitted with a center console and an automatic transmission received a Hurst Dual Gate shifter, also known as a "His and Hers." Several versions of this shifter had been manufactured since the early 1960s, but a new design was produced specifically for the GTO. A clever and stylish component, the cable-operated Dual Gate shifter was mounted directly to the transmission tunnel by four screws. The center console was then placed into position and a chrome finishing plate featuring a simulated wood-grain vinyl insert was affixed to the shifter via four mounting screws. A shift lever adorned with the Hurst name and topped with a black plastic shift knob completed the unit.

When no console was specified, the shifter for the TH-400 automatic transmission was mounted on the steering column. This combination is one of few examples of a GTO not featuring a Hurst shifter. (Photo Courtesy Eric Foehr)

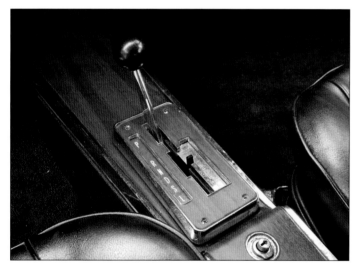

The addition of the TH-400 3-speed automatic transmission to the GTO's options list in 1967 provided Pontiac with an opportunity to offer a Hurst automatic shifter. The Hurst Dual Gate, also known as "His and Hers," offered both normal automatic function and a manual control. The manual aspect allowed the driver to shift gears at the desired RPM without fear of accidentally shifting into neutral.

The shift lever for the Dual Gate unit proudly displays the Hurst name and is topped with a plain, black plastic knob. In addition to its performance capabilities, it empowered Pontiac with yet another marketing angle, and was prominently featured in print advertisements and sales brochures.

This shifter allowed for typical automatic operation as well as full manual control, when desired. Manual control was achieved by moving the shifter into the neutral position, pushing the lever to the right, and pulling all the way back to first gear. Then, the driver could determine when to upshift by pushing forward and to the right for second and third gears. In manual mode, the design of the shifter eliminated the possibility of accidentally shifting into neutral and over revving the engine.

Stiffer suspension components remained standard equipment and kept the GTO firmly planted to the pavement. A road test by Motor Trend *magazine for the October 1966 issue claimed, "Not even a fast bend, sizeable hump, and wet road fazed roadholding of the GTO at test track."*

The combination of the stout TH-400 automatic and the performance-oriented Dual Gate shifter did not go unnoticed by the automotive press. The staff at *Car Life* magazine was more than impressed with its 1967 GTO test car fitted with these two components, noting, "Praise is due Pontiac for including the Hurst console-mounted automatic shift mechanism. This is one of the finest controls ever tested by *CL*. Manual selection of gears with this unit is positive, effortless and genuinely pleasant." Likewise, the January 1967 issue of *Motor Trend* magazine enthused, "The new GTO with Turbo Hydra-Matic throws down an exciting challenge to its 4-speed brother, as we found when we tested both."

A Hurst advertisement (proudly featuring a GTO convertible) from 1967 boasted, "Wouldn't you know Hurst would introduce its new automatic control wrapped in a '67 GTO? It's only proper. Hurst has been in GTOs since the first GTO was born. Now that they've kicked loose The Great One for '67, with a new engine, drivetrain components and a 3-speed Turbo-Hydramatic, Hurst is in there with something new of its own. A console-mounted Dual Gate control that's going to switch a lot of manual-shift lovers over to an automatic."

The Hurst print ad ultimately proved to be correct; because of the popularity of the TH-400 transmission and Hurst Dual Gate shifter, automatic GTO sales eclipsed manual versions for the first time in the car's history, with 42,594 automatics and 39,128 manuals sold in 1967.

Rear End

As in previous years, a 10-bolt rear end fitted with an 8.2-inch-diameter ring gear was used in all GTO applications. Gear ratio without air-conditioning was 3.55:1 for 335 hp, manual transmission GTOs (codes WT and WW), and 360-hp HO cars (codes YZ, WS, and WV). Cars fitted with the 335-hp 400-ci engine and automatic transmis-

sion (code YS) received 3.36:1 gears as standard equipment and 2.93:1 when equipped with air-conditioning. Like the 1966 cars, GTOs equipped with 3.90:1 or 4.33:1 gears were treated to the heavy-duty four-pinion limited slip differential. A 4.11:1 gear set was again available as a dealer-installed item. All Ram Air 1967 GTOs were fitted with 4.33:1 gears. The standard gear ratio for the new 2-barrel 400-ci models (automatic transmission only) was 2.78:1 when equipped with air-conditioning and 2.93:1 without.

Suspension and Braking

While many suspension and braking components were carried over from the 1966 model, there were some welcome improvements as well. The full-perimeter frame was retained, but the transmission crossmember was relocated for use with the TH-400 automatic transmission. Spindles were redesigned, with different pieces used in drum and disc brake applications. A threaded shaft with washers and nuts at either end was now employed to secure the front upper control arms to the frame (previous models used a bolt/washer/nut configuration).

Brakes

Although four-wheel drum brakes remained standard issue on all 1967 GTOs, power-assisted front disc brakes (code 521) were now optional equipment. At $104.79, the front disc brake option consisted of 11.12-inch vented rotors and four-piston calipers. Master cylinder bore size was increased to 1.125 inches for disc brake cars, compared to 1.00 inch for drum brake versions. Disc brakes are much less susceptible to fading in spirited driving situations and safer in wet conditions.

The dual-reservoir master cylinder was also newly introduced for 1967. Unlike the single-reservoir units from 1964–1966, the dual-reservoir design separated the front and rear braking systems and would retain at least partial braking ability in the event of a fluid leak. This design was not exclusive to the GTO; all 1967 and newer Pontiacs featured this important safety improvement.

After all the previous bemoaning by the automotive press about the 1964–1966 GTO's braking hardware, the August 1967 issue of *Popular Hot Rodding* magazine had high praise for their disc brake–equipped 1967 GTO, "Rounding out what has to be one of Detroit's best performance packages is the GTO brake system. After run-

For the first time in the car's history, power-assisted front disc brakes were available on the GTO. A $104.79 option, the disc-brake option included 4-piston calipers and 11.12-inch rotors.

The dual-reservoir master cylinder was a welcome safety addition that was used across the entire Pontiac lineup. It effectively separated the front and rear braking systems, and in the event of a fluid leak, the entire system would not be compromised. Black paint on the master cylinder is factory correct. (Photo Courtesy Don Keefe)

ning 100 mph at the races, we were able to make the first turn-off road, which is quite admirable. After 11 rapid-fire runs called for repeated stops from over 100 mph (we were driving past the finish line for brake test purposes) we experienced no fade or pull. Panic stops were accomplished from 60 mph with no fuss. The car stopped in a reasonable distance and failed to slide or skid."

The October 1967 issue of *Car Life* magazine was similarly enthusiastic. "The power disc brake system fitted to *CL*'s test GTO was outstanding. Fade was almost nonexistent, even after several stops from 100 mph at the end of the dragstrip. Perhaps more important, front-to-rear proportioning of this system was nearly perfect. . . . Pontiac is to be commended for an exceptionally fine braking system. Perhaps Pontiac and the remainder of Detroit manufacturers will see fit to match such performance in other models." Indeed, the 1967 optional power-assisted front disc brakes finally brought the GTO's braking ability up to the same level as the brute power and acceleration it provided.

Wheels and Tires

Wheel and tire choices increased for 1967, presenting the buyer with a wide array of options. Stamped steel 14x6 wheels adorned with dog dish hubcaps remained standard issue, although a second 14x6 stamped steel wheel (stamped DB) was produced for use with cars equipped with the disc brake option. Color-keyed wheels were standard on cars painted Starlight Black, Mariner Turquoise, Montreux Blue, and Seneca Bronze when fitted with dog dish hubcaps.

The wire wheel discs (code 452) were a $69.51 option for the 1967 GTO. They clearly impart a much more formal aesthetic than any other wheel or wheel cover choices. This car is fitted with modern radial tires.

The 1967 Deluxe wheel covers (code 461) were simple, yet stylish. At $16.85, they were the least expensive wheel/wheel cover option for the 1967 Pontiac GTO. (Photo Courtesy Alan Swearingen)

The 1967 Custom wheel covers (code 458) were attractive, mag-type pieces that featured a three-bar spinner center cap with a red PMD logo against a black background. (Photo Courtesy Alan Swearingen)

The handsomely styled wheel that debuted in 1965 remained unchanged from the 1966 version but was now officially named the Rally I (code 454). GTO buyers could opt for this wheel for an additional $56.87.

The Rally II (code 453) wheel made its debut in 1967 and was available on various Pontiac models. At $72.67, it was the top-of-the-line wheel choice for the GTO and provided a mag-type wheel option at an affordable price. Silver spokes against an argent surface yielded an eye-catching contrast. The polished trim ring presented the Rally II with an upscale appearance. The wheel ultimately became one of the most enduring factory wheel options of the muscle car era.

The Deluxe wheel covers (code 461) were a $16.85 upgrade. They were not radically different from the 1966 versions; the 1967 Deluxe wheel covers featured six cooling slots and six simulated slots, along with a PMD center logo.

Custom wheel covers (code 458) were also redesigned for 1967. They displayed six cooling slots against an argent face with a polished perimeter and three-bar spinner center cap. At $36.33, they were handsome pieces and an easy way to change the appearance of any GTO. Spotting a 1967 GTO with its original Custom wheel covers can be quite challenging. Throughout the years and, in most cases, several owners, they were lost or discarded in favor of Rally I, Rally II, or aftermarket wheels. In addition, neither the Deluxe nor the Custom wheel covers are currently being reproduced.

The Rally wheel, now officially named the Rally I, was unchanged from the previous year, retaining the black center cap of the 1966 version. The Rally I wheel (code 454) remained a $56.87 option for 1967 and was produced through the 1968 model year. Throughout the Rally I wheel's production from 1965 to 1968, it was only available in a 14x6 configuration and stamped KB. The 1965 wheel would be the only one to display a chrome-plated center cap, imparting a subtle, yet unique appearance to the 1965 cars.

New for 1967 was the Rally II wheel (code 453), available for an additional $72.67. A striking piece, the Rally II was a five-spoke design displaying five kidney-shaped cooling slots. For the 1967 GTO, the wheel measured 14x6 inches and was stamped JA. The center section and spoke perimeter were painted Dark Charcoal Gray, and the spokes were painted Argent Silver. Lug nuts were a closed-end design with red-painted centers, although some sources contend black-painted centers are correct. It should be noted that all cars equipped with Rally II wheels shown in the 1967 GTO/Sprint/2+2 brochure feature lug nuts with red-painted centers. A polished trim ring and PMD center cap (black with chrome accents and red lettering) completed the now-iconic design.

Pontiac Motor Division was able to keep manufacturing costs down by constructing the Rally II from stamped steel. An article by Terry McGean in the February 2010 issue of *Hemmings Motor News* relates, "The big difference between what the aftermarket was producing and what Detroit offered was the material: Cast wheels, be they magnesium or aluminum, were still fairly exotic in the mid-1960s, and guaranteeing their durability on an OEM level posed other issues. The solution was to produce attractive mag-styled wheels that were actually made from stamped steel, just like standard production

This 1967 GTO is fitted with the correct F70x14 Firestone Wide Oval reproduction tires, adding a small but noticeable detail to the overall restoration.

wheels." The relative low cost and beautiful styling made the Pontiac Rally II wheel a success from its debut in 1967, all the way through the late 1980s.

The Rally II wheel has been optional factory equipment on countless Pontiacs throughout its history, including GTOs from 1967 through 1974. Today, aftermarket companies such as Year One are reproducing the wheel in various sizes, including a modern aluminum version in both 17x8 and 17x9 configurations.

The vast majority of current 1965–1967 GTO owners choose to outfit their cars with either Rally I or Rally II wheels, even if not originally equipped. To them, they are a critical styling component for their beloved machines, and installing the factory-issued steel wheels and wheel covers is considered substandard. However, it is this author's opinion that spotting a 1965–1967 GTO with its original wheel covers, whether they are Standard (dog dish), Deluxe, Custom, or wire versions, is far more unusual, and therefore more interesting (standard hubcaps with correct color-matched wheels in particular) than the overused Rally I and Rally II versions. Using the original wheel covers is a simple and inexpensive way to assure that any Goat will stand out from the rest of the herd.

Tire choices increased for 1967, with new F70x14-inch Wide Oval redline tires becoming standard issue. F70x14-inch Wide Oval whitewall tires were a no-cost option. Other tires offered were nylon cord 7.75x14-inch whitewall or 7.75x14-inch four-ply versions. The staff at *Motor Trend* magazine tested three 1967 GTOs for its January 1967 issue (two were given the Royal Bobcat treatment, one remained in stock configuration). Of the unmodified GTO, they noted, "We liked the '66 GTO but we're sold on

For 1967, Pontiac introduced "The Great One" advertising campaign. It was born from necessity under pressure from General Motors to reduce or eliminate aggressive advertisements. The upscale appearance of the 1967 model corresponded perfectly with the new theme.

the '67. The car is church-quiet inside, mostly as a result of better weatherstripping around the curved, frameless side windows. Our 'town' car had optional heavy-duty suspension, which didn't shake or jar us in the least and gave firm, precise control at all times. Standard equipment Wide Oval tires plant themselves firmly to the road, doing their bit for good handling."

A period print advertisement for the Firestone Wide Oval tire depicted a 1967 GTO with the Indy 500 race roaring in the background. The ad proclaimed, "It's a passenger-car tire built like a race tire. Nearly 2 inches wider than an ordinary tire. To grip better. Corner easier. Run cooler. Stop 25 percent quicker. And like a Firestone race tire, it's built with rugged nylon cord for maximum strength and safety in sustained high-speed driving." Even though the Wide Oval tires were considered an improvement over the units available on the 1964–1966 models, tire technology has improved vastly in the past 50 years, and modern radial tires are still the best choice for performance and safety.

Advertising for 1967

By 1967, GM's renewed focus on safety posed yet another obstacle for Pontiac Motor Division. The screeching tires, high-speed hijinks, and aggressive tiger-themed imagery would be all but eliminated from Pontiac's bag of advertising tricks. Even though the new Rochester Quadrajet 4-barrel carburetor and redesigned 4-barrel intake manifold performed as well as, if not better than, three 2-barrel carburetors, the loss of the Tri-Power induction system was perceived as another promotional handicap for the GTO, which had become synonymous with the Tri-Power. Insurance companies had also wised up to the muscle car trend, and raised rates accordingly, so owning a GTO or any other high-powered automobile became increasingly expensive.

What may have seemed like insurmountable challenges ultimately proved to be fortuitous. They required Pontiac to evolve its marketing strategy. In an article penned for *High Performance Pontiac* magazine, notable

Pontiac expert Don Keefe wrote, "GM forced Pontiac to drop its extremely popular tiger-themed promotional campaign. In response, Pontiac's ad agency, McManus, John & Adams, scrambled to come up with a new slogan to use in GTO advertising and marketing. In a switching around of the letters G, T, and O, they came up with the expansion 'The Great One,' and it turned into a slam-dunk slogan for the '67 GTO." The Great One coincided with a slightly more mature GTO, with its expanse of elegant body trim, optional TH-400 3-speed automatic transmission and Hurst Dual Gate shifter, and the availability of a low-compression 2-barrel 400-ci engine.

In a television commercial for the 1967 GTO, actor Paul Richards walks up to a 1967 convertible in a dimly lit studio, coolly stating, "This is The Great One, the ultimate driving machine. And if you don't know what that means, you're excused. But if, when you see this car, you're seized with an uncontrollable urge to plant yourself behind the wheel and head for the wide-open spaces, then we're talking to you." As per GM's demand, there were no spinning tires, high-revving engines, or jungle cats prowling the scene, but the ad was nonetheless very intense. Richards's deep voice bellowed in a hypnotic cadence, challenging the idea of what the driving experience represented, and closed with, "The Great One is Pontiac GTO for 1967. Isn't it time you decided to ride the wide-track winning streak? The Great One is here." For the Pontiac enthusiast who has not yet seen this dramatic piece, it is readily accessible online and a great example of Pontiac's ability to adapt to the ever-changing demands of GM's strict policies.

The 1967 GTO/Sprint/2+2 brochure continued the theme, which depicted a Regimental Red hardtop and read, "The Great One. Pontiac GTO. The hardtop configuration. The ultimate driving machine. Made for people who know what that means. Others are excused." Even though the phrase, "The ultimate driving machine" is now closely associated with BMW, it's interesting to note

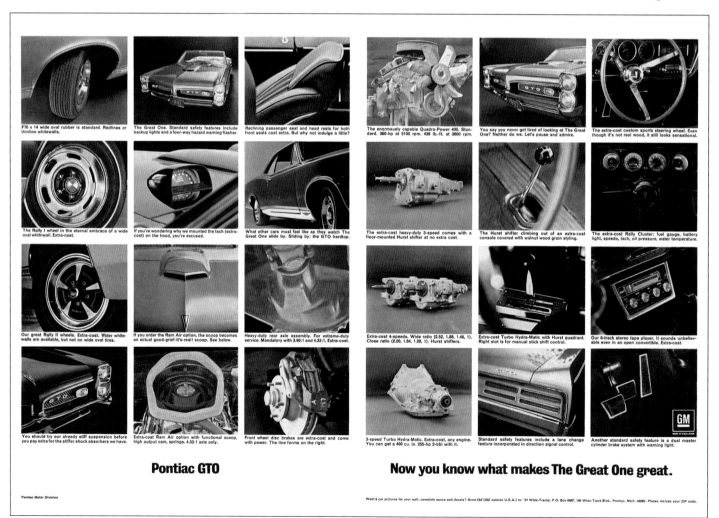

This print advertisement for the 1967 GTO focuses entirely on the car's hardware. Pontiac knew that the potential GTO buyer was astute, often comparing horsepower and torque output to offerings from rival manufacturers to make an informed purchase.

Gentlemen, start your engines.

GTO/Sprint/2+2

The 1967 GTO/Sprint/2+2 catalog was an eye-catching and informative piece of literature aimed at the performance enthusiast. Engine specifications and optional equipment were thoroughly explained. One of the lines used to describe the GTO called it, "The ultimate driving machine," a phrase now associated with German auto manufacturer BMW. (Photo Courtesy GM Media Archive)

There are few great moments in life.   This is one of them.

There is only one thing more spectacular than owning a GTO. That's driving one. Even if you don't own it.

For a GTO was made to drive. Relentlessly. In fact, the more you drive it, the more eager and responsive it becomes. Like a sleek cat that achieves perfection by being put through a hoop.

A GTO handles itself well because of its 400 cubic inches of powerplant and specially designed suspension. You can order a 255-hp regular-gas version (only with Turbo Hydra-Matic), the standard 335-hp or the 360-hp Quadra-Power 400. All come with the GM safety package which includes folding seat back latches and GM's energy absorbing steering column.

When you drive this driving machine, you will understand the ultimate conceit of our calling it The Great One.

The Great One by Pontiac

According to Jim Wangers, this now-iconic 1967 GTO print advertisement was as aggressive as management at General Motors would allow. GM's renewed focus on safety forbade certain types of action photography, and once more, the Pontiac marketing team was able to create memorable campaigns while (for the most part) following upper management's guidelines.

The Great One. GTO Hardtop. Need we say more?

Pontiac Motor Division

The incomparable GTO for '67 comes with 400 cubic inches of engine under a magnificently refined new skin. Or you can order the 255-hp version or the new 360-hp Quadra-Power Four Hundred. And for the first time you can order your GTO with our three-speed Turbo Hydra-Matic.

Our revolutionary 165-hp Overhead Cam Six is standard on all Le Mans and Tempests. You can specify the 215-hp 4-bbl version, a spirited 250-hp regular gas V-8 or its 285-hp premium gas cousin. Or you can step into the neatest grand touring car this side of the Atlantic with our OHC 6 Sprint package. Also new for this year—Executive and Tempest Safari wagons with walnut wood grain styled sides. All this plus the road-hugging security of Wide-Track on every Pontiac we make. See your Pontiac dealer right now.

Wide-Track Pontiac/67

You can add full fidelity sound by ordering our eight-track stereo tape player.

Leave it to Pontiac to come up with it first: now you can order a hood-mounted tach!

Somewhat of a departure for artists Art Fitzpatrick and Van Kaufman was the use of an abstract background. The car's tastefully exaggerated lines however, were a signature aspect of the duo's work.

that Pontiac had employed this line in 1967. An Internet search yielded this passage from the website, bmwstyle.tv, "The slogan was introduced during the 1970s and has captured the imaginations of BMW fans ever since. Bob Lutz, the executive vice president of global sales and marketing, developed the slogan while he was working with the advertising agency Ammirati & Puris on a fresh marketing campaign for BMW. Lutz had earlier worked with Ammirati & Puris when he obtained employment at Fiat before joining BMW. 'The ultimate driving machine' slogan became part of the company's marketing campaign in 1973 and became popular instantly."

Other articles give credit to both Lutz and Martin Puris, with the year of introduction varying from 1973 to 1975, depending on the source. Whether the idea was borrowed from Pontiac or developed independently is not definitively known. Perhaps Pontiac did not possess the desire or foresight to trademark the slogan; nevertheless, it is an interesting part of automotive marketing history.

One of the more forceful Pontiac print advertisements for 1967 depicted a GTO shot from a low angle, traversing a dirt road. Kicking up dust and appearing quite menacing, it read, "There are few great moments in life. This is one of them. The Great One by Pontiac." In his book, *Glory Days*, Jim Wangers commented on the piece, "From the first 1964 brochure, GTO advertising had always reflected a confident, almost arrogant attitude. This 1967 GTO ad was as close to showing action as we were allowed at the time."

The ad went on to proclaim, "There is only one thing more spectacular than owning a GTO. That's driving one. Even if you don't own it." It was a unique way to use motion photography and capture the buyer's imagination while not appearing overtly reckless or irresponsible.

Another great 1967 print advertisement featured imposing still photos of the Pontiac 2+2 (Big Brother), Sprint (The Great Imposter), and GTO (The Great One) with the ominous tagline, "Pretenders, beware." At the bottom of the piece were photos of available

The Great One is here.

This incredibly sleek mass is the 1967 Pontiac GTO. At rest. Four hundred cubic inches of engine under a magnificently refined new skin. In 255 and 335 horsepower variations. With even more of the distinguishing features that have made The Great One great. You can order things like our new 360-hp Quadra-Power 400, a 3-speed Turbo Hydra-Matic with manual shift control, front wheel disc brakes, eight-track stereo. Nor have we neglected its understudies—LeMans and Tempest. The 165-hp Overhead Cam Six is standard. A 215-hp OHC 6 (with or without the Sprint option) is available, as are 250- and 285-hp V-8s. New interiors. New colors. New options. New safety features, like a dual master cylinder brake system with warning light. And the road-hugging security of Wide-Track. 1967 may now begin. **Pontiac 67/Ride the Wide-Track winning streak**

This lesser known print advertisement for the 1967 GTO showcases the car's sleek profile, along with the available engines on both the GTO and Tempest models. The composition of this piece may seem peculiar today, but the 1960s were a unique time in American history.

This trio of 1965, 1966, and 1967 GTOs would be the envy of any Pontiac aficionado. It is evident that Pontiac Motor Division took great pride in style and performance, the two main ingredients to the GTO's winning formula.

engines and output specifications for both standard and optional powerplants. Shown for the GTO was the 360-hp Quadra-Power 400, most commonly referred to now as the 400 HO.

With action photography being used less frequently, Jim Wangers's prior insistence that artists Art Fitzpatrick and Van Kaufman focus on full-size Pontiacs became less relevant, and beginning in 1966, the duo began to paint a greater number of GTOs for use in print advertisements. One such piece showcased a 1967 hardtop over a somewhat abstract background, with a man and woman gazing into the distance. Titled "Wide-Track Pontiac/67" the rendering was accompanied by four still photos, each highlighting a specific detail on various Pontiac models. Page 29 of the 1967 full-line Pontiac brochure featured one of Fitz and Van's most recognizable GTO pieces, proudly displaying a 1967 convertible in an idyllic beach setting, with colorful surfboards in the background. A man coolly leans against the GTO, conversing with a woman seated in the back.

An intriguing ad for the 1967 GTO featured what appears to be a Montreux Blue convertible in a dimly lit studio, showcasing options such as the hood-mounted tachometer and Rally I wheels. A psychedelic-appearing female model poses curiously at the rear of the car (it was the 1960s after all), with the tagline, "The Great One is here," followed by the brilliant, "This incredibly sleek mass is the 1967 Pontiac GTO. At rest." In true Pontiac

tradition, the ad went on to state the numerous performance, interior, and safety options that were available for the 1967 model, closing with, "The road-hugging security of Wide-Track. 1967 may now begin." Pontiac may have been limited in the use of aggressive action photography, but they succeeded with clever, eye-catching advertisements that championed the GTO as a desirable performance car, capable of competing with the muscular offerings from other manufacturers.

The 1967 GTO is a favorite among both diehard Pontiac aficionados and casual muscle car fans. Even though the legendary Tri-Power was no longer available, the serious Pontiac enthusiast can provide a good case as to why the 1967 Goat is the best of the herd. Iconic exterior styling with optional, bulging hood-mounted tachometer, large 400-ci engine with superior cylinder head design, the availability of a true performance-oriented automatic transmission (TH-400), optional power front disc brakes, and the debut of the enduring Rally II wheel elevate the 1967 GTO into a cultural phenomenon. Pontiac expert Don Keefe summed it up nicely in the April 2014 issue of *High Performance Pontiac* magazine, "As far as the GTO is concerned, '67 was an iconic model year. It's the car many people recall when they hear conversations about GTOs in general. It seems like many Pontiac hobbyists have a bond to the '67 GTO, whether it was admiring one as a child, riding around in one as a youth, or as an aficionado or collector today."

APPENDIX I: 1964 GTO

1964 Pontiac GTO Production Figures

Body	Model Number	Production
Hardtop	2237	18,422
Sports Coupe	2227	7,384
Convertible	2267	6,644
Total Production		**32,450**

Production by Engine Type

Engine	HP	Production
389 4-barrel	325	24,205
389 Tri-Power	348	8,245
Total Production		**32,450**

Note: Transmission production figures are not available for the 1964 GTO.

Interior Color Codes

Code (with bucket seats)	Color
214	Black
215	Dark Blue
216	Light Saddle
217	Dark Aqua
218	Medium Red
219	Parchment

1964 Pontiac GTO Paint Codes

Paint Code	Color
A	Starlight Black
C	Cameo Ivory
D	Silvermist Gray
F	Yorktown Blue
H	Skyline Blue
J	Pinehurst Green
L	Marimba Red
N	Sunfire Red
P	Aquamarine
Q	Gulfstream Aqua
R	Alamo Beige
S	Saddle Bronze
T	Singapore Gold
V	Grenadier Red
W	Nocturne Blue

1964 Pontiac GTO Cordova and Convertible Top Codes

Code	Color
1	Ivory
1	Ivory
2	Black
4	Blue
5	Aqua
6	Beige
7	Saddle

Note: Cordova tops only available in Ivory and Black.

1964 Pontiac LeMans Options List

Sales Code	UPC Code	Description	S.R.P.
2227		LeMans Sports Coupe	2,480.00
2237		LeMans Hardtop	2,545.00
2267		LeMans Convertible	2,785.00
NOTE		After December 1963, base prices increased $11.00 due to seat belts being issued as standard equipment	
061		Basic Group with W62 GTO option: includes 392, 421, 471 (for manual-transmission cars)	92.59
061		Basic Group with W62 GTO option: includes 392, 421, 471 (for automatic-transmission cars)	90.44
062		Protection Group: includes 424, 512, 541, 572, 624, 633 (Sports Coupe and hardtop)	64.66
062		Protection Group: includes 424, 512, 572, 624, 633 (convertible)	43.14
081		Mirror Group: includes 441, 442, 444	17.48
084		Lamp Group: includes 404, 481, 482, 484, 491, 492, 494 (Sports Coupe and hardtop)	30.71
084		Lamp Group: includes 404, 481, 482, 491, 492, 494 (convertible)	18.02
382	W62	GTO Group (LeMans Sports Coupe, hardtop, and convertible only)	295.90
392	U63	Radio: Push Button with Manual Antenna (some PMD literature prices this option at $88.77 for convertible)	62.41
393	U63	Radio: Push Button with Electric Antenna (some PMD literature prices this option at $118.52 for convertible)	92.16
398	U60	Radio: Manual Control with Manual Antenna	53.80
399	U60	Radio: Manual Control with Electric Antenna	83.55
401	U80	Rear Speaker, Sepra-Phonic (not available with convertible)	14.15
402	C13	Wipers, Dual-Speed Electric	4.84
404	U26	Lamp, Underhood	3.55
411	A20	Front Seat Belts (prior to January 1964)	10.76
411		Wheel Discs, Wire	69.40
412	B50	Cushion, Custom Foam Front (not applicable for bucket seats)	8.07
414	A48	Seat Belt Delete, credit (after December 1963)	-11.00
421	C11	Dual-Speed Wipers with Washer	17.27
422	N25	Extensions, Tail Pipe	21.30

1964 Pontiac LeMans Options List

Sales Code	UPC Code	Description	S.R.P.
424	B70	Pad, Instrument Panel	16.14
431	K45	Air Cleaner, Heavy-Duty (standard with GTO package)	4.84
432	V01	Radiator, Heavy-Duty (included with air-conditioning)	15.06
434	C06	Power Top (standard with GTO package)	53.80
441	D34	Mirror, Visor Vanity	1.45
442	D31	Mirror, Inside Non-Glare	4.25
444	D33	Mirror, Outside Driver's Remote	11.78
451	Y91	Decklid, Remote	11.78
452	U16	Tachometer	53.80
454	N33	Steering Wheel, Tilt (requires power steering)	43.04
462	P01	Wheel Discs, Deluxe	15.60
471	T86	Lamps, Backup (manual transmission)	12.91
471	T86	Lamps, Backup (automatic transmission)	10.76
474	U84	Rear Speaker, Verbra-Phonic (not available with convertible)	53.80
481	U25	Lamp, Luggage	3.55
482	U27	Lamp, Glove Box	2.85
484	C86	Lamp, Dome and Reading (not available with convertible)	8.39
491	U29	Lamp, Courtesy (standard with convertible)	4.30
492	U28	Lamp, Ashtray and Lighter	3.12
494	U40	Lamp, Parking Brake	4.95
501	N40	Power Steering	96.84
502	J50	Power Brakes	42.50
511	N10	Exhaust, Dual (standard with GTO package)	30.88
512	B93	Door Edge Guards	4.84
521	P02	Wheel Discs, Custom	35.50
524	N34	Steering Wheel, Custom Sports	39.27
531	A01	Glass, Soft Ray: All Windows	31.20
532	A02	Glass, Soft Ray: Windshield	19.91
541	C50	Defogger, Rear Window (not available with convertible)	21.52
551	A31	Power Windows	102.22
564	A46	Power Driver's Seat	71.02
572	P17	Cover, Spare Tire	2.58
581	C60	Air Conditioner: Tri-Comfort	345.60
582	T60	Battery, Heavy-Duty (standard with air-conditioning)	3.55
584	C48	Heater Delete (credit)	-73.00
592		Special Request Items	Varies
601	D55	Center Console	48.15
602	D32	Mirror, Outside Rearview	4.25
604	U35	Electric Clock	19.37
612	Y96	Rally Handling Kit	16.14
614	K24	Positive Crankcase Ventilation (available after December 1963)	5.38
621	F40	Heavy-Duty Springs and Shocks (cars with W62 GTO option automatically received Heavy-Duty Springs)	3.82
622	G66	Superlift Rear Shocks	40.35
624	A49	Seat Belts, Front Pair	18.29
631	B32	Floor Mats, Front	6.24
632	B33	Floor Mats, Rear	5.81
644	K08	Fan, Heavy-Duty	3.12
671	K66	Transistor Ignition	75.27
692	J65	Metallic Brake Linings	36.86
701	G81	Safe-T-Track Differential	37.66
702		Standard Axle	No Charge
809	L71	389 Tri-Power Engine (GTO only)	115.78
77W	M20	4-Speed Synchromesh Transmission, Wide-Ratio (except 3.90:1 axle)	188.30
779	M20	4-Speed Synchromesh Transmission, Wide-Ratio (3.90:1 axle)	188.30
778	M21	4-Speed Synchromesh Transmission, Close-Ratio, Available after March 1964 (requires GTO package, Tri-Power, 3.90:1 Axle, Metallic Brake Linings, Safe-T-Track rear, Heavy-Duty Fan, and Heavy-Duty Radiator)	175.00
77J	M31	2-Speed Automatic Transmission	199.06
RTT		Two-Tone Paint (not available on convertible)	31.74
SPS		Single Color, Special Paint	40.19
SVT		Cordova Top (not applicable to convertible)	75.32

APPENDIX II: 1965 GTO

1965 GTO Production Figures		
Body	Model Number	Production
Hardtop	3737	55,722
Sports Coupe	3727	8,319
Convertible	3767	11,311
Total Production		**75,352**

Production by Engine Type		
Engine	HP	Production
389 4-Barrel	335	54,805
389 Tri-Power	360	20,547

Production by Transmission and Induction Type			
Transmission	4-Barrel	Tri-Power	Total
Automatic	17,518	1,456	18,974
Manual	37,287	19,091	56,378

Interior, Exterior, and Cordova/Convertible Colors

1965 Pontiac GTO Paint Codes	
Paint Code	Color
A	Starlight Black*
B	Blue Charcoal
C	Cameo Ivory*
D	Fontaine Blue
E	Nightwatch Blue
H	Palmetto Green
K	Reef Turquoise
L	Teal Turquoise
N	Burgundy
P	Iris Mist
R	Montero Red*
T	Capri Gold
V	Mission Beige
W	Bluemist Slate
Y	Mayfair Maize
1	Standard GM Paint, non-Pontiac color
2	Special Paint
3	Cadillac Firefrost
*Also used for pinstripes	

1965 Pontiac GTO Cordova and Convertible Tops	
Code	Color
1	White
2	Black
4	Blue
5	Turquoise
6	Beige
Note: Cordova tops only available in Black or Beige	

Interior Color Codes	
Code (with bucket seats)	Color
213-30	Black
216-35	Red
214-36	Turquoise
217-33	Dark Blue
215-34	Gold
218-3E	Parchment

1965 LeMans Options List			
Sales Code	UPC Code	Description	S.R.P.
3727		LeMans Sports Coupe	2,427.00
3737		LeMans Hardtop	2,491.00
3767		LeMans Convertible	2,726.00
061		Basic Options Group with W62 GTO Option: includes 392, 421, 471 (for manual-transmission cars)	92.59
061		Basic Options Group with W62 GTO Option: includes 392, 421, 471 (for automatic-transmission cars)	90.44
062		Protection Group: includes 424, 512, 541, 572, 624, 633 (Sports Coupe and hardtop)	64.66
062		Protection Group: includes 424, 512, 572, 624, 633 (convertible)	43.14
071		Mirror Group: includes 441, 442, 444	17.48
074		Lamp Group: includes 404, 481, 482, 491, 492, 494 (Sports Coupe and hardtop)	22.32
074		Lamp Group: includes 404, 481, 482, 491, 492, 494 (convertible)	18.02
342	C08	Cordova Top, Black (not applicable to convertible)	75.32
346	C08	Cordova Top, Beige (not applicable to convertible)	75.32
382	W62	GTO Group: (LeMans Sports Coupe, hardtop, and convertible only) includes: Heavy-Duty Synchromesh Transmission, 389-ci 4-Barrel Engine with Chrome Air Cleaner and Rocker Arm Covers, Special Hood, GTO Identification, Special Wood Instrument Panel Covering, Sports-Type Springs and Shocks, .937-inch Diameter Front Stabilizer Bar, Special Body Side Paint Stripe, 7.75x14 Redline Tires, Dual Exhaust, Heavy-Duty Battery, Special Seven-Blade Fan, and Clutch Assembly	295.90
391	U75	Power Antenna (with 393, 395, or 399 only)	--
392	U63	Radio: Push Button with Manual Antenna	62.41
393	U63	Radio: Push Button with Electric Antenna	92.16
394	U63	Radio: Push Button, AM/FM with Manual Antenna	136.65
395	U63	Radio: Push Button, AM/FM with Electric Antenna	166.40
398	U60	Radio: Manual Control with Manual Antenna	53.80
399	U60	Radio: Manual Control with Electric Antenna	83.55
401	U80	Rear Speaker, Sepra-Phonic (not available with convertible)	14.15
404	U26	Lamp, Underhood	3.55
411	N95	Wheel Discs, Wire	71.02
412	B50	Foam, Front Cushion (not applicable for bucket seats)	8.07

1965 LeMans Options List

Sales Code	UPC Code	Description	S.R.P.
414	A62	Seat Belt Delete (credit)	-11.00
421	C14	Dual-Speed Wipers with Washer	17.27
422	N25	Extensions, Tail Pipe	21.30
424	B70	Pad, Instrument Panel	16.14
431	K45	Air Cleaner, Heavy-Duty (standard with GTO package)	4.84
432	V01	Radiator, Heavy-Duty (included with air-conditioning)	12.91
441	D34	Mirror, Visor Vanity	1.45
442	D31	Mirror, Inside Non-Glare	4.25
444	D33	Mirror, Outside Driver's Remote	11.78
451	A89	Decklid, Remote Control	10.76
454	N33	Tilt Steering Wheel (requires power steering)	43.04
462	P01	Wheel Discs, Deluxe	17.22
471	T86	Lamps, Backup (manual transmission)	12.91
471	T86	Lamps, Backup (automatic transmission)	10.76
474	U84	Rear Speaker, Verbra-Phonic (not available with convertible)	53.80
481	U25	Lamp, Luggage	3.55
482	U27	Lamp, Glove Box	2.85
491	U29	Lamp, Courtesy (standard with convertible)	4.30
492	U28	Lamp, Ashtray and Lighter	3.12
494	U40	Lamp, Parking Brake	4.95
501	N40	Power Steering	96.84
502	J50	Power Brakes	42.50
504	U30	Instrument Panel, Rally Gauge Cluster with Tachometer	86.08
511	N10	Exhaust, Dual (standard with GTO package)	30.88
512	B93	Door Edge Guards	4.84
521	P02	Wheel Discs, Custom	37.12
524	N34	Steering Wheel, Custom Sports	39.27
531	A01	Glass, Soft Ray: All Windows	31.20
532	A02	Glass, Soft Ray: Windshield Only	19.91
541	C50	Defogger, Rear Window (not available with convertible)	21.52
551	A31	Power Windows	102.22
564	A46	Power Driver's Seat	71.02
572	P17	Spare Tire Cover	2.58
582	C60	Air-Conditioning: Tri-Comfort	345.60
584	C48	Heater Delete (credit)	-73.00
601	D55	Console, All with Bucket Seats	48.15
602	D32	Mirror, Outside Rearview	4.25
604	U35	Clock, Electric (not available with Rally Gauge Cluster)	19.37
612	N38	20:1 Steering Gearbox (not available with power steering)	10.76
614	K24	Positive Crankcase Ventilation	5.38
621	Y96	Ride and Handling Package	16.14
622	G66	Shocks, Super Lift Rear	40.35
624	A49	Seat Belts, Custom Retractable: Front	7.53
631	B32	Floor Mats, Front	6.24
632	B33	Floor Mats, Rear	5.81
634	U15	Speedometer, Safeguard, and Fuel Warning Lamp	16.14
661	F35	Heavy-Duty Frame (standard on convertible)	--
662	K68	Fully Transistorized Regulator (not available with air-conditioning)	10.76
664	F37	Rear Cross Member Reinforcement	--
671	K66	Transistor Ignition (with air-conditioning)	75.27
671	K66	Transistor Ignition (without air-conditioning)	64.51
674	K82	Alternator, Heavy-Duty, 55-Amp, (included with air-conditioning and heavy-duty battery)	--
691	P05	Wheels, Rally (with 7.75 x 14-inch tires only)	52.72
692	J65	Metallic Brake Linings (mandatory with Safe-T-Track rear, not available with aluminum front drums)	36.86
694	J60	Brakes, Heavy-Duty, Front Aluminum Drums (not available with metallic linings)	--
701	G81	Differential: Safe-T-Track	37.66
702	G94	Standard Axle	No Charge
704	G83	Economy Axle	--
708	G92	Performance Axle	--
742	M31	2-Speed Automatic Transmission: Water Cooled	199.06
744	M20	4-Speed Synchromesh Transmission: Wide-Ratio	188.30
778	M21	4-Speed Synchromesh Transmission: Close-Ratio (requires Heavy-Duty Radiator, Metallic Brake Linings, Safe-T-Track rear)	188.30
781	F40	Heavy-Load Springs and Shocks	--

1965 LeMans Options List			
Sales Code	UPC Code	Description	S.R.P.
788	A64	Standard Rear Seat Belts (requires code 624)	--
802	L71	389-ci Tri-Power Engine (GTO only)	115.78
	CC	7.75x14-inch Nylon-Belted, Red Stripe Tires (Standard on GTO)	--
	CG	7.75x14-inch Rayon-Belted, Whitewall Tires	No Charge
		Solid Paint, Special Color	40.19
		Two-Tone Paint (not applicable to convertible)	31.74
		Two-Tone Paint: Special Color (not applicable convertible)	71.93

APPENDIX III: 1966 GTO

1966 GTO Production Figures		
Body	Model Number	Production
Hardtop	4217	73,785
Sports Coupe	4207	10,363
Convertible	4267	12,798
Total Production		**96,946**

Production by Engine Type		
Engine	HP	Production
389-ci 4-Barrel	335	77,698
389-ci Tri-Power	360	19,063
389-ci Ram Air	360	185–190 (estimate)

Note: Some sources vary on 1966 4-barrel versus Tri-Power production figures, likely due to the uncertain number of Ram Air cars produced.

Production by Transmission and Induction Type			
Transmission	4-Barrel	Tri-Power	Total
Automatic	33,913	1,754	35,667
Manual	43,785	17,494	61,279

Interior, Exterior, and Cordova/Convertible Top Colors

1966 GTO Paint Codes	
Paint Code	Color
A	Starlight Black*
B	Blue Charcoal
C	Cameo Ivory*
D	Fontaine Blue
E	Nightwatch Blue
H	Palmetto Green
K	Reef Turquoise
L	Marina Turquoise
N	Burgundy
P	Barrier Blue
R	Montero Red*
T	Martinique Bronze
V	Mission Beige
W	Platinum
Y	Candlelite Cream
1	Standard GM Paint, Non-Pontiac Color
2	Special Pontiac Paint: Tiger Gold, Copper Blaze, Plum Mist, Fathom Turquoise, Ramada Bronze
4	Primer
*Also used for pinstripes	

Note: Cadet Blue (code F), Pinehurst Green (code J), and Sierra Red (code M) were available in 1966, but were not considered regular production colors.

1966 GTO Cordova and Convertible Tops	
Code	Color
1	Ivory
2	Black
4	Blue
5	Turquoise
6	Beige

Note: Cordova tops only available in Ivory, Black, or Beige.

Interior Color Codes	
Code	Color
219	Dark Blue
220	Dark Turquoise
221	Bronze
222	Medium Red
223	Black
224	Parchment

1966 GTO Options List			
Sales Code	UPC Code	Description	S.R.P.
4267		GTO Convertible	$3,082.00
4217		GTO Hardtop	2,847.00
4207		GTO Sports Coupe	2,783.00
061		Basic Options Group: includes 342, 371, 444	80.05
062		Protection Group: includes 431, 372, 382, 374, 381, 633 (Sports Coupe and hardtop)	50.66
062		Protection Group: includes 431, 372, 382, 381, 633 (convertible)	29.60
071		Mirror Group: includes 391, 392, 394	13.21
074		Lamp Group: includes 401, 402, 404, 411, 412, 414, 421 (Sports Coupe and hardtop)	35.45
074		Lamp Group: includes 401, 402, 412, 414, 421 (convertible)	17.65
082	V82	Medium Trailer Group: includes 622, 642, 661, 681 (Sports Coupe and hardtop without air-conditioning or Tri-Power)	51.50
082	V82	Medium Trailer Group: includes 622, 642, 661 (Sports Coupe and hardtop with air-conditioning or Tri-Power)	36.86
082	V82	Medium Trailer Group: includes 622, 642, 681 (convertible without air-conditioning or Tri-Power)	28.80
082	V82	Medium Trailer Group: includes 622, 642 (convertible with air-conditioning or Tri-Power)	14.17
291	C08	Cordova Top, Ivory (not applicable to convertible)	84.26

1966 GTO Options List

Sales Code	UPC Code	Description	S.R.P.
292	C08	Cordova Top, Black (not applicable to convertible)	84.26
296	C08	Cordova Top, Beige (not applicable to convertible)	84.26
341	U75	Power Antenna (with 343, 345, 349)	--
342	U63	Radio: Push Button with Manual Antenna	61.09
343	U63	Radio: Push Button with Electric Antenna	90.21
344	U69	Radio: Push Button, AM/FM with Manual Antenna	133.76
345	U69	Radio: Push Button, AM/FM with Electric Antenna	162.88
348	U60	Radio: Manual Control with Manual Antenna	52.66
349	U60	Radio: Manual Control and Electric Antenna	81.78
351	U80	Rear Speaker, Sepra-Phonic (not available with Verbra-Phonic or convertible)	15.80
352	U84	Rear Speaker, Verbra-Phonic (not available with Sepra-Phonic or convertible)	52.66
372	P17	Spare Tire Cover	2.53
374	C50	Defogger, Rear Window (not available with convertible)	21.06
382	B93	Door Edge Guards	4.74
384	D49	Delete Outside Rearview Mirror (export only)	--
391	D34	Mirror, Visor Vanity	1.68
392	D31	Mirror, Inside Non-Glare	4.16
394	D33	Mirror, Outside Driver's Remote	7.37
401	U25	Lamp, Luggage	3.48
402	U27	Lamp, Glove Box	2.79
404	C89	Lamps, Roof Rail and Reading (not available with convertible)	13.59
411	U29	Lamp, Courtesy, Instrument Panel (standard with convertible)	4.21
412	U28	Lamps, Ashtray and Lighter	3.05
414	U40	Lamp, Parking Brake	4.85
421	U26	Lamp, Underhood	3.55
422	A89	Decklid Release, Remote Control	12.64
431	A39	Seat Belts, Custom: Front and Rear	10.53
432	A49	Seat Belts: Front Only, with retractors	26.33
434	A48	Delete Front and Rear Seatbelts (not applicable with 431 or 432)	--
441	U15	Speedometer, Safeguard (not available with 448)	15.80
444	U35	Electric Clock (not available with 448)	18.96
448	U30	Rally Gauge Cluster and Tachometer (not available with 441 or 444)	84.26
452	N95	Wheel Discs, Wire	69.51
454	P05	Wheels, Rally	56.87
458	P02	Wheel Discs, Custom	36.33
461	P01	Wheel Discs, Deluxe	16.85
471	N34	Steering Wheel, Custom Sports	38.44
472	D55	Console, All with Bucket Seats	47.13
482	N25	Extensions, Tailpipe	30.23
484	J65	Metallic Brake Linings (731 mandatory)	36.86
491		Delete Pinstripes	--
501	N40	Power Steering, Wonder Touch (not available with 511)	94.79
502	J50	Power Brakes, Wonder Touch	41.60
504	N33	Tilt Steering Wheel (requires power steering, not available with column shift manual transmission)	43.13
511	N38	Steering, Quick-Ratio 20:1 (not available with power steering)	10.53
514	K02	Heavy-Duty Seven-Blade Fan and Clutch	3.05
521	V74	Traffic Hazard Warning Switch	11.59
522	T46	Liners, Fender: Red (four)	26.33
524	M09	Walnut Shift Knob, 4-Speed	3.69
531	A01	Glass, Soft Ray: All Windows	31.54
532	A02	Glass, Soft Ray: Windshield Only	19.49
544	P38	Delete All Tires (export only)	--
551	A31	Power Windows	100.05
564	A46	Power Seat: Driver's Bucket	69.51
568	A53	Strato Bench Seat, Notchback (special order only)	92.22
571	A82	Headrests: Passenger's and Driver's	52.66
574	A70	Strato Bucket Seats with Headrests and Reclining Passenger's Seat	84.26
582	C60	Air Conditioner: Custom	343.20
584	C48	Heater Delete (credit, not available with air-conditioning)	-71.76
591	W55	Speedometer Gear Adaptor (for special-order rear gear ratio)	10.98
612	K19	Air Injector Exhaust Control: California only	44.76
614	K24	Positive Crankcase Ventilation	5.27
621	Y96	Ride and Handling Package	3.74

1966 GTO Options List

Sales Code	UPC Code	Description	S.R.P
628	W61	Soft Ride Springs and Shocks	No Charge
631	B32	Floor Mats, Front	6.11
632	B33	Floor Mats, Rear (with 631 only)	5.69
634	G66	Shocks, Super Lift: Rear	39.50
642		Medium Trailer Provisions (with 082 only)	-
651	J62	Brake Drums, Heavy-Duty Aluminum, Front	49.08
661	F35	Heavy-Duty Frame (standard with convertible)	29.69
664	K68	Regulator, Transistorized Voltage (without air-conditioning)	10.53
671	K66	Transistor Ignition (with air-conditioning)	63.14
671	K66	Transistor Ignition (without air-conditioning)	10.53
674		Alternator, Heavy-Duty (standard with air-conditioning)	15.80
681	V01	Radiator, Heavy-Duty (standard with air-conditioning)	14.74
688	K01	Five-Blade Engine Fan and Shroud, Heavy-Duty	5.75
731	G80	Differential: Safe-T-Track	37.66
733	G83	Axle Ratio: Economy	-
778	M21	4-Speed Manual Transmission, Close-Ratio (requires 484, 514, 731, not available with air-conditioning)	184.31
782	M31	2-Speed Automatic Transmission	194.84
783	G94	Axle Ratio: Performance	-
784	M20	4-Speed Manual Transmission, Wide-Ratio	184.31
785	M13	3-Speed Manual Transmission, Heavy-Duty: Floor Shift Only	84.26
802	L71	Trophy 389, 3x2-Barrel Engine	113.33
		Ram Air Package (with 802 only: available 2/28/66)	
CB		7.75x14-inch Rayon-Belted, White Side Wall (WSW)	-
CC		7.75x14-inch Nylon-Belted, Red Stripe	Standard
CL		7.75x14-inch Nylon-Belted WSW Four-Ply Rating: Four-Ply	17.78
CG		7.75x14-inch Nylon-Belted WSW Eight-Ply Rating: Four-Ply	49.15
SPS		Solid Paint, Special Color	83.20
RTT		Two-Tone Paint, Standard Colors (not applicable to convertible)	31.07
STT		Two-Tone Paint, Special Colors (not applicable to convertible)	114.27

APPENDIX IV: 1967 GTO

1967 GTO Production Figures

Body	Model Number	Production
Hardtop	4217	65,176
Sports Coupe	4207	7,029
Convertible	4267	9,517
Total Production		**81,722**

Production by Engine Type

Engine	HP	Production
400-ci Standard	335	64,177
400-ci High Output	360	13,827
400-ci Ram Air	360	751
400-ci Economy	255	2,967

Production by Transmission Type

Manual	Automatic
39,128	42,594

Interior, Exterior, and Cordova/Convertible Top Colors

1967 GTO Paint Codes

Paint Code	Color
A	Starlight Black*
C	Cameo Ivory*
D	Montreux Blue
E	Fathom Blue
F	Tyrol Blue
G	Signet Gold
H	Linden Green
K	Gulf Turquoise
L	Mariner Turquoise
M	Plum Mist
N	Burgundy
P	Silverglaze
R	Regimental Red*
S	Champagne
T	Montego Cream
SPEC	Standard GM Paint, non-Pontiac color
2	Special Pontiac Paint: Coronado Gold, Verdoro Green, Mayfair Maize, Copper Blaze, Silver Turquoise, Sierra Red, Blue Charcoal
4	Primer

*Also used for pinstripes

Interior Color Codes

Code	Color
219	Dark Blue
220	Dark Turquoise
221	Medium Gold
223	Black
224	Parchment
225	Medium Red
235	Black with bench seat
236	Parchment with bench seat

1967 GTO Cordova and Convertible Tops

Code	Color
1	Ivory
2	Black
4	Blue
5	Turquoise
6	Beige

Note: Cordova tops only available in Ivory, Black, or Beige

1967 GTO Options List

Sales Code	UPC Code	Description	S.R.P.
4267		GTO Convertible	3,165.00
4217		GTO Hardtop	2,935.00
4207		GTO Sports Coupe	2,871.00
061		Basic Options Group: includes 342, 361, 474	89.48
062		Protection Group: includes 374, 382, 633 (Sports Coupe and hardtop)	43.92
062		Protection Group: includes 382, 633 (convertible)	22.86
071		Mirror Group: includes 391, 394	9.05
074		Lamp Group: includes 401, 404, 421, 422 (Sports Coupe and hardtop)	22.61
074		Lamp Group: includes 401, 421, 422 (convertible)	9.02
082	V82	Medium Trailer Group: includes 621, 642, 661, 681 (Sports Coupe and hardtop)	36.86
082	V82	Medium Trailer Group: includes 621, 642, 681 (convertible)	14.17
291	C08	Cordova Top, White (not applicable to convertible)	84.26
292	C08	Cordova Top, Black (not applicable to convertible)	84.26
296	C08	Cordova Top, Cream (not applicable to convertible)	84.26
341	U75	Power Antenna, Radio	--
342	U63	Radio: Push Button with Manual Antenna	61.09
343	U63	Radio: Push Button with Electric Antenna	90.21
344	U69	Radio: Push Button, AM/FM with Manual Antenna	133.76
345	U69	Radio: Push Button, AM/FM with Electric Antenna	162.88
348	U60	Radio: Manual Control with Manual Antenna	52.66
349	U60	Radio: Manual Control with Electric Antenna	81.78
351	U80	Rear Speaker, Sepra-Phonic (not available with Verbra-Phonic)	15.80
352	U84	Rear Speaker, Verbra-Phonic (not available with Sepra-Phonic)	52.66
354	U57	Stereo Tape Player (8-track)	128.49
361	K45	Air Cleaner, Dual-Stage (mandatory with 612 and 614)	9.43
362	B33	Mat, Rear Carpet Throw	7.90
374	C50	Defogger, Rear Window (not available with convertible)	21.06
382	B93	Door Edge Guards	4.74
384	D28	Delete Outside Rearview Mirror (export only)	--
391	D34	Mirror, Visor Vanity	1.68
394	D33	Mirror, Outside Driver's Remote	7.37
401	U25	Lamp, Luggage	3.48
402	U27	Lamp, Glove Box (standard on 4200)	--
404	C89	Lamps, Roof Rail and Reading (not available with convertible)	13.59
411	U29	Lamp, Courtesy, Instrument Panel (standard on 4200)	--
412	U28	Lamps, Ashtray, and Lighter (standard on 4200)	--
421	U26	Lamp, Underhood	3.48
422	U23	Lamp, Ignition and Starter Switch	2.06
431	A39	Seat Belts, Custom: Front with Retractors and Rear	6.32
432	A68	Seat Belt, Standard, Rear Center Seat	6.32
433	AL5	Seat Belt, Custom, Rear Center Seat	7.90
434	AS1	Shoulder Harness, Standard: Front Seat: 1 Pair (with 431)	26.33
434	AS1	Shoulder Harness, Standard: Front Seat: 1 Pair (without 431)	23.17
435	A85	Shoulder Harness, Custom: Front Seat: 1 Pair	26.33
441	K30	Cruise Control (automatic transmission only)	52.66
442	U15	Speedometer, Safeguard (not available with 444)	15.80
444	U30	Rally Gauge Cluster and Tachometer (not available with 442)	84.26
452	N95	Wheel Discs, Wire	69.51
453	N98	Wheels, Rally II	72.67
454	P05	Wheels, Rally I	56.87
458	P02	Wheel Discs, Custom	36.33
461	P01	Wheel Discs, Deluxe	16.85
471	N34	Steering Wheel, Custom Sports	30.02
472	D55	Console, Manual Transmission	52.66
472	D55	Console, Automatic Transmission (mandatory with 504)	68.46
474	U35	Electric Clock (not available with 444)	18.96
482	N25	Extensions, Tailpipe	30.23
491	900	Delete Side Stripes (special order)	--
492	A90	Decklid Release, Remote Control	12.64
501	N40	Power Steering, Wonder Touch (not available with 662)	94.79
502	J50	Power Brakes, Wonder Touch	41.60
504	N33	Tilt Steering Wheel (requires 501, not available with column shift)	43.13

1967 GTO Options List

Sales Code	UPC Code	Description	S.R.P.
514	K02	Heavy-Duty Seven-Blade Fan and Clutch (standard with air-conditioning)	3.05
521	J52	Power Brakes, Front Disc	104.79
522	T46	Liners, Fender: Red (four)	26.33
524	M09	Walnut Shift Knob, 4-Speed	3.69
531	A01	Glass, Soft Ray: All Windows	30.54
532	A02	Glass, Soft Ray: Windshield Only	21.06
551	A31	Power Windows	100.05
564	A46	Power Seat: Driver's Bucket	69.51
568	A53	Strato Bench Seat, Notchback	No Charge
571	A82	Headrests: Passenger's and Driver's	52.66
578	A70	Strato Bucket Seats with Headrests and Passenger's Reclining Seat	84.26
582	C60	Air Conditioner, Custom (not available with 664 or L67 engine)	343.20
584	C48	Heater Delete (credit, not available with air-conditioning)	-71.76
591	W55	Speedometer Gear Adaptor (with special-order gear ratio only)	10.98
604	P32	Delete Spare Tire (export only)	--
611	K21	Engine-Controlled Combustion System (with L65 engine only)	--
612	K19	Air Injector Exhaust Control (mandatory in California)	44.76
614	K24	Positive Crankcase Ventilation (included with 612)	5.27
621	Y96	Ride and Handling Package	3.74
622	F40	Springs and Shocks, Heavy-Duty	3.74
631	B32	Floor Mats: Front Pair	6.11
632	B33	Floor Mats: Rear Pair (with 631 only)	5.69
633		Floor Mats: Front and Rear (with Protection Group only)	--
634	G66	Shocks, Super Lift: Rear	39.50
642	V82	Medium Trailer Provisions (with 082 only)	--
661	F35	Heavy-Duty Frame (standard with convertible)	29.69
662	N38	Steering, Quick-Ratio 20:1 (not available with power steering)	10.53
664	K68	Regulator, Transistorized Voltage (not available with 582)	10.53
671	K66	Capacitor Discharge Ignition System (with 582)	114.80
671	K66	Capacitor Discharge Ignition System (without 582)	104.26
674	K82	Alternator: Heavy-Duty 55 Amp (standard with 582)	15.80
681	V01	Radiator: Heavy-Duty (without 582)	14.74
688	K01	Five-Blade Engine Fan and Shroud, Heavy-Duty	5.75
701	A49	Seat Belts, Deluxe: Front with Retractors	6.32
702	A48	Seat Belts, Standard: Front and Rear Delete (export only)	--
704	UB5	Tachometer, Hood-Mounted	63.19
731	G80	Differential: Safe-T-Track (except heavy-duty, not available with L67 engine)	42.13
731	G80	Differential: Safe-T-Track, Heavy-Duty	63.19
732	G94	Differential: Non-locking, Special-Order–Ratio (not available with L67 engine)	2.11
733	G83	Differential: Safe-T-Track, Special-Order–Ratio (not available with L67 engine)	2.11
734	G95	Differential: Non-locking, Economy-Ratio (not available with L67 engine)	2.11
735	G82	Differential: Safe-T-Track, Economy-Ratio (not available with L67 engine)	2.11
738	G92	Differential: Non-locking, Performance-Ratio (requires 781)	2.11
739	G81	Differential: Safe-T-Track, Performance-Ratio (not available with L67 engine)	2.11
778	M21	4-Speed Manual Transmission, Close-Ratio (requires 484, 514, 731, not available with 582)	184.31
781	M40	3-Speed Automatic Transmission, TH-400 (not available in Tempest or LeMans)	226.44
783	M11	3-Speed Manual Transmission: Column Shift Only	Standard
784	M20	4-Speed Manual Transmission, Wide-Ratio	184.31
785	M13	3-Speed Manual Transmission, Heavy-Duty: Floor Shift Only	No Charge
803	L65	400-ci 2-Barrel Engine (automatic transmission only)	No Charge
802	L74	400-ci 4-Barrel High Output	76.89
	L78	400-ci 4-Barrel, 335 hp (standard in GTO)	--
	L67	400-ci 4-Barrel Ram Air (requires 681, 731, and 778 or 781)	263.30
MC	PW8	F70x14-inch Nylon-belted, Red Stripe	Standard
MD	PW7	F70x14-inch Nylon-belted, White Stripe	No Charge
CB	--	7.75x14-inch Nylon-belted, White Line Four-Ply Rating: Two-Ply	No Charge
CC	--	7.75x14-inch Nylon-belted, Redline Four-Ply Rating: Two-Ply	No Charge
CL	N88	7.75x14-inch Nylon-belted, WSW Four-Ply Rating: Two-Ply	17.91
CG	T21	7.75x14-inch Nylon-belted, WSW Eight-Ply Rating: Four-Ply	49.15
SPS		Solid Paint, Special Color	83.20
RTT		Two-Tone Paint, Standard Colors (not applicable to convertible)	31.07
STT		Two-Tone Paint, Special Colors (not applicable to convertible)	114.27

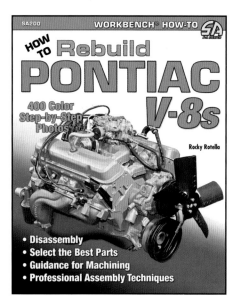

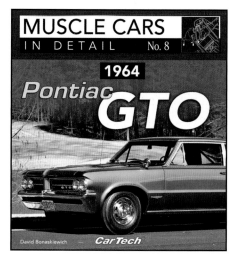